From G
Bipol

To Dan,

All the best mate
+ take good care

lookin forward to

the big game in
April!

George Wilson

regards

George

(219947)

chipmunkapublishing
the mental health publisher

George Wilson

Published by
Chipmunkapublishing
United Kingdom

http://www.chipmunkapublishing.com

Copyright © George Wilson 2019

Editor Michael Silvester

Ricky Simmonds for picture

Alan Hamilton management for bio on back

Back photography by John Quinn

ISBN   978-1-78382-4977

Quotes

Grange Hill

John Drummond (Trev)
"George is my oldest friend.
We've known each other for over 30 years and have enjoyed a shared sense of humour throughout that time, as well as a deep respect for each other.
We grew up together as teenagers and enjoyed every minute, from late night nightclub escapes to failed horse racing betting schemes! So many capers of which some I can't even remember, there were so many!
But I will never forget the day I saw him, shortly after he had come out of hospital the first time he was ill. I was devastated to see my friend looking so awful. Thin, pale and very nervous, almost afraid of his own shadow. In fact he was just a shadow of his former self.
Over the years I have seen him a couple of more times after a spell in the 'Cuckoo's Nest'. And every time I was as devastated as the time before.
But here he is, still alive, a father, a loving partner and with the same generosity of spirit that he has always had.
He is not defined by his mental ill health and however bad things may have been at times, it has not beaten him.
Mental health is still the 'elephant in the room' within society, with people either disbelieving of its effect on people's lives, or afraid to recognise or confront it.
I think it's because all of us have suffered at some

point in our lives, with the majority only briefly. But some are not so lucky, like my friend.
I'm so proud of him because it can't have been easy to write this, in his own words, without any filters.
I hope that this memoir encourages others to speak up and more importantly, encourages everyone else to remove the blinkers and accept that this is real and it's happening now to many more people, who desperately need help and support."

Erkan Mustafa (Roland)
"Mental health issues can affect each and every one of us, reading your story has been an insight to you as a person. I am so proud of you for being open and honest which is not easy. There is a stigma around mental health issues, which I hope will change one day."

Lee Macdonald (Zammo)
"From the first moment I met George all those years ago when he joined Grange Hill, I knew he was someone special! From day one he made me smile all the time and continued to do this until my last day. I did not know the issues George had until I read this book; how brave and honest to do this. I am so proud of you and hope this helps others who read your book, Thank you so much for sharing this. Love you G."

Ian Condon (Ted)

"I laughed out loud at parts and cried in parts and I mean cry. Reading this story has been over whelming; a mix of guilt and a lesson. If you read one story this year read this; a lesson in life."

Ruth Carraway (Helen)

"So proud of my dear friend for getting this story out - it's been one hell of a road for him at a time when mental illness was stigmatised... The sharing of his story supports his own healing as well encouraging others to get the support they need, that it's ok to be unwell, to speak out and to not be defined by their illness."

John Alford (Robbie)

"Me and George have been through a lot together and apart. I've seen him at his best and his worst, as he has seen me the same. He is like a brother to me. This book shows how you can hide behind your fame your true feelings. I hope people read this and realise yes fame is nice, but there is a price and also gives hope to those suffering."

Ricky Simmonds (Ant)

"When anyone ever asks me who is the funniest person I ever worked with - the only answer I ever give is George Wilson. On Grange Hill there were some good actors and there were some great actors. George was in another league. He was one of the best."

Gwyneth Powell (Mrs Mckluskey)

"I had no idea what you had been through, and was shocked and saddened by the tough time you've had in between Grange Hill and our meeting again on Pointless. I can't tell you how much I admire your honesty and courage in writing the book. It is a revelation, and I am certain that it will prove a best seller. How brave you have been, and how much love has been around you. God Bless, and keep you safe."

Lisa York (Julie)

"Such honest and brave words written. The best of times and the very worst! Mental health issues needs a voice and your voice in this book shines"

Fiona Mowlem (Laura)

"By the time we reach our 30's or 40's we begin to finally speak out about our mental health and in turn realise that most of us will suffer from one degree to another in our lifetime.

But there are many years beforehand when we don't speak out, not realising how prevalent mental health issues are.

George suffered in silence for too many years, amongst friends who adored him and had no idea of the inner turmoil he was going through. Within the Grange Hill Cast we really were one big, very happy family and we are all so sad that we didn't begin to see George's suffering and weren't able to help him.

This book is heartbreakingly honest and I hope will encourage other sufferers to seek help and turn their lives around as George has."

Aran Bell (Mr Scott)

"A brave and inspiring story from a Scouse survivor!'

Tim Polley (Banksie)
'A gripping read right from the off, funny and sad. An eye opener for people like me that don't quite understand Bipolar'

Fleur Tickner (Imelda)
"I really hope that George's story will encourage others to speak out about their own mental health. The highs and lows of George's life reveal that you never really know what's going on in someone's mind and life unless we all talk more. The dark times must be very lonely which is why it must be encouraged to confide in others. Well done George"

Alison Valentine Bettles (Fay)
"I worked closely with George for years and didn't have a clue he was feeling this way. Why do we feel the need to hide this!! Well done George for highlighting this and pouring out your heart and soul. A great read, which I hope can help so many people"

Mark Savage (Gripper)
"This is an inspiring personal account of the highs and lows of being an actor and of mental health, in particular, bipolar. George describes his experiences with humour and pathos, breaking down barriers of stigma and discrimination while offering insight, encouragement and hope. To recount uncomfortable life experiences selflessly in the quest to offer empathy, comfort and hope to others experiencing similar, is a display of strength of character. A must read."

Rachel Roberts (Justine)
"Unaware of many of the issues George had been dealing with, I didn't realise just how similar our lives have been in so many ways. Funny, heart-warming and frank, George's story is an inspiration to many of us who can relate to trying to deal with the daily struggles of poor mental health. You're amazing!"

Ron Smedley (Producer)
"Our George who tried his best - and succeeded."

Michael Silvester (Copy Editor / Webmaster www.grangehillgold.wordpress.com)
"By sharing his story with such candid honesty, George proves that the camera shows one story whilst real-life provides another. This should prove to be an inspiration to all."

Brookside

Jason Hope (Rod Corkhill)
"George's story is a compelling human journey, one that needs no apologies for being so."

Justine Kerrigan Frost (Tracey Corkhill)
"What a great book! Despite the difficult subject of bipolar, I found it very easy to read. I'm sure some mental health patients who are in recovery could benefit from aspects of this book. It's very honest and George's positivity outshines the negative aspects of his condition. Lovely memories too from when Grange Hill was in its heyday and some great laughs."

Steven Pinder (Max Farnham)

"George was a constant source of inspiration, working with him too! Reading it brings it all back"

Michael Starke. (Sinbad)

"I've known George since his early days in the business in Liverpool. His positivity and enthusiasm for everything he was involved with was always very infectious. He was a well-loved and valued member of the Brookside cast and kept us on our toes with his sense of humour and talent.

It's no surprise to me, and I'm sure many of his friends and associates that his honesty and bravery in opening up about the serious issues he has faced in his life, would show a side of George that the public might not have seen or would ever have suspected. Good for him that this book will address these things."

Various

Bobby Davro (Actor and Comedian)

"Well done to you sir! I wish you and the book well. I know you've had your past fame in the past. Grange Hill eh? I don't know how old you were when you were on it but I must have been the same age! I wish you well with life and good luck with your autobiography."

Ian Hulme (Chairman of Hillsborough survivors Association)

"Heart-warming and heart-breaking in equal measure; from reaching the stars as Ziggy, to the depths of witnessing Hillsborough, this book has it all and is such an inspiring read. It's been an honour for us at HSA to support George in his recovery and be a part of his inspiring journey"

Tony Hadley (lead singer Spandau Ballet)
"I just want to wish you all the very best, I heard about your new book coming out. It's gonna be brilliant and I hope it does really well. It will be gold! Take care always."

Jason Pegler (Publisher and Author)
'When I was younger my favourite programme on television was Grange Hill. One of the main characters was a guy called Ziggy from Liverpool who liked football. The actor who played this role is named George Wilson. Decades later he has written an amazing memoir describing his experiences from childhood celebrity to living with bipolar disorder. George Wilson writes with brutal honesty, wit, humour and energy that captures the reader at every stage. He recalls real life trials and tribulations including enjoying a beer with Chris Evans on a Brookside lawn, witnessing the Brixton riots, the Hillsborough Tragedy and standing up for what he believes in creatively and ethically. This book packs a punch literally. It made me laugh out loud and cry. The book will go on to help other people who live with mental health experiences and also help others to understand them better so we can co-exist in a happier world."

Eileen Woods (My Mam)
"George has always been a free spirit, going his own way, a risk-taker, difficult to pin down or guide along the way.

He has a warm, sociable nature and can be extremely funny (on stage and off).

Seeing him go through his psychotic episodes has been very painful over the years but he has also shown great strength in fighting it.

With age and maturity he now has a greater handle on the illness and able to live life to the full much more.

I hope this book can give some insight into this form of mental illness and help others see that there can be light at the end of the tunnel."

Mel (Partner)

"Before I met George like many people out there I knew nothing about Bipolar Disorder, however that was about to change.

Life has taken us both on an unexpected journey, we have somehow learnt and come to accept it is always going to be part of our lives.

Some mountains are hard to climb but the strength comes from within him. I have only been there to guide when the dark times come.

When you feel scared during your manic episodes I have never shown fear, as I have learnt that you are more petrified than me, but together we keep each other safe.

For anyone who finds themselves on this path, life doesn't have to be about 'Bipolar', you can make happy memories alongside the dark. One thing I have learnt is don't hide behind the word 'Bipolar' and never be afraid to ask for help; sometimes just talking about your feelings, can give strength, courage and hope."

Steve Hale (Close Pal)

"So proud of you for doing this book. It's a very brave thing to do, another show and rise of strength from you, my closest pal. Nobody can keep you down! My hat goes off to you. We have had many, many adventures together from 1987 to now and I will always cherish the great memories! I wish you all the luck in the world with this book, Scooter Son."

Introduction

The rise and fall of Ziggy, the true story of George Christopher, (real name George Wilson) a child star who had it all at one point. The highs unbelievable but, the lows after, unbearable.

This is the story of how you can go through the gates of Hell but find a stairway out, if you search your soul deeply enough.

It's hard to know where to begin and where to end with my story. I have seen many things good and bad and met many people good and bad. I have been to some wonderful places around the world and in England. Worked in television for many years of my younger life. Worked in other jobs later in life I detested.

I have had 5 spells in mental hospitals from the age of 21 to 43. I am now 49.

I got diagnosed with Bipolar Disorder 1 aged 43. Bipolar 1 in quick medical terms is - a large high followed by a large low. Bipolar disorder used to be known as manic depressive illness. A doctor suspected it when I was 21, after six months in hospital. He said it was probably Manic Depression (Bipolar) but they didn't like to label someone back then, especially at my age of 21 so it was hoped it was a one off. It took eight years for another episode.

Was I born with it or was my lifestyle the reason it surfaced out in me? The answer I don't know, and probably will never know. Once you read the pre breakdown lifestyle I led, of its highs and lows, a clearer picture develops. Was I heading for a fall or was it going to happen anyway?

Besides fellow Bipolar sufferer survival books, there are other books out there on the subject by experts and doctors, but does anybody really know what's going through the mind of a bipolar sufferer? They can observe and research but they don't feel it, live it and suffer it! Especially the manic episodes, and these I will try to explain best I can. It's strange how through all the madness and terror I remember so much of it, some I can't because I was either too out of it under sedation, or too far gone from reality.

I'm no expert on the subject and don't claim to be, I can only write about what's happened to me. More famous sufferers of this disorder have written books of their experiences which I applaud, including the likes of Stephen Fry who wrote 'The Secret Life of a Manic Depressive' and Carrie Fisher who had written a few books about her troubles. One book she spent 3 years writing but her PC crashed causing her to lose everything she'd written which led to a manic episode. Their bravery to write of their experiences opened a door for the likes of others and for me, as I felt why should I hide it?

I don't know the secrets of it all otherwise I'd have never been in a hospital, but I do know things that help prevent things, as you will read. Every bipolar sufferer goes through different events, what I have gone through and suffered will not be the same as Vincent Van Gogh, Frank Sinatra, Amy

Winehouse, Mel Gibson, Paul Gascoigne, Frank Bruno, Vivian Leigh, Spike Milligan, Maria Carey, Lou Reed, Russell Brand, Ruby Wax, Margot Kidder, Winona Ryder, Catherine Zeta Jones and Marilyn Monroe who certainly had some mental illness, and more than likely Winston Churchill, who are among just a few that we know about. My bet is there are more people in show business and other high-profile positions we don't know about as they keep it quiet, for their own reasons. All that these went through would have been different in their minds to me, but certain aspects I have been through would have been similar. It's an elite club when you look at this few from a list of many people of note who've suffered; all talented, intelligent or gifted in one way or another.

'Stars cannot shine without darkness'
DH Sidebottom.

The experiences I have endured are not pleasant but I figure I've spent over a 1000 days in different psychiatric hospitals so I know a thing or two, plus the healing process afterwards is never quick, but quicker each time. I have coping mechanisms in place now that I didn't have in the beginning. I learnt as I went along, self-taught, listening and watching. I've read little, but observed everything. Trial and error sometimes is the only way.

There are terrible lows, I've been so low I couldn't recognise my own Mother, but I will also talk of the highs before the lows and the highs after the lows. It's not to scare or shock but maybe give some understanding to not just bipolar persons but anyone with any mental disorder or form of anxiety, panic attacks (which I also suffer) or people trying to understand as they have a loved one suffering.

No matter how much you are in the dark, the light just hasn't seeped through yet.

I believe if I overcome all I went through, especially being a child TV star in days when it was more taboo, then anyone can if they can just believe in themselves and take certain steps. I control the illness now, it's not controlling me. In my past I've lost everything but gained everything too. I don't let it ruin my life. Bipolar is in the simplest terms a series of highs and lows, as is my story.

Chapter 1
The Rise

'Your future hasn't been written yet. No one's has. Your future is whatever you make it. So make it a good one'
Doc Brown.

1985 was a good year! Certain years I look back on stand out and 85 will always be significant to me as it was the year I got the part in Grange Hill and my life would never be the same. It wasn't easy by any means as I hadn't had a lot of acting experience compared to many others at the audition.

I did go the Liverpool Everyman Theatre with Jay Hope my close mate from school every Thursday to do improvisations. It was great all working class teenagers doing something we loved. That's where I met some good friends including John O Gorman, a natural ladies man who stayed friends for life, plus met amusing characters such as Adonis who was like the local Eddie Murphy. He'd come in with a ghetto blaster every week and blast 'White lines' before we'd start. John Dillon who later went into the army was also in our Everyman gang, plus Shaun Duggan who later became a successful writer for Television. Happy days as my agent Tommy would say.

I had a small part in a film 'No Surrender' With Michael Angelis and Bernard Hill. What an introduction to the film world working alongside those two. I thought 'Boys from the Blackstuff was the greatest bit of TV to come out of Liverpool. It surpassed anything I'd ever seen. That and 'One Summer'. I only had two days but to a fourteen year old on a film set for the first time, it was electric. Hearing tales of George Kerrigan who played George, who was also Justine Kerrigan's (Tracey in Brookside) Grandad.

I was pretty new in this game, a rookie you could say, but I knew I was good and just had a feeling one day I could show it. I was fifteen at the time of the audition, born on the 5th March 1970 in Fazackerley Hospital, Liverpool.

The only problem I had was my appearance at the time made me lack confidence. The main reason was the freckles on my face, I hated them. Around the time of the audition they were blatant and I thought myself ugly, but acting gave me confidence and somehow made me forget my hindrance.

So, I'm on my way to Manchester in a car with two other Scouse actors who I knew had more experience and had done much more TV stuff. I was the youngest, being 15 and when we arrived at a school hall full of maybe a 1000 kids I thought 'this is a waste of time. There's too many!' I looked around and saw confident, good looking and cocksure, convinced already lads walking the floor. Here's me freckle faced and inexperienced.

Then it began; I had to improvise being stuck in a lift. God knows what I did but I remember the two Scouse lads I went up with were eliminated quickly alongside a good many others. I remained. My memory fades of the next improvisation I did, but I do remember noticing the producer Ron Smedley constantly watching me. Even when I was waiting my turn to get up his eyes were watching my every movement. It made me a little more nervous but, looking back, I guess he was thinking I think I've found my boy, as before I knew it there was only two of us left ; me and a guy from Leeds. You see the character of Ziggy could have been from anywhere up North. The ratings I heard later had dropped in the north of the country. With Grange Hill being an all London school, it needed to get a northerner in, and I was almost there.

So I've a 50/50 chance now, but have to go to Brookside the next day to meet the series producer and creator, Phil Redmond, to let him decide.

But I have one problem; the guys who brought me have gone back to Liverpool and I'm due on stage in Romeo and Juliet in 2 hours for the show's last night. There were no mobile phones in '85 so my plan is to run like hell to the station and get the train. I should make it before curtain up. Except I don't know where I am and I don't even have the train fare, but I knew the importance of getting on that stage so I run, ask directions and get to the station only to miss the train that would have got me there on time.

So, I bunk the next train by sitting in the toilet, not locking it as a guard would see this; left vacant he won't check. The play begins at 7.00 and I run from Lime Street station to the Liverpool Playhouse like Forrest Gump and burst in at 7.10

to be greeted by the director screaming at me! I'd never had an adult speak to me so horribly and insult and belittle me as much as he did that night. I was told I'd never work in this city again. He had played my part that night and was furious. There was no point in explaining why I was late for his play and there was nothing I could say to make it better.

I walked out with tears in my eyes. I got home and none of my family were there as they were all in the audience waiting for me to come on. My dad rang at the interval and asked where I was. I told him about the audition and I might just have got the part. He was happy for me and said "Sod the play if you're not in it we'll come home." I was so relieved when they all came home that night as it had been an emotional day.

Meeting Phil Redmond (Later to be nicknamed Dr Reggae) was daunting, I knew he was the biggest producer in the city and it was up to him to pick me or the other kid. A mixture of fear, excitement and pure adrenaline was going through my mind and body. But it was so simple; all he did was ask me about 5 simple questions. I answered them all honestly. His way of checking me out. Then, the other kid went in. I sat outside, heart pounding as I wanted this. To play a part in Grange Hill was big time. Considering there were only 4 channels at the time, no Sky or Netflix in those days so every kid homed in on Grange Hill and rushed home from school to watch. I wanted to be a part of it. I wanted more than anything to show people I could act. Making money wasn't the major thing going through my head; it was to just act on Grange Hill and join the legacy left by Tucker, Benny, Alan, Tricia, Gripper, Suzanne, Stewpot, Zammo etc. and be on prime time TV; on a show that would go on to last 30 years!

"Well done George you've landed the part of Ziggy"
When Phil said that a 1000 things must have gone through my mind but I can't remember one! It was just relief and pure joy to hear those words. It was the happiest moment of my 15 year life so far. Everything that jumped up theatre director yelled at me the night before had now faded into insignificance. Incidentally I sent him a postcard a few months later from London!

I did it and it changed my life forever, for better or worse, but one thing is for sure; I would never have had the adventures I have had without it. Almost 35 years later, at a Grange Hill 40th event, I met up with the producer Ron. I spotted him in the corner; he was 94 years of age but I recognised him instantly. I sat beside him; he knew who I was instantly too. I told him I would never have had the life I had without him picking me out that day. It was an emotional few moments as so many years had passed since I'd seen him, as had so many things. For 35 years I often wondered why he picked me that day in 85 and I had to ask him why.
"Ron why outta all them people in that room did you pick me?"
He thought about it for a moment or two and replied "I really can't remember George!" I laughed

and thought 'great I'll never know now!'

Chapter 2
London Calling

'Nothing is certain in London but expense'
William Shenstone.

Although I'd got the part there were still a few things that had to be taken care of before any contract could be signed.

Firstly my Mum and Dad had to agree. There was no argument as they knew it was my dream, My Mother was a district nurse and my Dad worked on the docks, so to see their son have a chance to go into a job he loved, they all agreed. If you were to ask my Mother now though I'm not sure what she'd say, but nobody knew the future then.

Secondly, my school had to agree; West Derby Comp. The head was Mr Fraser, a man I hadn't had a lot to do with as I was hardly ever in trouble, but he knew me. He'd heard I was good at drama; word had got round. That's how I got into acting as I stood out in school at drama. Two teachers, Mr Ellis and Mr Maher, encouraged me to take it further, so I did. Simple as that. Luckily Mr Fraser agreed I could go and wished me well. He could have made things awkward, in fact put a spanner in the works, but he had seen that I had an opportunity to start a career in something I loved and I will always be thankful for his understanding and blessing.

The third hurdle was getting into a school in London. As I was just 15, I still needed to carry on my education, so a stage school was decided and Sylvia Young's the chosen one.

I would never settle at this school; I'd been so content at my comprehensive school. A stage school was totally out of my depth. I was like a fish out of water. The comp was rough and ready, I was used to chaos! I had the occasional problem with the odd bully but my ability to make people laugh got me out of many things.

Later on, my pal Jay, who was up there in the pecking order, was usually by my side as we went to the Everyman together. He too would go through fame and fortune soon with Brookside, playing Rod, so it was great we enjoyed it together. To have someone in my home town dealing with the same thing helped both of us. We would use this newly found fame to every advantage over the years.

However, life in a comp was totally different to life in a stage school. It was too arty for me. Singing, dancing, tap and ballet was not for me and it was as simple as that. I was no Fred Astaire! I got on very well with a girl called Fiona, she played Laura in Grange Hill and she really looked out for me during my brief stage school days. Probably my only friend, she got me out of many a jam. One day a teacher stopped everyone dancing and asked me how long I had been dancing. I turned to look at the clock behind and replied "about 10 minutes." I was bluntly told to stand outside the class as I heard nervous laughter behind. I just went a pool hall round the corner. "Sod that!" I thought.

Before I got that first train to London, nobody sat me down and prepared me for what was to come; I mean who could? I do remember my wonderful agent, the man who got me the audition, Tommy Mac, saying to me "Do your best". That's all he needed to say. What better advice could an old man give a young kid about to go on the adventure of his life other than 'Do your best'?

The first month in the smoke (London) was the hardest. I almost went home after 4 weeks. I felt so down in the dumps, I became despairing, in fact. The biggest problem I had was the BBC had put me to live with a family in Hackney. It was a small flat where I shared a room with another lad from the stage school, his mother and other kids she had, one adopted. The BBC were paying her to look after me too! I don't believe they knew the cramped conditions I was in or how nasty this old woman was to me, but I put up with it for a month as didn't want to jeopardise my working on Grange Hill, so kept quiet for the time.

My first day on the show, I felt stupid getting on the coach as the old woman made me wear my stage school uniform although it was the Easter holidays. Straight away I felt uncomfortable. There were kids mixed from various stage schools; Sylvia Young, Barbara Speake, Italia Conti and Anna Scher. Anna's were the kids I bonded with the most at first as they were more like me; went to comprehensives by day and Anna's in the evenings. Over time I became friends with pupils from the others stage schools.

The first to speak to me was John Alford and I instantly disliked him. He asked where I was from and who I supported, so I told him Liverpool. He was Arsenal. He called me a 'fucking scouser!' If you'd told me there and then he would become one of my closest friends for over 35 years, I'd never have believed you as I thought I'd best avoid this chap! Little did I know the scripts were written so that we would become best friends in the show too.

The first few days were fine. I got through the rehearsals no problem. I was a bit in awe of some of the older cast who I'd watched over the years; the likes of Roland, Banksie, Zammo, Jackie, Julie and Fay. I couldn't help but wish Tucker was there though as he'd been my favourite. Every kid idolised Tucker. I remember I couldn't keep my eyes off the girls that first day, especially Lisa York who played Julie. Most would say Jackie or Fay, but I fancied her the most. She was so pretty but I don't think she realized.

EastEnders was filmed at Elstree so you'd see the cast in the canteen every day. Leslie Grantham who played Dirty Den was the nicest. He always had time over the years for little chats. Being away from home, it was comforting for someone like him to take an interest in me. One female member I won't name, as she may have been having a bad day, was less friendly. I asked for her autograph for my sister Zoe. She was one of the biggest stars of the show but refused me saying she was sick of it and now getting asked for autographs at work! It hurt me, her saying this, but I vowed there and then I would never refuse an autograph when my time came. If I could go back I'd fling it at her and say "Sod ye".

Aran Bell, who played Mr Scott, was a great guy and a great actor. His father was the fabulous actor Tom Bell, who my Nan loved. Years later in 1990, I worked on a film called 'Let Him Have It' and worked alongside Tom Bell. I told him I worked on Grange Hill with his son Aran, so he made a fuss of me during the shoot and made sure I was alongside him in the Legs Of Man pub with all the other actors. We got a Polaroid pic together and he signed it to my Nan, she was over the moon.

Me and Alford, however, still had this underlying problem to be solved. He was what was known as 'Top Boy'; tough little north London kid from the Caledonian Road. I was a shy, Scouse kid from West Derby. It came to a point that after a few days we slipped off out of rehearsals, out of sight on the grass verge of Elstree to have a one on one. I remember thinking; "I'm not a great fighter, never have been. He's not top boy for nothing but if I don't face him he'll wind me up forever." He must have knocked me down 3 or 4 times. I just couldn't get near him! What pissed him off more was that I kept getting up to try again! It was our Cool Hand Luke moment. This seemed to go on and on until finally he said something like "Scouse you're game; Leave it now son!" Then we shook hands. From that day on, we have stayed very close friends and have never fallen out. In years to come, he would go through some dark days because of the News of the World newspaper. Between the paper and a fake sheik reporter, they sadly ruined his life.

Meanwhile, my problems in my new accommodation were getting worse. I was getting letters from family or friends back home and they were open! The old woman had been opening them saying she needed to know what was going on in my life. This was the final straw! The next morning, I packed my bag early and left for work. My plan was to tell the BBC I'd had enough and wanted to go home. This woman had got to me that much, I was willing to throw the towel in as it became unbearable.

I walked out of Marylebone station to wait for the coach with my head down. I was thinking it's all over; gutted but could see no way out. I loved working on the show but my new home life was killing me. Then, out of the blue, a long haired, thin man with glasses and a Dr Who type scarf draped round his neck, appeared. Geoff was his name, but I always wrote it Jeff. Me and the boys would call him Mr C. He looked like a taller version of Woody Allen and was the most laid back person I think I've ever met and more intelligent than he made out. If I was to go on 'Who wants to be a Millionaire' he would be that friend I'd call. He approached me in the rain, with his famous laid back south London accent "Wotcha!" He was a chaperone on Grange Hill but we'd never spoken. He said he'd heard I'd had problems living where I was, from a few other cast members I must have told. I spilled everything to him. He was that type of guy you instantly take too and I felt I could trust him to reveal all. After he heard my plight and plan to go home, he said he may have a solution. There was a spare big room in his house in Brixton where he lived with his wife, Dot, and daughter Emma Corleone. I was welcome there he said, if the BBC and of course, myself agreed. A huge weight had lifted already and I gladly agreed, we just had to convince big Ron!

Later that day, we sat in Ron, the producer's office. I told him everything about the other place and he said if my Dad agrees to meet Jeff and is happy then it wouldn't be a problem. Let's face it he had no choice; we were a month into filming. They'd have to find a new Ziggy, then settle him in. The solution was right in front of him.

So I went back to Brixton that night to meet his family. Within 5 minutes I knew this was the place for me. His wife, Dot, was a lovely lady from the off; his daughter Emma reminded me of my sister. Bob Dylan was playing on his record player. I loved Dylan as my mother played him before I could walk. They were kind, hippy types and I lasted 4 years living with them; my whole time doing Grange Hill. We would move to Mitcham a few months later, but there's a couple of things that happened in Brixton worth a mention. My dad met Jeff the next day and they hit it off. They barely talked about my welfare; all I remember being talked about was music they liked and the bands both had seen (Hendrix, Floyd, The Doors etc.) That was, I guess, my dad's way of checking someone out; the music someone liked. 'Oh if he likes Hendrix he must be alright!'

My three or so months in Brixton were great; sitting on Jeff's roof with an older hippy girl in the sun, strolling around the busy market, sitting outside the Green Man pub with Jeff enjoying a shandy etc. However, one night scared the life out of me. I had finished work and came out of Brixton station to a riot! The summer of 85 in Brixton, the streets were on fire! I stared from the station at chaos and destruction. I could smell the fumes of burnt out cars and could see lines of police waiting to charge. The only thing on my mind was getting home and it was about a mile away. I waited till it seemed quieter, then ran as fast as I could across the road. Other people, black and white, ran too. I remember getting about 20 yards and realising dozens of cops were giving chase behind. Then a white young woman beside me was hit over the head with a baton. She fell as blood rushed out of her head. I had to keep on running; even faster now as I figured my life could depend on it. I managed to elude the pursuing cops and found myself on the front line surrounded by a mob of tough looking blacks. These were the core of the rioters as I found out seconds later when one got a cloth out of his pocket, then a fat bottle. He lit the cloth and seemingly in slow motion, launched the twirling firebomb through a huge furniture shop on the corner. It went up in seconds, all three storeys of it. This image has stayed with me forever. It was like watching a movie, except I was in it. Time to go I figured and bobbed and weaved my way to Hinton Road where my new family anxiously awaited. When almost home, I did find a box of 50 plugs under a tree, so Jeff never had to buy a plug again for a long time! Nobody prepares you for that experience, but I understood why those riots took place in Brixton for a few nights, as earlier that day an elderly black lady, Mrs Groce, had been shot by police and paralysed during a police raid. It caused outrage in the community so the uprising began.

After Brixton, came Mitcham, where a whole new adventure began for me; four years in this tough little South London suburb. Many characters and friendships formed. This place opened up a whole new world to me, and a very exciting one to say the least.

Chapter 3
Mr C

'All God's Angels come to us disguised'
James Russell Lowell

Filming had begun in the April of 85. A few months earlier, I was running around doing a milk round with Pat 'Errol' Flynn, ex navy man who before he entered a room would shout "Permission to come aboard sir" to whoever he was meeting. I was freezing my nuts off to buy Bowie albums with my wages. We had some laughs though, and many of his sayings I used in Grange Hill. I would finish in the December and my first episode would air in the January of 1986. I had to commute from London to Liverpool every 2nd weekend and I'd have a few days to see my family and pals. The last train on a Friday night was an experience, full of characters who'd worked all week in London, like me but hard work. Builders mainly. If I was in the mood I'd drink and laugh with them around the bar, if not just chill to Pink Floyd or read the latest Viz comic. I had roughly 8 or 9 months of remaining anonymous to the 8 -10 million Grange Hill fans. I had seen the others get recognised and I couldn't wait; the attention seemed great. The day my 1st episode was shown, my life would never be the same.

The move to Mitcham came in the late summer of 85 and I knew nobody. All I had was Jeff and his family and I had grown close to them. They were peaceful, caring and intelligent people, not just about one thing but many things. There were new subjects I became more interested in now such as politics. Jeff was very left wing and despised Thatcher just like my own father. Their love of music was a big influence on me. They introduced me to an array of diverse music I'd never really paid attention to, such as Otis Redding, Sam Cooke, Led Zep, Johnny Cash (Years later Folsom prison blues became my Karaoke song) The Sex Pistols, The Kinks, Mott the Hoople, to name a few. There were also movies; every evening they'd settle on the sofa holding hands and watch either a movie he'd recorded or a TV show. 2001 A Space Odyssey, A Clockwork Orange, Orson Welles films, taught me about Dalton Trumbo who was blacklisted but wrote Spartacus, showed me Woody Allen films, Burt Lancaster (my favourite being 'The Birdman of Alcatraz'), and film noirs which later I'd become obsessed with. They had a bookshelf full of interesting & wonderful books like 'The count of Monte Cristo' or 'The catcher in the Rye' that I could pick up at any time. They introduced me to Art by the likes of Van Gogh and Salvador Dali. I learned of Kennedy, Martin Luther King, Malcolm X, Anne Frank. Even the universe itself could be a topic of conversation. Many nights till the early hours were spent chatting about anything you could think of.

Jeff became my surrogate father and I miss him dearly. He passed away in the bleak January of 2006 aged just 54 of heart failure. It broke my heart. It was the first big loss, except for my grandparents. We'd kept in touch till the day he died. Many times I'd knock on his door at some unearthly hour whilst visiting London and he'd always let me in. "You know where the spare room is Wilson" he'd say and go back to bed. I even turned up with 9 pals in 89 when LFC played QPR, we couldn't get a hotel so all of us crashed all over his house. He'd visit me if I was doing a play in Liverpool or my 18th doo, they were there. So when I got the call off his beautiful daughter Emma, I was outside a college doing a course, it was disbelief. I just cried and cried and went home cursing the world and asking myself why.

My pal, the Duke, brought a bottle of Jack Daniels round and 20 cigarettes, I lived alone at the time and just drank the bottle dry and smoked every last cigarette whilst playing only Bob Dylan. I believe old Jeff was an angel sent down for me that day he rescued me from going home at Marylebone Station. The last time I had seen him was about a month before he passed away. I was in London for a night out and descended on old Jeff around 3 in the morning. There was the usual greeting of help yourself etc., then I went to bed. In the morning we sat together; it was early as I had to catch a train. I had my last smoke with him and chatted about how we both were. When I got up to go, he gave me the biggest hug anyone had ever given me; he wouldn't let go. It was like he wanted to give me one last hug to remember. Maybe he knew this was the last time we'd hold each other, but one thing was for sure we never saw each other again. It crippled me for a long time. My guru, my Merlin, my Gandalf and my Ben Kenobi had left me. His family were heartbroken and shocked to the core. Years later Emma asked me to walk her down the aisle when she married Dave's nephew David, (Dave comes later). It was hard to step into old Jeff's boots so I mimicked him for the speech, I had to make em laugh, the only way I could do it. Luckily it worked.

To quote the Angel in It's A Wonderful Life;
"Strange, isn't it? Each man's life touches so many other lives. When he isn't around he leaves an awful hole, doesn't he"

No amount of money bought a second of time.

Once I got mugged by about 8 guys, when I going to meet Lee (Zammo) at his boxing gym he went in Hoxton, but whilst at the Elephant and Castle I got mugged. Wrong place, wrong time ~ story of my life! I wasn't badly harmed, but I was upset and shook up afterwards and came home cursing blacks. I remember old Jeff explaining not every black person was like this and I was just unlucky to meet these. I took on board what he said as it made sense; 'If 8 white guys had done it, would I hate all whites?' is the simple way to look at it.

John Drummond, who played Trev, I never instantly bonded with. It was maybe 4 or 5 months before something clicked. We had exactly the same sense of humour and before long he could have me crying with laughter and vice versa. Soon he stayed every weekend, right up to the end. I have about 5 or 6 people in my life who have the ability to make me cry with laughter and he's high in the pecking order of this.

One of the things we found amusing was Jeff's second name Cummantwood. His original name was Jeff Wood but he found it bland. So he took the first part of his Polish relative's name; Cummanski and combined the two, making Jeffrey Cummantwood his new found name. It was a name a few of us sneakily ad-libbed into the show.

I recall one afternoon, a BBC director named Clifford Bottomley was on the toilet in the next cubicle to me while I was reading the Daily Mirror. It was the quietest place if you wanted to read; the BBC lavatory. I heard the door open and then somebody climbing up the cubicle. The next thing I hear is someone saying "Oh you're big!" and the reply "Yes John" from the director! Drummond thought I was in that cubicle, so got the shock of his life when he saw poor Cliffy instead. We'd be working with him for the next month which made it even funnier. I remember laughing so much I almost fell off the toilet. "Oh you're big!" was just a silly saying amongst the lads, usually when unexpected, as Cliffy found. When you're a teen you have a weird sense of humour I guess.

Another time, Drummond was spending a weekend in Liverpool as he often did. He loved it up here; the nightlife, Liverpool girls and my family and pals always made him welcome. For some reason I wasn't with them, maybe I was off for a few days so my Dad took Drummond to Lime Street to get his train home. In the middle of the packed out station he grabbed my dad and began to scream "Please don't leave me Mr Wilson, I'll be your sex slave forever and ever!" all over the station! My Dad didn't know where to put his face with everybody looking over. That was Drummond; madness!

We went through a lot together in London. On the evening of 18th Nov 1987, we were very lucky. We finished filming at 6pm as that was always the wrap time. As usual we walked to Elstree station to catch a train to Kings Cross, only this time we were hungry so popped into the Wimpy for a burger. We both ordered, but I ordered a plain cheeseburger to the annoyance of Drummond as it took much longer in those days. This caused us to miss the train we needed so we had to wait for the next one on the cold platform. When it did come it never stopped at our station but all we could smell was the strongest smoke I've ever smelt. It continued to Moorgate. When we got off we heard the news that a fire had broken out at Kings Cross station; the underground stop where we would have walked through! The following morning the papers said 31 people had died.

This was the first disaster I narrowly missed being in the middle of, the second being Hillsborough, 2 years later. This I watched from the terraces.

I had not had a panic attack or any form of anxiety, breakdown etc. from any of these scary things so far but all were at the back of my mind and in my nightmares. I kept everything inside. They would come out in 1991 and other manic episodes I was to go through. It's like they were stored for a later date, in a memory drive of hell.

Chapter 4
Fame

'I know many fine feathered friends, but their friendliness depends on how you do'
Cat Stevens

The remainder of '85, even though I hadn't had the fame bit was still exciting for me. I remember, once settled, the odd Saturday night was spent wondering the streets of Soho. Either my pal John, from my Everyman days, would come up or my cousin, Jason. It was seedy and a dangerous place back then, but we liked it. You could walk into a booth and put 50p into a slot and a woman would undress for you. Aged 15 this was a big thrill for us to watch a naked lady touching herself provocatively. Don't get me wrong, I'd had a few girls back home, nothing major; mainly evenings just kissing in church yards or round the back of pubs in Huyton; anywhere it was quiet. So to see these women for 50p up close was an eye opener to say the least.

One particular night it went wrong though as me and John managed to get into one of the seedy bars. I can't remember the exact details but it was expensive for a drink and £5 for half of lager and we didn't have much money. Seeing the pretty women sitting about, we paid the money as we wanted to be there. Then we were joined by one of the girls, then another. Before long we were informed we had to buy them a drink for their time, but we were skint! A huge doorman was called and appeared and I thought we were going to be beaten there and then! The girl rambled on about how we'd tricked her, when the reality was we'd been tricked. Luckily enough this doorman could see we were young and foolish, he asked us to leave immediately. I cheekily downed my half lager and briskly walked out and planned never to return.

Another night with my cousin Jason, we foolishly spent all our money but this time missed the last tube home so we couldn't bunk the tube, which in those days was easy. You'd get up close behind someone going through the barrier and simply go through with them, or one pays and you'd do the same trick, working as a team, so it's easier. But this night we were stranded so had to walk from the West-End to South London during a snowy cold winter's night, going through every borough and some tough neighbourhoods. It was like the film 'The Warriors'. As we bopped our way back, the odd gang would spot us and we'd start jogging. We made it back unharmed.

Filming continued at the BBC and John Alford and I still hadn't bonded properly, even though we'd had our fight. There was a mutual respect but we never knew each other properly, until an episode came up where we had to film all around London together. The whole episode was just me and him. This was exciting for me as I'd only seen Brixton and Soho, so the thought of seeing these famous London landmarks was a thrill for me. We shot on a boat on the Thames and had to scrap on an escalator on the underground. He said he got the better of me during the scrap, which I agreed.

However the following year, I got the better of him scrapping on a barge during our filming on the Coventry canals. He ad-libbed "Hope you know ye messing with the Bemerton boys now, son" which was a gang he was in, and I replied with "I hope you know ye messing with the big boys now" which Neil says in 'The Young Ones'.

When people ask me what was my personal favourite episode, that one could be a contender. It's certainly in my top 5 for sure. It took a week to film that episode round the greater parts of London. I'd seen the major sites but more importantly I got to know John. That's was all it took. In that week we had a chance to talk of our families, our mates, music, football (mainly arguments over who was best Liverpool or Arsenal. Though LFC in 85 were the most dominant team in Europe, so he lost that one! Although many cockneys reminded me LFC got their team banned from Europe after Heysel.) He warned me what to expect once I got on telly, to be on your guard etc. I can safely say after that week, I really liked John, or Shannon as his pals called him. My stage name was George Christopher but real name was George Wilson, whilst his stage name was John Alford but real name John Shannon. That bond as I've said has never been broken. Ever.

I was still commuting back to Liverpool every other weekend to see everyone. One of the best was Saturday 13th July; Live Aid. It was a typical hot summer's day in July, I don't think anyone expected it to be as spectacular as it was. With the best musicians on the planet playing all day we should have known better! Most people say Queen were the best that day, and I do admit they were brilliant, but for me U2 stole it. Many people hadn't heard of U2 except for maybe the odd song, but after Live Aid everybody knew them. Bono getting the girl out of the audience to dance is one of my favourite rock moments ever.

Funnily enough, many years later in the mid 90's, I was in Dublin with my sister Zoe, her boyfriend Lee the Flagger and a Scandinavian lady friend of mine, Christine. Now I knew U2 had a night club called The Kitchen, so on the Saturday evening I rang the club and asked for the manager. I did a trick that I would often do to get into places and be looked after. I would pretend I was an agent and say that George Christopher was in town etc. Luckily Brookside had not long finished so I could use Grange Hill and Brookside now.

"Yea hi it's Eric Bingo here from Bingo Management, could I speak to the manager of the establishment please?" Once put through I'd continue: "Hi Eric here. All it is, I've got George Christopher from Grange Hill, and more recently Brookside fame, in Dublin right now with a couple of actors and actresses doing a movie, was wondering if you could possibly squeeze them on the guest list this evening?" Luckily the manager was a big Brookside fan and told me to ask for him. I told him "Mr Christopher will most appreciate this gesture."

I prayed U2 were going to be there and I'd meet

them, as I'd bought every album they ever made. The owner was great, he took us upstairs and said the words I didn't want to hear but some I did want to hear.

"Unfortunately the band are touring at the moment which is a shame because we all watch you on that telly up there" (pointing to a TV) "This is where the band sit (A beautiful wooden oak table) you guys can sit on it all night. This guy here is your personal bodyguard for the evening; he'll be no more than 5 yards away all night, oh and you don't buy a drink all night."

I was gutted the band weren't there that night, especially hearing they watched me but the free drinks all night was music to our ears. My sister Zoe was on Johnny Depp watch all night as she'd heard he was there that night, but we didn't see him. Anytime a man moved she'd be staring, hoping it was him. So none of us saw anyone famous that night, but we certainly got drunk!

During other trips back home, nights were mainly spent in a pub called 'The Barrys'. The reason was, it was the only one in West Derby village you could get in underage. We had our own little gang which grew over the years; not a fighting gang although when trouble did come our way the majority could deal with it. There were a few funny nights in the Barrys.

One particular evening, my oldest mate Fozz was drinking a pint of Guinness. This was a great opportunity for me when he went the toilet to slip my black sock in his pint. I thought he'd notice straight away to be honest but he never did! He kept sipping his Guinness whilst me and my other pal Buzz Williams laughed and laughed. Poor Fozz couldn't understand why everyone was giggling every time he took a sip. He was looking behind him, looking at his clothes, just never suspecting a horrific sock was in his drink. Only when he had got to the bottom of the glass he realised the nature of the laughter around him.

Pranks on Fozz had gone on from way back. When we must have been around 10 years old, there was a broken tree that hung over a muddy pond in Croxteth Park. It was a place we all loved as kids, as it had acres of fields, woods and ponds. There was about five of us; me, Stevie, Kunta Kinsey, Fozz and Kev. It was decided it would be a great achievement to climb the tree, shinny across to the other side and climb the other tree down, with the pond below. I did it first as loved these dangerous tasks, then the other two and finally Fozz. He was halfway across when I started shaking the tree frantically and the others followed suit. He couldn't hold on and fell straight into the pond below. Covered in mud he clambered out and couldn't even chase me as his keks were stuck together with mud and water. I remember shouting "last one home smells like Fozzie's Keks" then we all ran off leaving poor Fozz to have to walk through West Derby village drenched in muddy water.

Rewind even further to when we were about 3 years of age; my Mother took me and young Fozz to feed the ducks in Sefton Park. All was going well feeding the ducks on the edge of the lake until I slipped and fell in. However instead of just falling in I grabbed Fozz and pulled him in with me. This was his first water experience with me. Funny enough we are still close friends and later in life he played a part in what could have potentially saved our lives.

Moving forward now to January 1986 when my first episode aired. I was in London at the time and had been filming that very day. As I always did on the way home from work, I'd pop into the local arcade in Tooting Broadway. I played the oxo fruit machine games. I only put a couple of pounds in, nothing heavy. The show must have aired at 5.10 I believe, so I was in the arcade around 7ish after travelling from Elstree. I knew I was on the telly that evening, but thought nobody's going to recognise me after one show. How wrong I was, as a young black guy in the arcade said "Hey weren't you the geezer in Grange Hill tonight?" Then all his mates surrounded me. I didn't know what to say, especially with the Tooting/Mitcham thing going on. I just said "yes mate." He was over the moon and shook my hand, as did all his pals. Wow was all I could hear. I'm so glad the first time I was recognised was a wonderful experience.

To this day if anyone asks me if I was in Grange Hill or Brookside, I say yes and never deny it. If you deny it a few things can take place; they keep on asking you things or think you're rude not giving your time and denying it, can leave them puzzled for hours. So it's easier to just say yes!

Life was different now. Everywhere I'd go, anyone younger, my age or a bit older, knew me. I took it all in my stride. It was nice to be recognised. Mobile phones weren't about then and I think it would have been more of a pain if they were. Even to this day, people ask if they can have a selfie and it's no problem, if they are polite. It's no big deal as I was part of their childhood. I get it.

It's the jealousy I had to look out for. It didn't matter whether I was in London, Liverpool or on holiday in Spain, there was always one jealous bastard lurking somewhere. Learning to deal with it took time. Certain people I will talk about, looked after me in both cities. I became relatively safe but sometimes those people weren't with me so I was vulnerable and that's when the bullies strike; when you're alone. I was protected for years, one way or another but you cant be 24/7.

I even got slashed on one occasion in my local in Liverpool. That escalated to a doormen being knifed afterwards because I knocked the slasher down after he did it. Something was said about Brookside, next thing my neck is pouring with blood. He came looking for me with a machete but I was in a separate room being cleaned up by the bar staff and Big Al who missed it. For 5 minutes I was on my own, all it takes. Thankfully a large family from Anfield who controlled the doors sorted this problem, and I thank them. To think I'd drunk in the back streets of Marseille, drunk on the Falls Road in Belfast, Sandy Row, Toxteth, The East End, the Gorbals in Glasgow, walked through the Bronx etc. but I was to get slashed in my own village, just missing my jugular! The Dr told me I was very lucky as he stitched me up afterwards.

My Nan used to always say "Be most on guard in your own backyard." How right she was. So it's not all glamorous. When I walk in a room I check everyone out within 20 seconds. Any potential threats or past nutters, I'm out of there now, too old for all that. I wore a baseball cap by day and still do so I can tilt my head if see a potential threat coming. Regardless of this, I can honestly say 99% of people have been nice over the years.

I know I'm not the only one who's had to deal with the jealousy; Alford and Drummond did too. Mark Savage, the guy who played Gripper, got it worse than anyone as he was a racist character, so imagine the life he had as a kid. My mate Jay, who played Rod in Brookside and went the Everyman with me, had constant battles because he played a cop. I'm sure countless many others have been through it too. I just went to many rough and ready places, so I was bound to come across members of the bum of the month club. I'm more careful now plus I can't drink due to the medication I'm on, so pubs don't interest me as much. Like I say, fame can be a wonderful thing if you know how to handle it.

The trick for me is to get on the level of the person who approaches me. I try and suss them out quickly and whatever makes them tick, keep it ticking! Make 'em laugh usually a good one to avoid a possible unnecessary scrap.

Everyone has a level, whether I'm talking to a millionaire like Phil Redmond, or a homeless guy like Skully who resides in a wheelchair in town, I find their level.

To quote Bob Dylan; "Being noticed can be a burden. Jesus got himself crucified because he got himself noticed. So I disappear a lot"

Chapter 5
Gypsy

'It's easy to be a tough guy when no one's going to come knocking on your door.'
Pete Hamill

The following 4 or 5 years were probably the most exciting time of my life. I'd done my first year on the show and was being kept on so I was happy. I could handle living away from home, I had friends in the show and girls were showing much more interest. I had money in the bank, nice clothes, holidays abroad, the best stereo system I ever wanted and every Bowie album. What was there not to be happy about? But things got more interesting once I'd been on the actual TV, as that's when I encountered even more interesting people and places.

1986 was an important year for Grange Hill as it had the heroin storyline with Zammo. They cleverly showed how you can overcome the addiction. Lee Macdonald played this to perfection. He had done his research and when it was aired, shocked a whole generation. This is testimony to his performance. Years later when I played Little Jimmy in Brookside, I was killed off to show how dangerous it can be to get involved. Also that year Grange Hill won best children's tv programme. I remember the producer Ron telling me and a few of the boys he was lining up to meet Princess Diana. I asked what was she like. He replied "She's more beautiful up close than in any tv or newspaper you will ever look at"

So you've got the whole Zammo thing going on, then 'Just Say No' kicks off and goes to no 5 in the charts. Nine of the cast went the White House, but not everyone can go. Sadly I didn't but I wasn't connected to that storyline, so it was mainly the older ones and a few younger. It was the ambassadors of the show and sadly, me, Alford and Drummond were not! I mean, would you really want to take a man to meet the president's wife, who on occasions, would ride the subways and when the tube comes into a packed station would drop his trousers and push his naked buttocks up against the window so it would glide past the awaiting commuters, like Drummond did once? We were a bit pissed off we weren't going as I always wanted to see America. Many years later I would go, with my partner Mel, to New York which was amazing, and again to take our son Kirk for his 18th. So I did get to see the USA in the end, and thought it was the most exciting place on earth.

So it's all crazy, all go, and all good. I still hadn't made any friends in Mitcham as I'd not really gone out round there. All my mates were back home and me and Drummond hadn't explored Mitcham yet. One night, I thought sod it, I'll go and play pool in the local called the Nag's Head. Before long I got chatting to a couple of lads. One of them was huge and a good few years older than me. Colin I believe was his name. They invited me to go to a club with them called the St Helier's Arms in Carshalton. Now I thought the hatred between Tooting and Mitcham was bad, but the rivalry and hatred between Mitcham and Carshalton was much worse. These two boroughs hated each other as I found out that night. On one side, you had all the Mitcham people and the other the Carshalton crowds. You could cut the atmosphere with a knife. Within an hour of being there, Colin started fighting the bouncers. He was picking them off like flies. I don't know what it was over, but remember my heart was pounding as I'd come in with the guy!

They somehow got him out. I felt uneasy as his mate had vanished too, so figured I'd best cut loose now. It was very uncomfortable to say the least, sitting in the middle of two rival gangs. I got outside and walked about 20 yards. To this day I can still feel the feeling that struck me from behind, like a train. A local from Carshalton came from behind me and punched me so hard in the face I hit the ground. My legs were like jelly; I couldn't stand up if I tried. I just stared at him as he shouted 'Mitcham wanker.' He was quite big too, much bigger than me.

I was waiting to be finished off, when out of nowhere a few lads from Mitcham came over. London Gypsies I was to learn afterwards. One of them was quite a well-known fighter in his day with the wonderful name of Eddie Crockett. He chased my attacker with a big gypsy who became a good pal called Big Les, from a massive family; the Harding's. The others asked if I was ok and that's when I first met Nev from the Young clan. Three gypsy sisters fussed over me, wiping the blood from my lips.

They somehow got me to my feet and into a cab. We went straight to a gypsy site and into a beautiful caravan where the girls lived. This caravan had crystal chandeliers, a beautiful drinks cabinet, lovely glass tables, outside Mercs were parked up, not what one would of expected. There I was made welcome, as an old gypsy woman, their grandmother, gave me a brandy as I got cleaned up properly. Months later she would read my palm, at the time it made no sense, it does now 30 odd years later.

Me and Nev were driven home; turned out he lived opposite me. Nev was to become my first Mitcham pal and I still see him to this day. They didn't know I was in Grange Hill when they saw me slumped on the floor surrounded by this bully and his mates. Once I'd got up and spoke, they recognised me, but it didn't matter who I was. They had seen someone in distress and outnumbered. If they hadn't come when they did, he would have gone in for the kill, and I would have been beaten much worse. I laughed to Nev the next day saying "I wouldn't mind, I'm not even from fucking Mitcham!"

So once I'd met Nev, or Ned as I called him, he introduced me to all his friends; male and female. I have many fond memories with these people. The gypsy girls had a tendency to be wild, but were great fun.

The one gypsy who stood out the most though, and wilder than anyone I'd ever met, was Dave or Mr T as I called him. He was somewhat of a local legend. I would hear stories about him for years off different people. To have him as a friend was very valuable to me being famous and him for different reasons. He was once King of the Gypsies. I'd been told by many the old fair grounds wouldn't let him in. They had posters of him to keep out because he'd turn up and get in the ring and knock the gypsy out who you had to beat to get a £1000 cash. Dave kept turning up at different fairs in his prime and making a quick buck. He'd done time a few times for armed robbery. He was also famous for balancing a pint of beer on his head and doing 50 press ups without spilling a drop. Everyone in Mitcham knew him, loved or feared him; take your pick. You can see after the night I'd had outside the Arms why I needed people like Dave, and he liked to show me off too so it worked both ways.

The night we met was in a pub called the Buck's Head. He was always immaculately dressed. He had a black suit with an open white shirt and gleaming leather shoes, plenty of expensive gold jewellery and very short cropped hair, not shaven. He wasn't a particularly big man but wiry stocky and athletic. You knew by looking at him you wouldn't want to get on the wrong side of him. He reminded me of Bob Hoskins in the Long Good Friday. My favourite British gangster movie.

So Nev introduced us and we hit it off. We got on and he asked about the incident in the Arms the weekend before, so I told him. He said come with me tonight. We went. The first thing I noticed was the doormen who were all skinheads, all looked sheepish. Not one asked for the admission into there. They all put their heads down; about 10 big skinheads! Nor me, because I was with him.

Once inside it was like Goodfellas; people coming over to him, drinks passed over, the owner shaking his hand and mine. "See this little man, if he ever comes in here without me make sure he's alright" he told the owner. I liked all this. It felt good to be in this man's company. Within an hour, we must have had 50 people in our company. They were mainly Mitcham people, some my age, some his age (which would have been about forty). Mostly gypsy folk, but all looked like they could handle themselves. However he was the main one and they knew it, as did he.

The kid who knocked me down was in the corner with about 10 of his mates. He looked like he'd seen the devil. He was putting his head down every time I looked over. Maybe wondering if I recognised him and if I did, had I come to get him badly beaten (which he more than likely thought)? I went to the loo. I hadn't pointed him out to Dave and this huge gathering of gypsy hard men I'd suddenly found myself in the company of.

Whilst I was washing my hands he came in and approached me. He had fear in his eyes and apologised profoundly for what happened. He blamed drink, thought I was someone else and blah blah..... I had two choices; tell him where to go because you're getting it or shake his hand and say forget about it. I took pity on him and shook his hand and said don't ever do it again but tell all your Carshalton mates, as next time I won't be so forgiving.

My mate Nev could never understand why I never let him get beaten up that night, especially after putting me through the hardest punch I've ever received, but it just wasn't in me. Like I say I hate fighting, unless I really have to. To have a whole gang of gypsy lunatics beat him up and not me would be unsportsmanlike of me. To quote Gandhi "An eye for an eye will leave the whole world blind." which I kind of understand but don't fully agree with. If someone harmed a member of my family would I let it go? But it's still a great quote and the only way to get world peace, but someone gotta let go...

So Dave was in my life and he took me out of Mitcham and introduced me to other places and people. The Old Kent Road was one. We had many a night in the Frog and Nightgown or the World Upside Down. Occasionally, another was the West End, where you had the Hippodrome and Stringfellows, although I was never fond of the Stringfellow establishments as it was all money money money and it bored me.

Dave looked after Freddie Starr on some tours so I met Freddie a few times. He was very funny as you'd expect, but always taking the mickey out of me. I liked Freddie. Dave soon introduced me to his family, including his brother Mickey, who gave me a gold watch for appearing at his kid's birthday party.

I liked the Gypsy people, loved being around

them. Constant laughter. You see documentaries on tv and it doesn't always paint the picture of how they really are. I'm not a gypsy but they looked out for me. Yes it impressed other people when they saw them with a Grange Hill star, but there were plenty of other moments away from the nightlife; like sitting in some of the caravans for an afternoon. Not scruffy little caravans, I'm talking about big ones with beautiful chandeliers and expensive glass tables, drinks cabinets etc. The only thing I didn't like was some had little birds in very small cages hanging outside their immaculate caravans. I never knew why, I never asked. Good luck maybe? They certainly took me under their wing and I embraced it, because I could go in any pub or club in the area and people left me alone. They would shake my hand, and say hello; no more jealousy, no bullies, no more knock downs, in fact no one bothered me whilst I was around these folk!

One night, I was so drunk and I could be a pain in the arse in this state (like a lot of men with too much ale in them). Some idiot was annoying me. I can't remember why or what was said but I wanted to confront him and Dave looked into my eyes and simply said "You don't get paid for fighting." Looking back he was right, whether you win or lose nobody is gonna come up to you and give you a wad of cash. It took a few years to sink in, but it's right.

One particular afternoon I sat in Dave's apartment, I had tons of fan mail in a bag I'd been given by the BBC earlier. He started browsing through them, then picked up the phone and began ringing these young fans one by one, pretending to be from the BBC and saying "We got your letter for Ziggy here, he wants to say hello". They couldn't believe it, some thought it was a joke but most when they heard my voice got excited or cried in shock. It was the last thing these young fans expected. It was a nice touch by Dave boy, we must of rang about 20, I would never of thought to do that. One more thing about this character was I never saw him fight; he never had to. I saw him balance a full pint of lager on his head and do 20 press ups in the middle of a cheering pub but never saw him throw a single punch.

Chapter 6
The Baby's Bottle

'I know not with what weapons World War III will be fought, but World War IV will be fought with sticks and stones'
Albert Einstein

One of the things I enjoyed on my weekends home was to have a drink on a Sunday afternoon with my Grandad (Jeepers I called him) He was born in 1912 and my Nan always said there was 2 disasters in 1912, the Titanic and the day my Grandad was born. He always had two pals Jack and cousin his Pip with him. My Dad would join us too and he kept this ritual up until my Grandad drew his last breath. These were men who'd been through the 2nd World War and had been through much worse than I have. They barely spoke of it, at least not to me, whatever horrors they had seen they kept to themselves. Especially Jack. He was one of the soldiers who liberated Belsen (Nazi concentration camp). My Dad said when he arrived home from Belsen and went the pub to meet my Grandad and cronies, they asked him how it was and he replied "I don't want to talk about it, don't ever ask me about it again." So they never did, and he never spoke about it for the rest of his days.

My Grandad was a very careful man with his money. He stashed his money up chimneys as never believed in banks. My sister Zoe went to America for 3 weeks (to Hawaii, San Francisco and Fresno) to see the Wilson family who emigrated to Fresno in California, on the Lusitania in the early 1900's. My Nan Evelyn went in the 60's, so Zoe was following her steps. I've never been. My Grandad gave her a fiver towards her spends. This I believe sums up just how careful this man was.

One time, my Dad comes in with a Liverpool Echo and my Grandad had already bought one; so he rushed the shop to take it back! When he was younger, my Dad remembers seeing my Grandad getting ready to go on holiday. My Dad noticed Grandad was fiddling with his own underpants and asked what he was doing. He said he was sowing his money to his underpants. My Dad curiously asked why and got the response: "If any French bugger wants to rob me, he'll have to saw my leg off." My Dad was to learn he'd done this in Africa and India during the war, and continued all his life.

My grandad had many a story from when he spent time in North Africa in the RAF. One day he got a telegram saying 'Jimmy is dead come home.' This was a shock, but the shock was a confusing one as he had two Jimmy's in his life; an Uncle Jimmy and his brother Jimmy. Now you wouldn't want to wish anyone dead, but he could only pray this was his Uncle not his beloved brother. So for two days, which is what it took to get back to Liverpool, he prayed and prayed it was his older uncle not his younger brother who couldn't go to war because of his sight.

The Grafton a dance hall at the time, but underneath was an air raid shelter, at the top of

Tuebrook near Kensington were all my family were from. The Wilson family were all gathered in the air raid shelter; my Auntie Winnie, my Nan Evelyn, Jimmy, my Grandad's brother and his baby (also called Jimmy!) and a few others. "Oh no I've forgot Little Jimmy's bottle" said Winnie. Jimmy said he'd go and fetch it as it was quiet. They all pleaded with him not to go, but he rushed off saying he'd be fine. He got to near their family home on Vivian Street in Kensington, then the Luftwaffe dropped a bomb. Jimmy was killed instantly. Just like that - over a baby's bottle. This was the news that greeted my Grandad when he returned home from Africa; the outcome he dreaded. My Dad told me this, as his mother, my Nan Evelyn told him. My Grandad George never spoke of it to me.

Forward in time to 11th Sept 2001. I had an Uncle Martin who worked on Wall Street. He was a very clever and successful business man. My Grandad loved him, worshipped him as he'd done well. All my family had worked hard all their lives, but he lived in the Big Apple and travelled all over the world on business so he'd love to hear his tales, like mine. So Martin is due for a meeting in the World Trade Centre, around 9am and on time. He had his baby girl in the back of the car; she was to go in a children's crèche either in one of the towers or nearby, I'm not sure. He got halfway there, still on time, then realised he'd forgotten the baby's bottle! He had to turn back and make his way to his apartment to retrieve it. This delayed him long enough not to be anywhere near the North Tower which was engulfed in smoke from the worst terror attacks in human history. He could see it as he was stuck in traffic on one of the avenues with the baby's bottle on the seat beside him.

So those days spent in a bar, in the Adelphi, were fully enjoyed; old gentlemen always smartly dressed telling stories and jokes. There is one story about him I love which shows the man he was. It's known as the Zulu story.

He was in Durban during WW2 at one point and when he arrived saw a Zulu standing by the port with an old wooden rickshaw. He decided this man could be handy here, as after hours or maybe days of travelling he needed a drink. He asked the Zulu to take him round all the bars in the rickshaw to wet his whistle, so to speak. He went to the first bar but noticed the Zulu never followed him in. During a conversation with the bar man he was told they weren't allowed in any bars. So my Grandad orders a whisky and starts drinking, but keeps looking back at the Zulu outside on his own in the heat. He figured he'd get him a whisky and took it out to him. They finished their drinks and my old Grandad Jeepers climbs back in the rickshaw to the next bar, and same again, gets him another whisky. I don't know how many bars were visited this day, my guess around eight to ten. At the end of it all the Zulu was so wasted he couldn't stand up. He was three sheets to the African wind. Jeepers had to put the Zulu in the rickshaw and take him back to his village, to which he somehow pointed the way! Now I don't know how many white men walked into this Zulu village in the past but I'd bet none with a drunken member of their tribe in a rickshaw. Apparently his wife and half the village were all waiting for this man as he was expected home hours earlier. My Grandad, the man that he was, paid his wife for the tour and made his way to base camp. That is my favourite story of Jeepers and I have a black and white photograph of the drunken Zulu sprawled out in his rickshaw with my Grandad holding it up, grinning profoundly.

In 1992, me, a surfer looking girl I was dating, my Mum and Dad, sister Zoe & her crazy boyfriend Ashley and Buster the Jack Russell all went to live with my Grandad. It was like the Walton's. In 1990 My Nan had sadly passed away, peacefully as she sat up in bed. I had to tell my Dad who was walking Buster that day. Twice I've had to tell someone close that someone has died and it's one of the hardest things a person can do. Anyway, we all moved in to Darley Drive. My poor Grandad had years of peace and quiet but now he had madness, but I like to think it kept him going. Me and my Dad were with him the night he died. Sitting beside his bed; he left us like he lived his life, peacefully aged 91. I'm glad I was with my Dad that night and he wasn't alone. I liked to think his brother Jimmy was waiting for him at a platform on the other side.

Chapter 7
A Tale of Two Cities

'Life was meant for good friends and great adventures'

The last few years living in the smoke went as smoothly as could be. There were no real problems I can think of. Weekends were usually going out around Mitcham with Drummond or Chalk Farm where he lived or Camden Town, which I loved.

There was a massive difference I noticed between Liverpool and London which was fashion. You could wear what you wanted in London especially around the likes of Camden or the West End. In Liverpool, everyone kind of wore the same outfits, just different colours. Men mainly as girls were a bit more adventurous. My pals and I used to wear suits to go out in the late 80's and early 90's. We felt smart, but if we went out of town on Liverpool away matches we'd stand out in a pub. Locals wouldn't be suited and booted like us so it caused problems from time to time.

I recall in 1989, in Norwich, about 9 of us sat in a pub. We drove up in a mini bus we hired, driven by my pal Hagan. He was the toughest of us all but it didn't matter in here. We sat down with our drinks, suited and booted; hair gelled back except Molly who was bald and nicknamed Kojack. We were ready to go to a nightclub later, chatting and laughing away, doing no harm to anyone, when all of a sudden the biggest feller in the pub or maybe

Norwich for that matter came over. He had long scruffy blonde hair and an unshaven ugly face, was built like Hulk Hogan and stood well over 6ft. He said "You Scousers fuck off! " I just remember looking at him thinking "shit". The first to speak straight after was my pond dwelling friend Fozz who told him we were only having a drink etc. The big yeti wasn't having any of it; that's what we nicknamed him afterwards 'The Yeti'. What was worse, we were surrounded now by maybe 30 local lads, all scruffy like him in white woolly jumpers and jeans. Hooligans it turned out as we'd walked straight into a notorious hooligan lair and obviously this Yeti was the leader! The whole pub looked over and fell silent. More locals surrounded us. There was no way we would get out alive if anyone threw a punch or said the wrong thing. Even Kojack kept quiet as he knew this was a no win situation and he liked a scrap now and then. So we stood up - it was an Animals situation 'We Gotta Get Out Of This Place!". The drinks were left - except Fozz he couldn't resist downing his Guinness! We walked to the door close together but then they came at us. Punches were coming at us. It was a bit of a scramble but we got out. My pal Dools also known as Big Al caught one of them with a fine right as he held the door outside which luckily had a handle. (Big Al was with me the night I got slashed many years later on my neck, on the other side of the pub so missed the chaos but had the bright idea to get me out which in effect caused the doorman to be knifed and not me.) We dived into the minibus one by one. Big Al let go of the door and ran towards the vehicle as dozens came out behind giving chase, "Hurry up

Turkey legs" shouted Whitty, the philosophical member of the firm. His long legs literally dived into the back of the minibus and we razzed off to safety. Me, Swifty and Kojack mooned them as we drove away. Anyway LFC won 1-0 in the fight to win the league the next day. As Rik Mayall's final words in 'The Young Ones' said "phew that was close!"

We weren't hooligans; going to see LFC was an adventure. We loved a laugh and joke more than anything, going to new towns or cities, visiting new pubs and clubs, meeting different girls etc. The same gang would go Tenerife, Benidorm, Magaluf, Malia, Ibiza etc. and those holidays were some of the funniest times of my life; every night out for usually 10 days or 2 weeks. These holidays had everything you could possibly imagine, and everyone looked out for each other.

Fozz, as usual, was unfortunate a few times. In 1989 we were all sitting in a packed irish bar in San Antonio 1989 called Joe Spoons. It was a great place with live music. All of a sudden a guy ran in and across the pub. There must have been about 80 people in there but he stopped by Fozz and threw up all over him! This caused great amusement to the gang. He also had to trek back to the hotel to get changed; poor Fozz.

He had good luck one night in Malia, Greece in 95. We had both copped off with a couple of girls and left the boys to go back to the hotel in the early hours. We got to the lift and there were about 4 lads waiting for the lift. We were only on the 4th floor or something low so I said let's walk up as I couldn't be bothered waiting for the lift and it would have been packed, I hate being closed in; hate packed lifts.

The following afternoon we saw the lads who were waiting for the lift. They'd been beaten black and blue; one even had a head brace. You see, what had happened shortly before we arrived at the lift a few lads had pushed some local Spanish bikers' bikes over. They were outraged and followed them to our hotel. They waited until all four were in the lift, then sprayed them with CS gas before battering them with fire extinguishers. This time I saved Fozz's ass, without knowing it at the time obviously.

One pal I do miss is Brian. He was top boy in our school, In later years this was to become in handy for me as on many an occasion something would happen on a night out in town, especially during the Grange Hill heyday. Big Bri would usually sort situations out. He'd try and reason with these idiots first; he was a good negotiator of trouble. The odd time he couldn't reason with people, he'd have to use his fists. 9/10 times he'd knock them clean out with one punch. But he never liked to talk about it, all that much.

The town was a tricky place in the late 80's for me. There was always someone dodgy, so it was safer in numbers. I always felt safer in a pack; to go to town with just a girl was tricky. I'd only go where I knew the doormen. Hardman Street was safe for me.

All my life I have to be careful were I go. Even at a Space concert a few years ago, a coked up idiot started going on at me, trying to bait me, I was with Fozz again and had told him earlier to move as sensed trouble but he thought it would be ok. It never ends I always have to look over my shoulder. But I made that deal with the devil in '85. As I say though, 99% are fine, and to quote John Lennon 'Nobody told me there'd be days like these, strange days indeed.' You just gotta learn how to deal with it and like my illness it got easier over time.

When I was young I was foolish, especially when drunk. I know I was a nightmare at times. I believe many would be the same with all the money and fame I had. It was bound to go to my head sooner or later. When it ended and my struggles began around 89 to 91 I soon calmed down. By the time I did Brookside in 96, I was more prepared for the fame again as I'd gone without for so long; seven years in fact. I was so grateful and appreciated every moment and penny earned. I rented a house and moved to South Wales etc. Years earlier I would have just blown it in a few months, if that.

One of the greatest things about doing Grange Hill, was between 86-89 I did many personal appearances (PA'S) all over the country and got paid lucratively for this. It was also a great way to visit other parts of the country I'd probably never see normally. All I had to do was turn up at a nightclub full of screaming girls. There were a few lads here and there but mainly female fans of the show. I even had a separate agent who booked these gigs, which in average paid £500 to £1000 for a few hours work. Soon they became every weekend plus the odd week night. Besides this great new income, it also opened up trips away for myself and certain people. My Dad and his best pal Pape came on most if I was back home. Pape was an amusing character, quite quiet but could charm a lioness with his subtle words. One of the most down to earth guys you could wish to meet. A few pals might come too, usually Brian as if there was any trouble before or after the gig he'd resolve it one way or another.

John from my Everyman days, was always a handy man to have around; not for any fighting abilities but his way with women! He was more a gangster of love, a handsome slim fellow with a look of Paul Newman. He couldn't go wrong. In fact it was him that introduced me to girls when I was 14 around Huyton. He knew them all so simply let me know a few. You have to remember I'm a 17 year old kid, in under 18's discos with hundreds of girls who all fancy me because of me being on TV. Life was good! If in London, Dave would drive and a few London pals would go. I visited Corby which was the first, then Scotland, Yorkshire, Birmingham, Portsmouth, and Manchester. It was sometimes tricky as the football rivalry was still rife then so a good few of us would do them but I never had a problem there.

I did Sheffield once and it was just after Hillsborough in the summer of 89. It was an emotional one because I was at that fateful day in

April. I made a bit of a speech saying if any of your mams and dads let any Liverpool fans in to use your phones, to let their loved ones know they're safe (which I'd heard happened), thank them for me. Then the whole crowd of young girls and lads started chanting "You'll Never Walk Alone" I had a tear in my eye I won't lie.

We went on to, Leicester, Essex, Nottingham etc. etc. So we travelled up and down the country a merry band on occasion and most times stayed over in hotels. I'd spend a fair bit of the PA Money those nights or sometimes on weekends, living it up and getting to know the locals so to speak. Some days they'd be 5 on the bounce in different villages and towns; great for all involved.

The only problem was one of Pape's skills in life was he could play tunes out of his arse, I've never met anyone before or since that could actually break wind and make a tune out of it. People would gather round him at parties as he would demonstrate his skill. This was all very well but if you were stuck in a car with the man for long journeys which we were, it was hell on earth. Windows were constantly opened during all weather. On one particularly long journey from Hull Pape played his Bohemian Rhapsody with his arse, with others joining in, but it was my mother's car so she had to drive to work the next day, in total horror.

In '88 my mate Brian and my Dad's mates Kenny, Pape and Wally would all go to Manchester Maine Road, Man City's old ground to see Pink Floyd. It was the greatest concert I have ever been to. A warm summer's night packed with Mancunians and scousers mainly and not one ounce of trouble. The music, the light show, the fireballs coming from the stage, a huge pink inflatable pig flying above in the sky. I recall a huge joint being lit when 'Wish You Were Here' come on. I have seen some great gigs since including Ray Charles with Jay, Oasis alone, Amy Winehouse with our Zo. McCartney with Jay, Lynard Skynard with my Dad. U2 in 93 with my friend Nicola, Dylan with my Mam and Mal, UB40 with Mel etc.

I was never bored in-between living in London and Liverpool, always holidays abroad or just the Lake District or North Wales. Bunking in Butlins was a great laugh. Like in The Great Escape, we'd wait till dark and when a security guy would go for a walk we'd climb the fence one by one, whistling the next one when it was clear, then he'd climb over. We'd meet our red coat mate Steve who'd have a room organised for us. All we had to do was get in, and it never went wrong. On the way there once, we were driving up a steep hill in Wales. Jay was driving and Brian was in front, me and Fozz were in the back. Brian very rarely mooned, but he'd seen an opportunity he couldn't resist. A farmer was riding his bike up the hill, peacefully minding his own business when Brian put his window down and positioned his arse right out the window. As I looked back through the window he'd fell off through laughing. He was on the floor beside his bike in hysterics. It wasn't the reaction we expected from this moon; he'd seen the funny side as well as us I guess.

Years later on with Liverpool away matches, moon patrols came in place! We'd go through villages in a mini bus with 8 different arses out of 8 different windows. How we never got arrested I don't know. It just became part of life, mooning on trips away.

Pape sadly passed away in about 2004. He was 58, way too young, but got cancer. It broke my Dad's heart to see him deteriorate so rapidly and watch him go. I was again beside my Dad in Pape's living room where he spent his final days when he died. He lost his closest pal whom he'd known since school and had been through thick and thin with him. I was sad too as I looked up to him as well as loved him. I mean he'd been around all my life. My Dad still mentions him every day and misses him like a brother. Every man has one mate he confides in the most; Pape was my Dad's and he wishes he was here so much. As do his 6 daughters and son, and wife Doreen.

Chapter 8
Roamin' and a Gloamin'

'I spent a lot of money on booze, birds and fast cars. The rest I just squandered'
George Best

When I was in the Grange Hill limelight I did a fair bit of clubbing. One of the first night clubs I ever went to in Liverpool was called The Coconut Grove. This was in a pretty tough neighbourhood and was surrounded by equally tough places such as Norris Green, Kensington, Old Swan and Anfield not far away. You had a mix of gangs of lads and girls from these areas downstairs, but upstairs you had a few Liverpool and Everton players, local actors and local gangsters.

I must have been 17; it was 1987 but I looked younger. I got in and it was the in place to be at the time. I was just chatting to Fozz and Buzz, Brian etc. when a man in a smart dark suit called me over. He asked how old I was, so I told him 18. I didn't know who this man was but he looked dangerous, not a big meat head type but the type who had a face and aura about him that you wouldn't want to get on the wrong side of. He laughed when I said 18 and pressed a bit more. He guessed I wasn't and I guessed he was the owner. I'm on the telly in Grange Hill I told him. I'm here as everyone says it's the best club around. Now he was interested in me, although he'd never watched Grange Hill. The fact that a new face had come in his club from the TV appealed to him. He asked a young barmaid did she recognise me and she luckily said "yea he's on Grange Hill". So, I told him a few tales of living in London etc. and he said "I'm Bobby, you'll be safe in here, come with me".

We went for a walk to the entrance where he introduced me to the head doorman; one of the biggest doorman I think I've ever met. He was as big as a mountain and his name was Brummie. He told Brummie if I ever come again, I don't pay from now on. VIP they called it. It did embarrass me every time I went afterwards as Brummie would shout "one VIP coming through" and everyone would look.

Now, I didn't know at the time but soon learnt Brummie had the reputation of being one of the hardest men in the city. Not many could stand toe to toe with this man. I should have known by looking at him. Although he had this tag he never threw his weight around though. He never talked about fighting as most real hard men don't have to. Like my pal Brian, he would try and do things diplomatically. If it failed, God help them.

Now you hear this and hear that about people, but I saw another side to this man not many would have seen. I take people how I find them, not others. Once I'd got to know him over the few years of going, he asked a favour of me. Now when a man like Brummie asks a favour no matter what it's gonna be I was gonna agree. "Sure Brum what can I do" was the most likely reply. "I have a very sick niece in Alder Hey, she has leukaemia. Will you come with me to visit her and the rest of the kids on the wards. It will cheer them up you being on the show etc.?" I never had to think, of course I agreed.

So, the following Sunday, he picked me up and we went to the hospital. I took some publicity photos in case needed and walked to the ward. His little niece was no more than four years of age. He made her laugh and giggle, this big giant of a man playing around with this beautiful poor sick child. Jenny was her name; I'll never forget it. It was a heart-warming sight. After a while he kissed her goodbye, then we ventured into an older children's ward. Most of them knew me so I signed and gave out my pics. Some were too weak or drugged to know what was going on but I'm glad the ones who did I cheered up that day. When we got outside, I felt gutted after what I'd seen, but the biggest toughest man I probably ever knew had tears pouring from his heartbroken eyes. He couldn't bear to see his little niece in there. I can't remember the conversation we had on the steps, only that I tried to console him, I just remember thinking you're human after all. All the folk stories didn't matter; you were a better man than all the tough guys around you. It wasn't my idea to cheer those kids up; it was big Brummie with the even bigger heart. Sadly he passed away April 2019 and I go to his funeral in two days. There I will say my goodbyes to one of the last old school doormen of the city.

Other places of note me and my pals frequented were the Cavern, The original Bier Keller where the brilliant band Groundpig played, The Wookie

Hollow, The Pen and Wig, The Cabin, The late Terry Philips Club, Huyton Rugby Club, The Broadway Club, The Casablanca, The Blue Angel, The Montrose, Ferrari's, The Underground, Plummers, Streets, Kirklands, The Gladray and The Pivvie in Toxteth for a late drink, The Yankee Bar, Pickwicks, The Paradox, Charlie Scott's, The Buzz, The State, The Quadrant Park and The Grafton, when needs must be. These are just the clubs, to name the pubs I'd go on forever, but in all these places many great nights happened when we were all young free and single!

A couple of times though, I was confronted and attacked if I strayed away from my pals during drunken nights. All because I was on TV. Alone I was vulnerable; in a pack so much safer. Walking home from town alone for me was my worst fucking nightmare in the 80's. As everyone left nightclubs at the same time (2.00 am), it was a free-for-all to get a taxi. Unfortunately the odd jealous drunken bully would spot me, usually with a gang so I had no chance.

Besides the PA's there were always other big events I'd have to do, such as the televised Soap Aid at St Helens Rugby ground and The Soaps cup at Goodison Park Everton FC. These were the biggest two of many events me and the cast got involved in.

Soap Aid was amazing at the time as you had all the major soap stars from Brookside, EastEnders, Grange Hill, Crossroads, Emmerdale Farm and Coronation Street. That was it back then, you didn't have as many as now. On this particular occasion I took a heavy mob; my Mum, Dad, sister and my Nan Eileen. She was a massive soap fan and loved them all except EastEnders. She was in her element sitting in the VIP lounge backstage chatting to all the soap stars she'd loved for years. She even looked like a soap star herself, so a few thought she was as she drank wine, feeling mighty fine.

We had to mime to 'Just Say No' which I wasn't looking forward too in the slightest but you had to do these things. Before we went on I noticed Ian McCulloch from Echo and the Bunnymen sitting there as they played that day. I wasn't into them at the time so never made the effort to talk to him. Years later, around 2015, I would get into them and seen them live at the Philharmonic Hall on my own. I just went off the cuff and got a ticket outside. After Pink Floyd this was to be the 2nd favourite gig. Although on my own I danced and sang along right through it. They were awesome live and so damn cool. I was on a massive high after this concert so my partner Mel had to bring me down for days. I would have been bouncing round the house blasting their songs had she not been there to be the sensible one. Being bipolar you can go too low or too high and considering I had no drugs or alcohol, I was as high as the sun, the moon and the stars afterwards. He sat right by me at the Soap Aid and I barely spoke to him. Even more insulting I never watched their set that day, what an idiot I was!

So, with my Nan and family settled, including my sister (also in her element meeting the Brookside and Corrie heartthrobs) me and the Grange Hill gang went out to do our mime! There was a good few thousands in the crowd that day. We went out one by one. I remember my heart pounding seconds before, but once out there I was flying like any stage I've trodden.

Then we had the Soaps Cup at Everton's ground, which was a special day. All the soaps from the time played. We lost to EastEnders in the final, even though we had Liverpool keeper Mike Hooper. They had ex Arsenal players running amok; we never stood a chance despite Hooperman's best efforts.

Me and Drummond wrote "EastEnders is shit" on the wall outside the EastEnders studio on our last day of filming to avenge this and all the moaning some of them did because of the noise we made over the years!

The girls won the women's cup and paraded a silver shield around Goodison as long as they could. So Grange Hill took something home that day. Great day!

So many days and nights were spent roaming and a gloamin' around the country doing various exciting things. I made a lot of money doing the personal appearances but blew it all soon enough.

I never wanted for anything but if I'd have been

more careful, I'd have wanted for nothing a lot longer. That's when my life became harder; when the money I was so accustomed too finally ran out.

Chapter 9
Over and Out

'How lucky am I to have something that makes saying goodbye so hard'
A.A. Milne

People have often asked me what are my favourite Grange Hill moments or scenes. There's a few, but to be honest it took me a while to get going and find my character. Plus it was freckle mania so I didn't feel 100% confident on camera at first. By the time I got to 16, they seemed to just go overnight. Sitting in the sun I got colour and soon they went. I got my hair cut shorter as it was long and scruffy when I started. Being in London, I dressed differently, smart trousers or Levi 501's with a blue silk shirt (I thought I was Mick Jagger) and black boots. Girls were starting to take an interest in me and fan mail was telling me this. So naturally I was more confident now, and it showed on the screen.

From my personal view, my scenes in the later years are better. I added lines from Heroes, a few of Rick's from The Young Ones, The Cuckoo's Nest, The Godfather, Fawlty Towers, Oz from Auf Weidersen, Bob Dylan songs, The Long Good Friday and Eddie Murphy laughs. We threw in endless sayings we had at the time and got away with it - how I don't know! After a while the directors just let us do it. I think it was only natural, kids imitating famous people in a playground, nothing venomous about it.

Drummond looked and felt better later on too with his red hair gelled back and smart suits. He even wore a brown overcoat at my 18th at the Limelight in town, owned by Ricky Tomlinson. That was a great night. It was a mix of my family including my Auntie Brenda. She was a model in her younger days and was high up in the Labour party mingling with the likes of Tony Benn in her time. There was also my cousins, Helen Shapiro who show jumps, and Justine who lives in Kent running her business. All my grandparents were alive. Zoe and her lovely best mate Kathy who sadly died in a car crash aged just 20 (a beautiful girl so missed). My Liverpool mates, my London mates (including Jeff and family), Grange Hill mates, Brookside stars and other random actors who just turned up to be nosy, were all there. There was also gypsies and a welsh rugby team (who sang to me). Jay's brother Gary from New York turned up in a Dr's gown with the drip still hanging as he escaped from the Royal Hospital to attend. Also there was a hypnotist, a doorman from the Coconut Grove Big Mickey dressed as Rambo, plus a few Liverpool gangsters dotted about. It was one of the best nights of my life and not an ounce of trouble considering the combination of characters. It was nice.

All my grandparents were alive then and they loved the whole thing too. Jeff and Dot were treated like royalty as they knew they'd looked after me for nearly 4 years. Jeff joked to me at one point, saying it was like the wedding in 'The Godfather'. You couldn't move in there and Ricky said to me years later, the most money the limelight ever made was on my 18th. That's fame! If I wasn't on Grange Hill, I probably wouldn't have half-filled the place, looking back now.

Later on that year, in the summer of 88 (my favourite year by the way) me and many of the cast went to the Isle of Wight to film for 10 days. This was probably my favourite memory. But it began with a memory that frustrates me to this day. We met the coach at white city and I needed to go the loo before we set off so I jumped off to shoot into the BBC toilets. I remember standing at the urinal and hearing the door go. A guy stood over the urinal beside me. I never looked at him. I mean why would I want to look at a man pissing? In a rush I quickly washed my hands and dived back on the coach.

"Did you meet him?" asked Alford. The coach departed.

"Who?" I replied. The boys were all listening now too.

"David Bowie you mug, he walked in the bog after you!"

I felt sick as I loved Bowie ever since I was about 8. He was my childhood hero and I could have met him. He was filming Top of the Pops at White City. I wanted to turn back and run in just to say I play Ziggy, named after you. I guess I'll never get another chance now. Years later, when he died he was one of a few superstars that i actually cried over when heard the news.

It was scorching hot when we arrived. We stayed at the Treetops Hotel. I got in the sun right away by the pool to get tanned for the scenes ahead.

There isn't one particular memory that makes it my fav, it's the whole 10 days of it. It was just a constant laugh with the two Johns and the rest of the guys and girls.

The first night I remember me and Drummond ended up in a nightclub and the owner recognised us. So the usual treated like royalty takes place and he kept giving us bottles of champagne, plus Tequila slammers every few minutes. I Don't normally drink champagne, a pint of lager and the odd JD and coke done me. Anyway I'm drinking this champers and tequila like there's no tomorrow.

At some point we've got 2 girls in our company and one's Chinese. I'd never been with a Chinese girl before, so made my move on her. Drummond was content because her friend was very pretty too. We left the club and decided it would be romantic to sit on the beach, under the moon and the stars with the sea coming in. Everyone is up for it.

I sat with this girl on the sand whilst Drummy wasn't too far away. I remember hearing his greatest jokes and stories with his booming cockney accent. I must have talked for 10 minutes then I started feeling a bit dizzy. I'll shake it off I thought. I was just about to kiss her, then from nowhere I threw up all over the place; the sand, my top and jeans and couldn't stop! I felt terrible, definitely the worst I'd ever been so far in my life.

I was so bad Drummond had to carry me across

the beach and back to the hotel, leaving the two poor girls behind. Obviously he wasn't happy about this, but got me to the hotel and to our floor. I felt like I was going to be sick again. There was no toilet and we were a fair distance from our room so I had no choice I staggered into someone's room they'd left open for some reason and I threw up in their bin. God knows who was in that room and what the reaction to this was, but Drummond got me outta there quick and into the room we were sharing. God also knows how I got up for filming at 8 in the morning. One thing is for sure, at all the parties, weddings or events over the years I have never drank champagne again, ever.

The other thing I remember fondly was something I'd never seen before. I was free for a few hours and wanted to spend some time on my own, so I sat against a rock, looking out to sea. I had my Sony Walkman and was listening to Pink Floyd's new album 'A Delicate Sound Of Thunder' whilst smoking a cigarette. It was the song 'Learning To Fly' that I was listening to, when a flock of geese; maybe only 7 in total appeared across the horizon and began to fly across the sea. It was like slow motion again, except a sight of beauty and not a man launching a petrol bomb across the Brixton horizon. I couldn't keep my eyes off them till they were a distant blur. The mix of Floyd, enjoying a smoke, geese majestically gliding across the seas of the Isle of Wight was a great sight. I never told any of the lads about watching the geese. They may have laughed but it was my little moment so I didn't want to ruin it.

One night was just spent with Ruth in the hotel room watching 'One Flew Over the Cuckoo's Nest'. Nothing raunchy about it, but Ruth had just lost her mother so was going through a terrible time. At the time I was obsessed with this film and the character Jack Nicholson portrayed. Ruth loved it too. The video was packed in my case so we watched it together that night. Me and Ruth were good friends by '88 and that's the way we kept it. It would have ruined our friendship if we took it any further. There was no capers even if we secretly thought about it. Strange though, that that film was to be my favourite 3 years before I'd set foot in any mental hospital myself. I probably watched it once a week and found it hilarious and tragic at the same time. I knew all Nicholson's speeches and funny quotes, and I used to impersonate him everywhere I went. Maybe it was warming myself up for what was to come, without knowing it.

One nice memory during that break was when I met a blind girl in a nightclub. I never knew she was blind until we stood up to leave and said "Hold my hand I can't see a thing" I would never have known until she said this. She was very pretty and confident and her eyes looked perfect; how would I know? We went back to her house overlooking the sea. Once in the bedroom I turned out the light and said "Now we're both blind."

Towards the end of our filming in the Isle of Wight signs were showing I wasn't 100% mentally fit. I began to break down crying for no reason. In the hotel room or during a scene I'd begin to lose it. I'd get away quickly so nobody would see. I remember looking out the hotel window whilst Drummond slept, sobbing my eyes out. I rarely cry, so this was strange behaviour for me. Once back to London I was fine; call it the Isle of Wight blues! This was my first warning sign. It would take another three years to fully manifest.

Another of my favourite moments was filming on the canals in Coventry in 86 for a week. More cast went on this and it was fantastic too. Not as memorable as the Isle of Wight but a good time was had by all.

The scenes around London which I've mentioned are up there too. Also an episode with a large black girl babysitting I look back fondly on. She was great considering her character was the last resort I go babysitting with. She took it all well and respect her for that, looking back.

Finally I also loved the episode running around the school at night with myself, Alford, Mauler, Ted and the caretaker Mr Griffiths looking for the Grange Hill ghost. Mr Griffiths was played by a man in his 60's called George C Cooper. He was an experienced actor, who'd done loads over the years. Everybody loved George and the boys loved his stories. My favourite story he told a few of us one day was just before 1964 he went for the audition to play the colour sergeant Bourne in the epic film Zulu. He got the part and was over the moon. It was only when he learnt the dates he would have to go and shoot in South Africa, coincided with the date his wife was due to give birth. He told them he couldn't do it. Nigel Green replaced him but old George stayed at his wife's side to make sure all went well for his first child. That's the type of man he was. So filming with him that night and the other 3 lads was a great laugh. That night, was one of my final shoots for the show.

Mr Bronson played by Michael Sheard was different from George, not as friendly but Alford and a few others liked to play poker with him when we were sitting about. I believe he cleaned the lads out a few times as he was bloody good at it. I never was; I always got mixed up what beats what, so just watched them. Michael had a go at me once for being late. It wasn't the first time, so I deserved it looking back, but I had to get a bus to Tooting, a tube to Kings Cross, and then a train to Elstree before walking a mile to the studios every day. Over 16 you make your own way now. So when he shouted and cursed in front of the whole cast, I wanted to bury my head in the sand. I knew I couldn't argue as he was right, I was late and everybody was waiting on me. Luckily Alford was late a good few times so it wasn't just me. Michael passed away on the Isle of Wight in 2005. He loved it that much, he retired out there. One thing I am so glad I did happened a few months before he died. I got his email off the internet somehow and thanked him for that day he yelled at me. I told him I've been punctual ever since thanks to him. He replied saying he was so glad to hear it. During my Grange Hill days I didn't respect him, but in later life I certainly did.

Saying my goodbyes in London was hard. I spent the last 6 months with a girl called Lorraine, she was 27 whilst I was 18. I would meet her outside Waterloo station with flowers I'd buy off the once great train robber Buster Edward's earlier. I found him a nice guy and was saddened 5 or 6 years later to hear of his death, and the way he died. Me and Lorraine were close but not close enough for one to make a move in either ones city. Still a nice girl and we had some laughs.

 I don't know who was the hardest; the lads from the show or Jeff and his family. It had been 4 years. I could have stayed and done a 6th form but I wanted to come home and leave on top. Whether it was a wise choice, I don't know but all I wanted was to be around my family and friends back home, now nearly 19 years of age. As they say, all good things come to an end. So, with a van packed full of my stuff I'd amounted over 4 years, I left. I didn't know it then, but I was leaving the best 4 years of my life behind.

Chapter 10
Fear

'Everything you've ever wanted is on the other side of fear'
George Addair

I always liked the element of danger. From an early age I was always the one to climb the highest tree or climb the conker tree from the top and shake the branches for the boys below. I was the first to cross a pipe about 30ft up across the old deserted railway. I would call bigger tougher kids names, so I could outrun or outsmart them someway.

The gang was Fozz, Brian, Jimmy, Ste, Kev, James, and Kunta Kinsey. There were other hangers on but that was the crux of our little gang. We were inseparable aged ten. Croxteth Park was our playground and we knew every inch of it; the ponds, the woods, the dens we made, the hiding places if need be and the old crypt at the back of St Mary's church we dared enter at times. We knew every tree in that park. There was usually four to seven at the most playing manhunt or hide and seek, climbing massive trees and causing Fozz to fall in ponds!

All my memories playing down there I look back at fondly. Except one time I came unstuck. The first was in 1980 when we were ten years of age. There were five of us to begin with but I threw a muck bomb at Fozz so he stormed off sulking. He was the lucky one. We usually stayed up the West

Derby end but this evening, probably about 7pm, we ventured further down into the park, which we'd never done this late in the day. It just happened without realising, we were out of our comfort zone by Croxteth hall. This was the first time I felt real fear.

Within ten minutes, we were surrounded by about fifteen older and tougher kids on bikes. I just remember hearing "Get them!" It was every man for himself. We just scattered and ran for our lives in different directions. I was always fast as a kid but this situation was to take wits as well as speed. As I ran I noticed my mate Jimmy being beaten by a stream; they got him first as he was closest.

Luckily I was a fair bit back so had half a chance. I spotted two huge hedges that ran parallel for a long distance. Me and my mate Kev ran down it; Kev was in front. Within moments of running down this hedge tunnel two of the gang were behind me giving chase. My heart was pounding as I didn't want to be beaten up, it had never happened before. I'd had scraps with Fozz since I could walk, but nothing compared to this sudden terror upon me. We got to the end of the hedges and Kev ran out first. He was grabbed instantly by I don't know how many and took the blows. I looked behind and saw the two gaining on me but couldn't turn back, so I stepped out surrounded by the rest of the pack. I knew I couldn't win. I was the smallest and weakest and had not the slightest chance against this crew. So I used the only card I knew to play, the sympathy card. Looking the biggest lad in the eyes who was sitting on a bmx bike I cried "I want my mum!" hoping they'd feel pity. The two behind had caught up and we're just about to grab me, when the big lad on the bike yelled "nobody touches the little one." The relief was immense, the momentary big baby act had got me off the hook. The leader took pity on me and I was saved from a sure beating that sadly the other three got that night. We never ventured that far again. Ever.

Croxteth Park was our playground but West Derby village was our base. There wasn't a lot to do but hang around. The wall of the church was a favourable spot to sit; out the way, high up and overlooking the church grounds.
We weren't in any Cubs, Scouts or Boys Brigade. There was no place to play pool or snooker. The only real place to hang around was Mr Young's video shop. He opened in about 1982 when I was twelve. James was the first to get a video player. I was so excited the first evening he got it! Me, James and Jimmy all watched 'The Life of Brian' We howled with laughter all the way through. I begged my Dad to get one and he eventually did. Mr Young's shop was only small but he had every film you could think of. How he fitted them all is anyone's guess. He also had two arcade machines in there, which he swopped games every so often. Mr Do's Castle, Mario Brothers, Dragons Lair, Dig Dug, Track and Field and Donkey Kong to name a few. Hours were spent taking it in turns playing these games, trying to get the highest score. Whilst waiting for my turn I loved looking at the videos and reading the back

to see what they were about. I knew every film on his shelves and one by one, I tried to watch them all until London called in 85. That was the only place our little gang could go inside of an evening; Mr Young's video shop.

Roll forward to about 1997, me and my good pal Stevie and a few others, Big Foot and Davey, were in Magaluf sitting outside a bar. I had seen this bald German looking feller I thought walking up with a girl. He had a tight pair of leopard skin trunks on; hence I thought no Englishman would wear them! Plus with a long beard, he had to be German. He was very muscular; the type that trains every day. So as he walked past, I shouted "Hey steroid head!" Bad move. He looked back, his face raging, but carried on walking. Maybe he can understand English I thought. It was forgotten about as he never came over thankfully.

A week later, back home me and my old mate Jay were in a nightclub in town. Jay went to the bar as I waited by a table. Suddenly I was grabbed, frog marched away and thrown into an empty room. It had remnants of blood on the walls. This was the place people would have been taken for beatings over the years. I stood up to face a stocky bald doorman who wasn't happy. "Remember me?" he kept saying. I kept looking at him and replied constantly 'no'. Then he put something round his hand, some kind of leather strap. I thought "Jesus, I'm gonna get crucified here. I can't fight this fellow. He's like a bulldog; hands bigger than his head!" I looked on the floor to see if there was something I could hit him over the head with as I knew I couldn't go toe to toe with him, but there was nothing. He was just too big and wasn't a doorman for fun. It didn't matter who I knew; all the London or Liverpool gangsters, doormen or Gypsies couldn't save me now! I was alone, besides if I named one, they could be his enemy or have hurt him so I'd get it worse. That's when it dawned on me, when it comes down to it you're on your own. Who you know means fuck all.

"I was in Grange Hill and Brookside maybe you're getting me mixed up with that mate," I hoped would work as people often think they know me not realising I've been on TV.
"I don't give a fuck, remember me?"
I still said "no" as I generally didn't know him at this point.
"Think back to last week" he yelled.
I instantly replied "I was in Magaluf last week"
He gave a chilling smile and said "So was I!"
That's when it dawned on me it was the muscular bald guy who I thought was German, who I'd insulted. The odds of this I don't know but the odds weren't going through my mind. What was going through my mind was how to get out of this one alive! Now I guessed he must have recognised me from the TV when he looked over that night, but I was pretty sure he never knew who shouted it, as it was quick. So I had to think quickly. I assured him "Listen, I swear I never shouted that, that night. It was my pal Davey." I said his name because I knew he never came out with us. So I continued "He was totally out of order. I even told him afterwards. I can only apologise for this cunt."

He looked at me unsure it was the truth. My heart was still pounding as he was right in front of me. He could have head butted me he was that close.

"You'd ruined my holiday" I remember him saying. Then finally I heard the words I wanted to hear "Go on fuck off" and unbolted the steel door to my freedom.

The relief filled my body as I walked out to Jay, who was wondering where the hell I'd been. I've never drank a JD and coke so fast after he gave me it! Shaking, I told Jay what happened. Then, one of the biggest gangsters in the city at one time called Charlie Seiga saw me looking all shook up. He came over and I told him what happened. He said "Stay by me all night. He won't touch you now" I'd met him once before, but this night was to reunite us and spark a friendship that would lead to him saving me a few times and vice versa, but in totally different circumstances. One thing is for sure, I have never shouted 'steroid head' at anyone ever since, and neither has Davey.

An unexpected great day in 88, was when me and Jay went to Wimbledon. He liked his tennis and was a decent player, I however was awful and wasn't overly keen on going to watch it. He convinced me it would be a great day and as usual talked me round. We got the train down there and queued up like everybody else. We waited in the line for a good few hours then we paid in.

We watched a few games in the cheap seats we'd paid for, then Jay had the idea to try and get into the more exclusive areas. He had a couple

Channel 4 passes on him which he's used at some Brookside event down the line, so we tried our hand. We called it the Jedi manoeuvre; find a weak willed security type and show the passes with every belief they are fine. You have to show no signs of nerves. We'd done similar tricks at the Grand National years earlier so this was similar. Star Wars is not far from the truth; there are people you can use your mind over matter on them, you just have to 100% believe yourself.

Before we knew it we were sitting not too far from royalty, actors and actresses. We were sitting among the elite of the country and it felt great. We even went into their eating area in a huge canopy outside where we enjoyed strawberries and cream with the upper classes. On a table not too far away, we watched Cliff Richard holding court around a table. Everyone was glued to his every word. He never came up for air!

The Lakes 88 was me, Jay and John, three days of pure bliss. All 18 years of age. Me on Grange Hill and them on Brookside. There's no need to go into the girls we met and those adventures as I've never boasted over those things. It's obvious we weren't choirboys and were young free and single so we lived life to the full. Some celebs or rock stars boast that they have been with a thousand women or more; so what?! If you've done it you've done it. Why the need to boast about it and make yourself look a twat? Nobody will shake your hand after hearing it; nobody's bothered except them.

I always said 88 was my favourite year, so many

good things happened. I can't remember one bad thing to be honest. But whilst in the Lake District, we were sitting outside a lovely pub by a river when we got chatting to a group a local lads. We had a laugh with them and one said "you can't come the lakes without doing the tree of death." We didn't have a clue what they meant but after a few light ales went with them down the embankment.

We came to a huge tree that had steps made out of small bits of wood leading to the top where a wooden ledge awaited. From the ledge you can leap into the river. My guess is that it was 100ft high. I just remember Jay saying "you do it first". So, the cocky one out the gang that suggested it, climbed up and without hesitation leaped into the river below, avoiding a few rocks below. No problem. Now Jay had to do it. He'd never backed down to anyone or anything in his life. So he climbed up and got to the ledge. He couldn't do it; he stood on the edge for what seemed an eternity but the height and risk of missing the river must've been playing on his mind. So I stepped in and started to climb. He was unaware and halfway up.

I said "Come on Jay we'll do a Butch Cassidy and Sundance kid"

This made him panic more "No No George get down for God's sake" he yelled.

I went to retrace my steps down but one of the Lakes boys told me you can't come back down, it's impossible, you gotta jump too! I didn't know whether I was intending to jump or just wind Jay up, but now I had no choice it seemed. I had to hold onto the big old tree until Jay jumped. Luckily he did not long after. He hit the water and got back with the crowd. I got to the top as carefully as I could and thought if I think about this like he did I'll never jump. I've just gotta do it. So I did; I got on the ledge, gauged the distance from the rocks below and did the leap of faith. If you asked me today, I would rather fight 10 gypsies in a field than do that now.

The next day, we were walking along the lakeside and got chatting to a couple who were canoeing for the day. They'd just been out so were relaxing. We asked if we could have a go in their canoes and they gladly obliged. Stupidly, without realising I got in my canoe backwards. John was beside me as we paddled out but after about 3 minutes when trying to excel in speed, my canoe began to turn over. I was underwater, again my heart pounding as for the 2nd time in my life I thought I was gonna drown.

The first time was as a young kid in Benidorm. I fell into a swimming pool, unseen by my parents. I struggled as I couldn't swim but luckily an old lady appeared and pulled me out gasping for air. The first Angel in my life.

So now, I'm gasping and struggling in a deep lake. I somehow Eskimo rolled up and saw John on top of his canoe, do the greatest dive off it; like he was Johnny Weissmuller in Tarzan. But he got too cold after swimming a few yards and headed for land. I'd gone under again, but this time and I don't know how, I wriggled out of the canoe. The couple who lent us their canoes, and Jay, were watching from the shore confused and in shock. I swam back to them catching my breath and fell on the stony ground relieved I was ok. However, the two canoes were floating away so the poor couple had to go and retrieve them. We joked about it all later in a pub high up on a mountain. But at the time, it was a frightening experience and I've never got in a canoe since.

The next time I would have to face water, and fear, again would be 32 years later in 2019 on holiday in the Caribbean. I was on a jet ski with my 19 year old son, Kirk. Both on together, I was upfront, no problems. We were a good few miles out when he asked to take control. I foolishly let him and within 10 seconds he spun it too fast and we were both treading water and the jet ski was upside down. My last words before we hit the water were "For fucks sake Kirk what have you done?"

Since the age of 9, when my Dad took me to see Jaws, I have had a fear of being in the sea. The film Open Water never helped either! I never expected this to happen as I'd ridden a jet ski many times in Spain years earlier with my pal Steve. I'd never come off, so the thought never entered my head that I'd go in. I froze in the water; the only thing on my mind was I gotta get out quick but how? Luckily my Kirk is in the Royal Navy and his training in water took over and he said "We gotta tip it over dad." So we pushed like mad, using every bit of strength I had, until it flipped over. I dived on in less than 2 seconds. He was on a little after. This was in St Lucia and when we arrived in Barbados I asked a local guy known as Chicken George if there were any sharks in Barbados. He said "No you only get the big dangerous sharks in St Lucia. Great whites been spotted and many bull sharks" I went cold knowing I was in that water for at least 3 to 4 minutes. Fear again, but knew what had to be done and dealt with it. I will never get on a jet ski with my son again!

I'm not a religious man, but all my life I've felt I've had somebody or something looking out for me. Maybe a guardian angel, maybe God, or maybe I'm just lucky. A lot of sliding doors. Even this year I went to play a charity football match for a young postman called Tony Lochrane who died of a brain tumour in Middlesbrough. The guy who arranged it, Mark, met me in a place called Saltburn by the sea. I noticed it had a really high cliff called Hunts Cliff. I wanted to go the top and look out over the sea; my tradition. I noticed on the way up many little plaques saying things like 'remember you are loved' or 'in remembrance of those who took their lives on Hunts Cliff' etc. I felt sad reading these messages, realizing this was a big suicide spot. Anyway, we got to the top and the view was incredible over Saltburn, a beautiful sea town. We looked like Frodo and Sam at Mount Doom in Lord Of The Rings, standing there. I wanted to get a photo near the edge. As I walked towards the edge, my foot went into an unseen hole not far from the edge. I lost my footing as my heart sank, but luckily I fell backwards, not forwards. In flip flops it could have been the end as it was slippery.

The drop was 550ft I found out afterwards. It made me think maybe not all the suicides were suicides but accidents like I almost had. I won't go that near a cliff edge again that's for sure.

Looking back one of the scariest things I've had to do was in about 2009 in Turkey. Me and my partner Mel and son Kirk aged 10 hired Quad bikes. On the brochure it looked a peaceful event on a beach. Kirk was on the back of mine as Mel rode shotgun with a Turkish chap. It was great at first but then we started going up a mountain higher and higher, there was no way of turning back and you could see the tops of the trees below whilst I drove this big quad up and up a narrow winding path, with my 10 year old son on my back. One false move and we're both finished. I've never concentrated so hard in all my life. I told Kirk "just dont speak to me till its over" My heart was pounding every second of what seemed at eternity journey. This was fear i had to contain as my son was holding on for dear life too..

Chapter 11
1989

'*On the 15th April 1989 24,000 Liverpool fans went to a football match, 96 never returned*'
Fact.

If I could wipe out one year off my life and never have seen a day of it, it would be 89. Grange Hill was over, I was home and living in my converted loft which me and my Dad had done. It was my sanctuary. It had everything I needed, but also gave me isolation from the world, which later was to be catastrophic to me.

The year started off well as I was invited to go on the Wogan show, live! Me, my lovely friend Ruth from Grange Hill and Sean Maguire, who later did hit Hollywood. He says I taught him everything, but I kept some things from him. I took my mum on this one. I figured my Dad had been on enough trips so wanted to treat her.

So we gets to the BBC and waiting in the green room I spotted Julian Lennon. I couldn't believe it, the son of one of my idols. I knew my Dad had war medals belonging to his great uncle George, so I figured that would be a good excuse to say hello and meet this fellow. We spoke for about 10 minutes. I liked him. He was a quiet, shy unassuming fellow, very down to earth and looked the image of his dad. The medals didn't really interest him. In fact many years, on my pal, the Duke, would see him regularly in Spain and tried to see if he wanted to buy them but he never did.

So I do Wogan; I was a bit nervous beforehand, being a live show; praying I wouldn't swear or say something stupid, but I never did. In fact, I had the audience laughing; relief..

Pretty soon the personal appearances ran dry. What money I had was spent on nightclubs, bars, casinos, hotels and holidays with the lads. After a while, the well run dry. Besides working on Grange Hill and my other bits in showbiz, I'd only had one job and that was doing the milk with Pat.

At nearly 19 I thought I could just walk into Hollywood but it wasn't gonna happen as I soon learned. I got a few mundane jobs that year but I couldn't get used to people saying "Why's Ziggy working here?" To be honest, I felt embarrassed. Years later this wouldn't bother me, but at the time it hindered me, so I never lasted long in any of these normal jobs.

My Dad was on my back at the time and it caused many arguments. Only years later I understand why he was on my case.

I had followed Liverpool to most of the home and away games in the FA cup that season with my pals and our hired mini bus. So naturally, the semi-final with Forest at Hillsborough was a must see game. It was down to Fozz to get the tickets for me and him. I said to him to get them in the standing area where we always go on away matches as the atmosphere was always better. He said "No, not this time. I was in the Leppings Lane the season before and it was horrific, I was crushed so I wanna sit down for this one." I trusted his word and agreed so he got us in the West Stand, right in the middle and directly in the middle of the stadium. It overlooked everything. Just me and Fozz went that day and from the off it had a bad feeling about it. From the second we got off the train, cops were dragging us out from walking down, searching and manhandling us for no reason. It didn't feel right, then.

I don't want to go into too much detail of what I saw that day or what I really think, as there's a blanket of silence right now as legal proceedings still go on almost 30 years on. All I can say is it was like watching the aftermath of a 16th century battlefield not a football field. I saw dead bodies being carried on makeshift stretchers by Liverpool fans. I saw the injured laying helpless, loved ones trying to find loved ones, people bemused and confused as to what was happening. I saw the without hesitation bravery and commitment of those Liverpool fans trying to give life on the pitch by mouth to mouth or CPR as there was nobody else until too late. I saw fans run with advertising boards used as stretchers. I witnessed about 50 cops standing the length of the halfway line doing nothing but fold their arms. I saw Hell on Earth. I saw what nobody should have had to see.

The only way to describe it was like watching the worst horror film imaginable, unfold in-front of my eyes. I had tears in my eyes and felt helpless, which is something that has played on my mind ever since. Why didn't I run down and get on that pitch and help with the other Liverpool fans involved when nobody else was? The families of those who died, the injured, the traumatised, the whole city of Liverpool in fact were let down afterwards by the Government, Police, the Sun newspaper and countless bastards since who've had their unwanted say in the media. Everybody in Liverpool knew what happened that day and who was to blame, but it was made so much harder by certain bodies. The loss was horrific enough but to be told they were to blame is inconceivable. The Sun hurt the city more than they will ever know...

There are so many great men and women who stood up against this injustice:
Terry Burkett and his lovely wife Anne who lost their son Peter.
Anne Williams who lost her son Kevin, has done more than anyone in my eyes. Her daughter Sara continues the justice campaign.
Sheila Coleman - I never met a more determined woman than her to fight the cause.
My good welsh pal Dean, who I met in a bar distraught after a memorial, marched to Downing Street with a petition for Anne Williams.
John Herbo, a survivor and constant thorn in the side to the justice system.
Jerry from the HJC shop who worked every hour God sent to raise money until he passed away recently.
Pete Carney, a survivor and constant campaigner also helped me deal with things I'd blocked. Trevor and Jenny Hicks who lost two daughters Victoria and Sarah.
Ian Hulme the chairman of the survivors group called the HSA, who wrote books and goes

beyond organising help for victims.

Margaret Aspinall, who is the chair of the Hillsborough Family Support Group and lost her son James, never stops.

John Glover who fought for justice till his last breath for his son Ian.

Amanda Tootle who lost her beloved brother Peter.

Lance and Matt who wrote the Hillsborough play,

Steve Rotherham the labour MP,

Andy Burnham the mayor of Manchester,

journalists like Tony Barrett and Andy Hunter,

singers like Pete Wylie and Mick Jones from the Clash who came up from London on the 12th September 2012 to be in Liverpool when the courts ruled in the families' favour.

These are just a few of the people I know or have had the pleasure to meet. There are countless others, including all the families, survivors and people all over the world who joined in the fight. To list them all I'd fill the book.

It took many years for the truth to come out, 23 years in fact. On the steps of St George's Hall me & Fozzie watched Anne William's, Sheila Coleman and Margaret Aspinall salute the crowd after the panel said the fans were not to blame, the police were. The truth that everyone knew all along. The whole thing would have been brushed under the carpet. There was a banner at some point in the Kop that simply read 'You messed with the wrong city' and they did. The fight still goes on as I write this 29 years later....

None of us talked about this day afterwards. All

our gang where there spread out around the ground. That night sitting in the Coconut Grove, we just sat in silence, no joking or messing round or chatting girls up. We just sat in a corner in disbelief at what we witnessed and went through. It's hardly ever mentioned to this day amongst the lads.

The following day, the whole city was shell shocked. Only three times have I witnessed this eerie silence of pure disbelief in my city and that was the day after Hillsborough, the day after beautiful toddler James Bulger was murdered in 93 (by two ten year old animals, and even that's a polite word) and finally in 2008, when innocent 11 year old Rhys Jones was shot dead. Each time, the whole city was silent and in disbelief. In all the three cases, silence turns to anger when the truths came out. Everybody was affected by these incidents including me. I wept with the rest for all those families above.

I have never spoke publicly about Hillsborough to any media, or my Bipolar for that matter. This is the first time I have spoken about these things except with those involved. Years later, in 1998, my lovely agent Cathy Toner got me in a play called 'Waiting for Hillsborough'. I didn't want to do it at first as thought it would bring it all back. I didn't want to re-enact what I heartbreakingly saw. but after meeting the chairman Terry Burkett (who I immediately took to) and the rest of the HJC group, and a great cast I decided to do it. The cast included my pal Steve, Danny Taylor who was also at the disaster, my good friend Gozzy and

Paul Codman (who I didn't appreciate at the time but working with years later, realised how talented he really was). It would help me come to terms with what I had seen and had many nightmares about since. The main aim was to bring awareness of what happened. It was the hardest play I have ever done. The tears I had to shed on stage every night were for real. I never had to act, they just flowed as I wasn't acting, I was talking about something that affected my mind deeply.

Later that year, I got myself in trouble with the police for the first and last time. I was foolish looking back. I lit a joint in a club that was full of off duty cops called The Cabin. The Rolling Stones 'Sympathy for the Devil' came on and I couldn't resist sparking it up. If I'd have done what he told me to do, there wouldn't have been a problem. Every now and then I liked the odd joint to relax me and to music as it enhanced it for me. So this fat cop says "Put it out or I'll arrest you" but instead of putting it out and ending the situation I replied "You can't arrest me, you haven't got your hat on." This infuriated him and he called his boys over. Jay, my mate tried to calm the situation but ended up scuffling with a few. Meanwhile I'm dragged out to a waiting police van as he'd called for backup.

I spent the night in the cell and was released the next day. The main thought going round my mind sitting in that cold cell was 'I hope this doesn't get out in the press'. Walking home that morning looking slightly rough, I went into my local newsagent to get 20 Regal ciggies only to see myself on the cover of the Liverpool Echo saying 'Grange Hill star arrested for Drugs' with a stupid picture of me grinning. The cops knew who I was and one of them tipped the press. I didn't want to go out after this, but my pals told me you gotta get out, don't let the bastards beat you. Face the music. Everybody thought I was on heroin, as never said what drugs were involved.

It hit the family hard this one, especially my Nans and Grandad's who'd been so proud of me over the years. A moment of stupidity and madness caused shame for a good few years. A momentary lapse of reason caused by myself. Certain Nightclubs wouldn't let me in for a while thinking I'm some drug baron or something. All I did was lit a joint. Some people who were normally respectful in the past turned their back on me.

I was glad when 1989 was over. The only good things I can remember were Wogan and me and the boys going to see Scottish band Deacon Blue. It was an amazing concert and I'll never forget a little speech the lead singer Ricky Ross gave saying how sorry he was about what happened at Hillsborough. It was a speech straight from the heart. The response was the whole crowd sang 'You'll Never Walk Alone' back. I know I had a tear in my eye and I'm pretty sure all my 8 pals did too, along with most of the crowd on that exciting and emotional night.

Years later I stopped smoking the herb, I remember Pape saying to me "it's brought nothing but bad luck to you" so I knocked it on the head.

A strange thing happened a few months later in The Cabin one night (I'd talked my way back in!) As I sat there with Jay and my Dad, two big burly guys who looked like army or cops ran in and beat the shit out of the cop who'd arrested me; beat him bad. All his so called cop-friends stood in a circle and watched, doing nothing. He obviously upset someone else. I never saw him from that day on.

Not long after I decided to get away from everything; Liverpool, my family and friends, to go and live and work in Guernsey on my own. Liverpool, for the first time, had got too much for me. I needed a break from it all and everyone around me. For the first time, Liverpool was sucking the life out of me.

Chapter 12
Guernsey

"Sitting on a cornflake, waiting for the van to come"
The Beatles

Even though I was going out with a pretty barmaid at the time, and the envy of every man in the village (she even made gay guys question their orientation!), I decided I had to get away. I was working in warehouses stacking shelves, whilst older lads in a click would shout "Ziggy" and snigger every so often. It was not what I wanted.

So Guernsey it was. I'd heard from various sources there was plenty of work for Scousers if you found fellow Scousers once you arrive. Head for a pub called the De La Rue as that was the Scouse headquarters.

I boarded the boat and remember getting very drunk with a bunch of Navy lads. I had my own little room, so had a great night living it up in the bar, sharing tales with these naval folk, then staggered to bed. I awoke in the morning to an empty ship in France. After some fuss with a crew member, the captain under some laws had to turn the ship round and drop me back in Guernsey. Not a good start.

When I got off the ship at Guernsey a few hours later, I was strip searched as I looked suspicious apparently. When I finally got to my destination, it was chaos; massive street parades, every pub rammed and bands playing. It was their Independence Day.

I joined in the activities by pub crawling and meeting locals and before long found a builder who offered me work to help build a wall for a rich local fisherman. I'd never done labouring before but I'd soon learn. The builder I helped was a stonemason, maybe the rarest in the building trade as it's a very specialist job.

Granite rock would be used and chipped into desired shapes. Every morning for my first month we would go to the quarry and collect large pieces of granite rock, have it weighed, then pay and off to our fisherman friend. We'd park as near to his huge house on the hill as we could. My job was to mainly carry this heavy rock up the hill all day, so the stonemason, Dug, could chip the pieces into shape and cement into the wall. Mixing cement was part of the day too.

High up on this hill I quite enjoyed this job, although in the heat some days it was exhausting but I needed the £50 a day, which back then was good money. I felt I earned my money doing this and spent it wisely. I stayed in a one man tent not far away on a little camp whilst I worked for Big Dug. When the job finished he wanted his tent back, so now I had no job and nowhere to live.

The next few months, I had to live on my wits, but not a night went by where I didn't have a bed to sleep in. The Guernsey folk I found ok, but very wary people. They weren't as trusting as my

Gypsy friends or London pals in the past.

I worked in bars, restaurants, hotels and finally the back of a chip shop peeling potatoes with the leader of the local Hells Angels type's son, called Kirk. A few warned me to steer clear of this fellow as he was dangerous, but I liked him. Riding on the back of his Harley at some speed across the island was an exciting, but also quite frightening, experience. The reason I liked this job the best was we'd start at 5am and be finished at midday so I had the rest of the day to enjoy myself. Go drinking, sit on beaches etc.

Oliver Reed lived on the island. I knocked on his door once, and his door knocker was a large brass penis which I found amusing! I wanted to ask him if he could recommend a good agent to me. I knocked about 3 times, then I heard a huge yell saying "Fuck off! " I figured I don't want to get on the wrong side of Olly so I left it there. I never got to meet him. Whilst on the island I heard many stories about him including one that every now and then he'd turn up at a pub, throw a grand on the table and if any man could beat him in an arm wrestle they could keep the grand. Apparently the only man who ever beat him was Stan, Kirk's dad and the leader of the local Hells Angels type gang. I met him a few times with Kirk, he was a big bald scary guy. Not the kind of guy you'd shout 'steroid head' too, that's for sure!

What I liked to do on many occasions was ride a motorbike Kirk lent me for my last month, to the highest point on the island, right by these German bunkers that had been built when the Germans occupied Guernsey during WW2. There I would park up and watch the sea coming in for the afternoon, alone with a pack of cigarettes. The calming of the sea plus the various sea birds on display was a great way to relax after work. I would do this often on my travels abroad; go to the highest point I could find and sit off to watch the sea come in.

One time in Greece in 94 with my pals, we hired Vespa bikes out and in formation turned a corner, but Junior, the younger brother of Fozz went straight into a pensioner on a push bike. There was blood on the road as the old man's hip was half out. This was a bad situation as local angry Greeks gathered round us. The five of us stayed close to Junior trying to explain it was an accident. Soon the local police came and took Junior away. Hagan went with him, as he was the best negotiator on this trip. To send Kojack or me would mean he would still be there now.

Meanwhile, the old man was taken away in an ambulance. Hagan later said poor Junior was chained to a radiator in a corridor. We got back to the hotel and arguments broke out between ourselves. Big Fozz was stressed and worried for his now locked up brother, so naturally tempers boiled. I rode off, up, up as far as I could go; up the hills above the town to the highest point again. I sat myself down and could see a beautiful Greek town below with the beach in the distance and the clear blue sea coming in. The traditional cig was lit as I distanced myself from the stressful scenes in our hotel miles below.

Luckily for Junior, when the pair got breathalyser tests the old man was way over the limit. We hadn't been drinking, Junior was as clean as a whistle so they had to let him go. He was 5 years younger than us, so this shook him up a bit for the rest of the holiday. He was alright as his best mate, Wheels, pointed out it could have been a lot worse if he'd had a drink and not the old man. They'd have thrown the book at him in the summer of 94.

Another time on a Vespa in Tenerife with Brian and Buzz Williams I nearly got knocked off the bike and over a cliff by a bunch of mad Spaniards in a car. I must have cut them up by accident and next thing the front wheel of the bike was almost over the edge of the cliff! My heart pounded and I saw my life flash before my eyes. Then I said to myself "this is not the end" and revved it to the right, going in front of the car and slammed on the brakes. 'Thank god I'm alive' I thought as the car carried on. Brian looked back and shouted "what the hell happened now?" Aged 17, it shook me up, but I drove back the villa to tell the tale to Buzz who never came; he was chilling by the pool in his trunks with a bunch of West Ham fans we'd met.

Besides the chase in the park, the riots in Brixton, the fire at Kings Cross and being knocked down outside the club, this was probably the next biggest scary thing to have happened to me. Like the rest I simply blocked it out my mind, as I was to do with everything scary.

Back on Guernsey, I was alone on this island. I'd go out in the evenings with whoever I was working with at the time; from fellow barmen, builders, Navy lads or sons of Hells Angels. Some nights I'd have to go out alone and just meet people. Being recognised helped make friendships on this island off the coast of Normandy.

One particular night I was in a nightclub alone, sipping a cold bottle of beer. The music had been pretty shit so far that night, so I just sat watching girls dance, missing home and my family and wishing my pals were with me. Then a song come on that I'd heard and loved from back home by the Happy Mondays called 'Step on'. Me and my pals danced to this in the clubs back home, so it felt only natural for me to get up and dance to it similar to Bez style. I danced for a few minutes then noticed loads of people were watching, some trying to copy. You see the indie scene hadn't hit the island yet. This may have been the first time the song was played. It was released in 1990, but I must admit I hadn't heard it on the island before. It was a buzz being surrounded and teaching these locals, girls and boys how to move to the Mondays. Little did I know then that six years later I would befriend the Happy Mondays. I don't think I got round to ever telling Shaun or Bez that I taught the locals in Guernsey how to dance properly to their music, but I did.

After 3 to 4 months of living there, I wanted to come home. I became lonely, although I was meeting people, it's still not the same. If I had a mate with me, I would have lasted longer I guess, but alone you're always a one man show. It was a small island and everyone knew your business. My wits were running out, but the main reason was I missed my family and my real pals. As Dorothy says in 'The Wizard of Oz' 'There's no place like home.'

My last night, I took a girl to the top of the mountain to sit on the German bunker. to look out to sea. She had the most incredible green eyes I'd ever seen. You were hypnotized staring into them. That was my last night talking under the Guernsey stars to the girl with kaleidoscopic eyes. Looking out I was homesick, tired and eager to get home, but there was something else. I was starting to feel nervous, much more than normal. I sensed I wasn't 100% but couldn't put my finger on it. Just butterflies in my stomach for now and I never knew why. I just knew I had to come home. I was sitting on a cornflake waiting for the van to come. In the morning I was gone.

Chapter 13
The Fall

'I should never be left alone with my mind for too long'
Libba Bray

After three adventurous months in Guernsey, in 1990 I lost my first Grandparent; my lovely Nan Evelyn. She was nicknamed Dolly on account she was so pretty she looked like a doll. To sum up the kind of woman she was, a few years before she passed away, we were both studying the horses one afternoon. I said I fancy this one called 'Garsid' Checking the results the next day it won at a decent price, maybe 10-1 and my Nan had about a fiver on it. so won a few bob. In 1990, £50 odd was nice. Anyway the next time I saw her, she gave me a watch she bought with her winnings; every penny she won went on this lovely watch for me. That sums her. She was the kindest person I've ever known.

When my Nan passed away, my Grandad was working on the 1991 film version of Robin Hood starring Uma Thurman. He was only an extra playing a peasant but he enjoyed doing extra work in his old age. He never went in the day my Nan died but the next day he figured there's no point in moping around so made the effort. The film crew heard what happened and fussed over him and word got round. They were filming in a forest I forget where but my Grandad was sitting alone smoking a cigarette on an old log when Uma Thurman approached him. She said she'd heard what happened regarding my Nan and offered her condolences, then invited him to her trailer to keep warm for a while and drink coffee and chat some more. She warmed an old man more than she will ever know that day. That small act of kindness he never forgot in his last 10 years on earth, and nor will I.

The rest of the year I don't remember much. I probably spent it going out with what little money I got off the dole. For the first and last time, I collected benefits as there was no work for me; no acting, no auditions to act and I'd foolishly left my agents Tommy, Ronnie and Ricky Tomlinson. I left because they said I was going to be typecast for a few years and it would be hard to get me work, so I figured what's the point in staying; I'd find an agency who can find me work. The truth is, I never found a better agency than those three. Art Casting they had every Liverpool actor under the sun and started many a career.

By the time 1991 came, I was approaching my 21st birthday, and things started happening to me that I couldn't understand. I went to a birthday party and had the idea it was a surprise party for me. When I realised it wasn't, I was upset. I felt weird but was unsure why.

A few days later I was taken to a Born Again Christian church by one of my friend's mum and dad. After listening to the pastor for a few minutes, out of nowhere I stood up and screamed at him, in front of his flock. "You're a fucking liar! Hypocrite! You know fuck all what you preach you bastard" and many other obscenities I can't quite recall. Everybody was stunned, including me. I don't know where it came from. Just came out in a manic rage. It had begun.

Being an outgoing and sociable type I hated staying in. If I had money I was out, but suddenly I didn't want to go out. I would rather sit in my loft listening to music and think things over and over. Maybe there was a bit of agoraphobia too. My mother tried to get my friends to come round and get me out. They'd knock or ring but I wasn't going anywhere. Many times my Dad rang Big Al, Hagan or Brian to get them to try and talk to me, but I just talked jibberish or cried for no reason.

My mother took me to my GP when I was first showing signs of rambling, feeling emotional and on the edge, but he wasn't much help.

Nobody knew what was happening to me; why I was this way. The loft was my sanctuary and I felt safe. I recall going over things from the past in my mind; feeling bad about things I'd done. The way I'd treated women for instance. I'd never physically hurt or hit a woman but I knew I'd hurt some by cheating or never ringing them back again after a few dates. I'd insulted a few drunk and this upset me and I felt guilty and a horrible person for it. Then the failure thoughts kicked in. I always thought I was going to be a big star and now I'm on the dole with no money, no job. I never had a pot to piss in or a window to throw it out of.

Then when I got worse, my mam asked the GP to

recommend a consultant and they paid privately for a consultation. He put me on antidepressants but I was much worse after that. Things got heavier as they went along. I began to imagine things, going into dream like states, but not pleasant things.

Hillsborough was one. I kept seeing the faces of the fans crushed up against the terraces, like I was there amongst it all. I would scrunch my face into the images I had seen, feeling the pain. Those images of terror were now haunting me. I imagined whilst talking to my dad, that he was the devil and he wanted me to go out and kill. All this seemed so real but it was all in my mind, I thought I had AIDs, as that had been on the news recently. I believed I had it. I knew I'd had sex without a condom a good few times, so my mind teased me that I had caught AIDs, to the point that I cried and cried about it. I vaguely recall my Mother playing the Travelling Wilburys album one night hoping it may calm me, but when the song 'The Devils Been Busy In Your Backyard' and '7 Deadly Sins' came on, I I cried uncontrollably imagining it was a message to me. Telling me that the Devil had been busy and I was to feel the forthcoming wrath of it, or I had committed the 7 deadly sins etc.

Delusions were constant; every one sad or terrifying and getting worse. My normal mind was now playing tricks on me. Then one awful night in March, just before my 21st birthday, I remember the footballer Gazza who I admired had been in the news lately having been set up. Somehow I must have thought the same thing was going to happen to me. I was screaming "They done it to Gazza and now they going to do it to me". I grabbed my favourite huge framed glass picture of two dolphins jumping out the sea and threw it out of the loft window. This always represented beauty and freedom to me but ironically these were the two things soon to be taken away from me.

Now I'm out of control. Now I don't know what's happening or what's real and what's not. I'm just crying, screaming and howling. Now I'm in a world of hell. The risk for bipolar suicide is highest when patients are in an impulsive or mania state. Although I may not have thought it or attempted it yet, I could have easily harmed myself without intending, as I didn't know what I was doing. I wasn't me.

It's hard to describe exactly how frightening all this was. If I look back on all the things that had frightened me in the past and future, nothing compared to this. My heart was beating a thousand miles per hour. My head was racing from one scary thought to the next. The fear inside me was at its peak; sheer terror going through my mind like was possessed. Having a very vivid imagination anyway, probably made it worse. Darkness had taken me and I had strayed out of thought and time.

Every bad thing that ever happened all came flashing back during this terrible night in my home in West Derby. I smashed my beloved loft up; all the beauty, things I'd collected, gifts given, anything I could grab. The climax of the illness was upon me; it had come out in a confused rage. This is mania.

It's important to know that mania is not what it seems. It's not a super high or being extremely happy. It's not a joyful experience, no feeling on top of the world. You're at the bottom of Hell looking up with no way out. Mania is overwhelming, terrifying, unpredictable and totally exhausting. At this point I had completely lost touch with reality.

My mother rang the consultant and he told her to bring me to his clinic straight away. By this time I could hardly function. I could barely walk. My whole body was breaking down and he admitted me right away. I arrived in a wheelchair to Rathbone Psychiatric hospital.

I awoke in this strange environment; a Psychiatric hospital! A cuckoo's nest! But this was the best place for me, although I didn't see it like that at the time.

One of my first memories was being surrounded by these quite big male nurses. I was ranting and raving telling them I'm going to do this and that, I was like an animal possessed, just pure aggression and hate for anyone around me. I never threw a punch at any of them thankfully but the same scenario took place for a while.

At some point near the beginning, I had another meeting with a psychiatrist. I vaguely just remember giving him lines from 'One Flew Over

The Cuckoo's Nest' They were all coming out, probably not making sense but the film had come back to me, realising I was living it.

I was closely watched for the first few months. I found this intimidating and couldn't understand why everywhere I went, someone would follow. I despised all the male nurses, who were only doing their job. Only one nurse somehow broke through the barrier with me; a nervy chain smoking female nurse called Mandy, from St Helens.

She had a way about her that could calm me down, make me see reason amongst the madness. I remember one day whilst looking at a newspaper there was an article about a man wanted for raping and killing women. I started crying non-stop, tears pouring down my eyes. Mandy came over to see what was up and I told her "I gotta hand myself in." I believed I was this horrific person responsible for these acts. She assured me for over an hour I had nothing to do with any of it, it was all in my mind, and that I was just sick. She'd hold my hand whilst comforting me in these moments. I owe so much to that kind and caring nurse. She knew I was Ziggy, but that had nothing to do with how she went out of her way to comfort a man at the lowest point of his life. She helped immensely to get me through my 6 months in there; another little angel sent down maybe.

A few years later, I heard Mandy passed away from cancer. Life can be so cruel. She was no more than 25. She was the finest nurse I've ever known, a natural. Without her, God knows how I'd have coped in there in the early days.

During these dark days, where I was to spend my 21st birthday I was on all kinds of medication; trial and error. I was still not in touch with reality. I turned on my own father. He came to visit me and I screamed for him to go away. I didn't want to know him. The man I looked up to more than anyone in the world, more than any mate, actor, gangster or gypsy, was my Dad, I worshipped the ground he walked on and still do, but during these suddenly unexpected times, I didn't want to know him. So it wasn't just me suffering, now my family are suffering. Dad's suffering because his son is in a mental hospital and to make it worse he can't visit me now.

Anyone who throws the word bipolar round saying they have it, when really all they are a bit low but think saying bipolar can help get them off work or claim benefits; spend 6 months on a psychiatric ward and see how it really feels.

My mother (God bless her) came in every day without fail. Whether in her breaks or lunchtime or in the evenings, she found time every day. I even had to say to her towards the end "you don't have to come every day Ma" as I felt sorry for her rushing round to see me. I never turned on my mother, I needed her. You loved me before seeing me.

I had an early day out one afternoon, I was taken to the Royal hospital for a brain scan, as my condition was so severe. I was not responding to

any medication and still rambling in a private world after months. It was thought I may have a brain tumour or I was hit on the head at some point in the past. I remember laying down and going into this long machine. There was dazzling lights around my head, I liked it; it was very trippy to be honest. Anyway the results came back and that wasn't the problem.
Thank God.

After a few months of this monotony; of sitting round wards, sitting in the small courtyard to smoke, same awful food every day, old men having to have their nappies changed, the heat, the screaming in the middle of the night, watching new patients come in and kick off, chairs launched as your enjoying your breakfast, guys pinned down after kicking off, the occasional suicide on the ward and the sheer and utter boredom, I decided I was going to escape. I'm out of here. Like the line in Shawshank Redemption 'Some birds aren't meant to be caged.'

The plan wasn't easy as I had to be watched all the time. I'm manic and in this state you dont know what your doing, I tried to slit my wrists a few days earlier, a dark moment I have never mentioned till now. My mind was so tormented this seemed my only way out. So I needed 24 hour watch. I knew the night would be easier as it was quieter. I had one big nurse Brian watching me. I walked up and down the same corridor and into the dining area over 20, maybe 30, times. He followed no more than 10 feet behind me.

I never got on with this nurse. He was probably a really nice guy, but during my sickness, I looked at him as my enemy. So I walked and walked waiting for him to slip up once, and he did. He never followed me into the dining area the 31st time. He figured I'd just come out as usual. But I never came out of the dining area that night.

In the few moments I had, I instantly picked up a pretty heavy chair and launched it through the window, leaving a hole big enough to jump through and run across the fields to a deserted railway beyond. It was my Chief in One Flew Over The Cuckoo's Nest moment. I was free. I looked back from a distance to see if he was chasing but he wasn't. I guess he was ringing the police. I didn't care as for the first time in a while I was under the stars and could see the moon clearly instead of through a hospital window pane. I was out and had plans but I was still manic, still very ill.

I wanted to go to London and see Jeff. I thought he could help me; cure me from this fucking craziness. The drop from the top of the old railway was about 30ft to 40ft and the only way down I could find was a black electric cable wire leading to the bottom. In this condition you have no fear. I grabbed the top and began lowering myself down but halfway down, I lost my grip and went down at some speed, burning my hands terribly. I then hit the floor about 10ft from the bottom as I couldn't hold on any more. I thought the police would maybe looking for me and I knew there were no trains at this early hour of the morning, so I jogged a while until I found a dark empty tunnel. There amongst the odd rat crawling about, i could hear but not see them, which I don't know what's worse. I sat against a wall, couldn't see a thing except when I lit a match for a cig. My hands burning, feet killing, mind wondering, I just sat in dark silence looking back on how I'd got to this point. How did my life get to this, being on the run from a mental hospital with nobody but myself. I looked on the old days, the laughs with Drummond and the boys, all the good times and glory days but the more I thought the more i sobbed. I felt 2000 light years from home that night. This was one of the lowest points of my Bipolar, I was literally in a hole. Views of looking over beautiful oceans from the highest point were a million miles away. I soon closed my eyes and drifted to infinity until i come back again.

Morning had broken and I needed clothes if I was to go to London, so I headed to the family house, My mam and Dad were at work, but my sister Zoe was in. I didn't mean to frighten her that day, but I know I did. I was acting manic whilst packing my kit bag. I never harmed her in any way just the random gibberish that came out. I remember her crying saying "Don't go to London, Georgie" but you can't reason with a man who doesn't know what he's doing. It was fate that I told her my plan of London because as soon as I left she got hold of my mother - clever as there were no mobiles then.

Before I got to Lime Street, I remember a nun seeing me crying not far from a church. I had tears in my eyes, talking to myself. She came over and said some kind words to me. I can't remember exactly what she said, but something like "go home son you'll be ok, be with your family." But I couldn't go home; the only place I'd end up if I did, was back in that hospital which I despised.

I got to the station and walked through the crowds. I had money and bought my ticket and headed for the platform. Then my mum called me from behind, telling me I have to go back, please Georgie please. My poor mother had been frantic when Zoe got word. She rushed out of work knowing if I got to London in this vulnerable and manic state anything could happen. She rang my dad but he couldn't deal with it anymore. I remember a guy intervened saying "has this guy robbed you love" as my mum had hold of me and it looked like she was trying to get something back. In the end I listened, I seen sense during the confused madness of it all. In hindsight it would have been disastrous going to London in that state. I rang Jeff every day from the hospital anyway so I guessed I'd just have to keep on doing that. My mum rang the organisation 'Mind' not long after the great escape, she said they were really helpful and put her at ease about my Dad saying most men can't deal with their sons going like this, it's difficult for them, especially when I'd turned on him so ferociously, he couldn't handle it simple as that. In time he could, now he's much more understanding, like anything you learn with experience I guess.

There was talk of me having ECT treatment, electric shock treatment. My mother didn't want this so when it was discussed it was decided not to be done. I don't know whether it would of worked, I know it works for some people. The success rate is quite high I believe but thankfully my condition began to improve, so I didn't have to go through this trauma.

A new patient arrived, a little old feller called Alf, if it wasn't for Alf I would never have got through the next four months as easily as I did. He gave me a new lease of life. Maybe another one of them Angels I keep meeting and then vanish when their work is done with me. I and old Alf became inseparable. I looked after him made sure nobody harmed him, but he didn't need looking after. He first came in like me kicking off, wanting to fight everyone especially the big intimidating nurses. Shouting and hollering with his walking stick. I cried laughing at this sight because he was so small and old and the insults that came out of his mouth. Like everyone eventually he calmed, his medication would kick in. Then he became Alf the wise, no longer was I the protector of him, calming him down all the time, he suddenly got back to his real self which was a very clever, wise and thoughtful man. He was like a mini Gand~Alf in lord of the rings. For hours and hours we would sit up all night talking, telling our stories. He was like me as an old man I always thought. I Loved Alf and later on we were allowed days out accompanied. So when my Dad picked me up one day for a drive, yes thankfully I'd got over the hatred and we were fine again.
I brought Alf along so all three of us had a day on Crosby beach. We got a train once to Southport

for the day, I recall as we got off the train Alf lifted his walking stick up like he was holding a rifle and shouted "Charge" as he ran down the platform. It was funny to watch, my Dad commented later that he probably had a flashback from when he was in the trenches or in battle during the 2nd world war. Like me he went into his little worlds too, Visions from our past.

Obviously other things happened in there over the six months and I could go on and on about it, but it's nothing to write home about, time in the beginning was spent so drugged up I just slept a lot of the time, moped about. Time progressed and whilst on some drugs I remember my mam and her Mum, my Nan Eileen visiting me and I was very humorous, like Jim Carey going on and on but they laughed and laughed so there was laughter at some points. Playing chess or pool with the guys in there, I was very lucky to have my Grandad Albert, he was a very intelligent man, a draftsman in his day who drew up the plans for the cavern believe it or not. He done the original plans before anyone knew who the Beatles where. He was in the RAF in this country but never got based abroad. He probably taught half the RAF to play chess during quiet moments known him! My other Grandad taught me about being careful with money, drinking and telling stories or jokes. This other Grandad, Albert, taught me more useful things in life, like how to play chess, snooker, look after my teeth, my money, dominoes, draughts etc. by the age of ten I could do them all except the money part, that took till I was 48. He was a very patient man who for hours on end would teach these games, I mean how do you teach an eight year old to play chess, keep still and listen and learn, especially a hyper active one like myself? That was Albert. Always by my side In Rathbone was little Alf, he became my closest pal in there and when we both came through our worst would laugh constant.

Looking back yes it was hell at first in there as I didn't understand why I was locked up so to speak, but once time progressed it got easier as I grew better. For months I just rambled, made no sense.

When I was about seven or eight during a wet afternoon in Blackpool with my Mum and Dad. We took shelter in a movie theatre to see 'Lord of the rings' the cartoon. Many years before the big Hollywood trilogy starting in 2001. I loved it, all these Hobbits, wizards, elves and orcs etc. It blew me away, not long after someone bought me the 'The Hobbit' book and I read a chapter every night before I went to sleep dreaming of this strange and wonderful world. My Godfather Chris, my Dads good friend and reason my middle name Christopher bought me the 'Lord of the rings book' for 14th birthday. I got about 2 chapters in but it was too much, I just couldn't get into it, it was the thickest book I'd ever tried, looked daunting before I tried. So I left it somewhere in Chapter 2, until now in 91 for some reason wanted to give it another go. My Mam brought it in, the same book I had in 1984 signed to me by my Godfather. Every night I read a chapter, I'd go to bed specifically early so I could read more of this, as I knew I'd get drowsy soon with the meds. I read every page of this fantasy epic by JRR Tolkien. I got into that world he created probably better than I could of if later down the line out of hospital. In my room there was no distractions, nobody bothered me, still unwell and all my feelings magnified this book lifted my spirits, not like the films were it's done for you, I had to imagine these characters, places and battles etc. I must admit it kept me going in there, and felt at the end it was an achievement, I'd read 'Lord of the rings' in a psychiatric hospital amid all the chaos. There was always a line I remembered in the cartoon in Blackpool were Aragorn the toughest of them all says to Gandalf "Don't take me to the dark place Gandalf I beg you". Well I was in a dark place but found some solace in this fantasy book.

During my stay at Rathbone we got switched to Broad-oak in Broadgreen. Mandy and old Alf kept me going, and a black nurse called Joe, looked like Jimi Hendrix, but other patients kept me going too, there was an x millionaire, a teacher, an x doctor, a huge builder called Paddy, kids no older than 18, a female actress I will not name, as she was as ashamed as me at the time, a postman, solicitor etc. Anybody can end up in them places, it doesn't matter what you do for a living.

I walked out one day at 98 pounds (seven stone). Although I was out, I wasn't 100% right by far. I wasn't manic but jaded, yes. I looked the worst I've ever looked. Gaunt, thin, white, pale and down trodden. I went down the village with Fozz on the first proper weekend home. I never even got into the pub, as a guy came from behind and punched me to the floor. I tried to get up despite there being two of them, twice as big as me and Fozz. Fozz as usual said his piece, "Please mate he's just got outta hospital" but there was a reason for this dig, and looking back despite his bouncer like frame, it didn't hurt half as much as that one in London when I was 16. I had to take this one on the chin and keep quiet.

A month earlier, on weekend leave, I went to the village with a gangster's son who also spent some time in the hospital. After a few drinks mixed with my medication, I went into that world for a few minutes and started shouting at all these young lads, who turned out to be gangster's sons and future gangsters themselves. It caused chaos, fighting at the taxi rank and teeth flying out. We were outnumbered, but my pal hurt a few of them before they could get at him. It was so unnecessary. I shouldn't have been allowed out. I wasn't ready. Those lads were just having a drink. They weren't harming us, but in my madness I caused mayhem. Luckily, I was just warned after my knockdown to let things lie, as I believe I threatened them with gangster names, which in normal circumstances I would never do. It's been well forgotten over the years and I see some of these guys out and about and we are fine with each other. I hope they know it wasn't me that night.

To sum up the first experience, it basically crept up on me like a tiger in the jungle, there was no warning. I had no inkling as to what was happening to me once it attacked. I was helpless in its grip and just had to experience this hell as it got worse and worse. If you can imagine standing on the savannahs in Asia and you see a tiger running towards you, or your snorkelling off the Great Barrier Reef and see a Great white rising up, that feeling of terror a man would have is how I felt the night before I got committed, both in Liverpool and another horrendous night in South Wales. It's a pure adrenaline rush of uncontrollable fear. All your fears and scares hitting you at once in a jumbled up mess.

If you look Bipolar disorder up in the Oxford dictionary it simply says 'Characterised by both manic and depressive episodes, or manic ones only.' This doesn't give you a great insight into the illness. I mainly go high, so high I'm untouchable. I'm unpredictable, unapproachable, delusional, aggressive, petrified and all at once. The lows are just before the manic episodes and after them, when I'm recovering, the comedown so to speak. That's the low, but for me the highs considerably outnumber the lows, and are far more serious and dangerous.

One thing worth noting is during breakdown number one right through to number five, I never saw anyone that was not really there. I don't hear voices telling me what to do like a schizophrenic might. It's all in my mind not in my eyes or ears.

To define, Schizophrenia 'Is a mental disorder characterized by abnormal behaviour, strange speech, and a decreased ability to understand reality. Other symptoms include false beliefs, unclear or confused thinking, hearing voices that do not exist, reduced social engagement and emotional expression, and lack of motivation.' What I have is frightening enough but to see things too, I can't imagine how unbearable that would be.

John Nash whose theories are widely used in economics, shared the 1994 Nobel Memorial Prize in Economic Sciences and suffered paranoid Schizophrenia, had a film made about his life. It was called 'A Beautiful Mind' and he was played perfectly by Russell Crowe. Nash sadly died in a taxi cab, aged 86, in New York with his wife.

'It's almost as if a demon might have passed from one host to another' –
John Nash.

This quote is not far off when I have an episode.

The main fear that I had, when I left the hospital, was will it happen again? I wasn't to know back then that it would, eight years later, as stress and a chaotic lifestyle would ultimately catch up with me again.

I still have the same worry today, yesterday and I will have it tomorrow; will I end up in hospital again? I may not live to excess anymore; I'm very careful in that department. My nights of heavy drinking and partying are over. In fact I don't drink, and haven't for five years, I don't get into debt. I keep busy working so I'm not sitting round thinking things over ;not too much only part time as that suits me. I don't take things on that are too much (writing and producing Titanic plays for instance - even though I pulled it off, it took it out of me). I don't even smoke anymore; I stopped when last in hospital in 2014. So I live a totally different life than when I was twenty one. I have found new interests, hobbies and things to do. I have stopped certain things I know now had helped cause it. Maybe life is not as exciting as roamin' and a gloamin' the world with my pals partying and meeting women, but it keeps the psychiatrists from the door and me out of hospital. To me that is more important than anything in the world, but it took many years to realise this!

When I first came out of hospital I existed, but I did not live. I was a shadow of my former confident self for a long time. Maybe two years till I felt myself again.

At one point I got so low I attempted suicide again, only this time I bought 100 strong pain killers and took the lot. Only by fortune, my Mother found me vomiting over the toilet, then I was rushed to A&E to have my stomach pumped. This is a dark moment I regret so much and I'm so glad it never worked. The heartache it would have caused for my family I can't imagine. The things I would have missed out on in life are uncountable. The main one looking into the eyes of my son for the first time when he was born 8 years later in 1999, and seeing myself.

You have to understand this is how low and vulnerable I was after going through all I went through during this breakdown at 21 years of age. I never thought I'd recover, so didn't want to spend my days as this fragile, frightened and numb person I'd become. I can't turn back the clock on this night, but I can tell anyone who is thinking or considering doing what I did, that just because they think their situation is forever, it's not. I am living proof that over time a man's situation and feelings change. There's always another way out and that is life, choose life, don't waste the gift. Like I say, I thought I was doomed but the reality is I wasn't, it was only temporary. Nothing lasts forever...and I've never attempted it again.

The remainder of 91 was spent mainly recuperating, getting my head back together. Taking life a lot slower for a while. The top Dr in Broadoak said it could be manic depression caused by the lifestyle I'd led over the last few years. London, fame, no fame, drinking, things I'd seen etc. or it could be a one off and never happen again. I wish it would have been the latter, to go through it once was horrific enough but another four times!

The gap was good though. From 91 to 99 I stayed out of hospital and lived a normal and exciting life again. Over the years I forgot about the dreaded breakdown in 91 where I spent my 21st birthday. I never forgot my pals either who came to visit me every week without fail. They know who they are and my gratitude is beyond measure as they had me laughing when I needed it. You can always rely on your close pals, no matter what you're going through, to somehow make you laugh, especially when all together.

In 1992 a local actor called Danny from Huyton, who'd been in Brookside for a while and had visited me many times, went into the offices of Brookside and pleaded or demanded (I'm not sure which) to give me a chance in Brookside. Now most people only remember me in it during 1996, when I played a drug addict called Little Jimmy. Well, I also played Little Jimmy in 92 for 4 episodes thanks to Danny. It helped get my confidence back. Although not in it long I felt better about myself; I can still do it!

It also showed the man on the street that I wasn't a failed ex-actor druggie. Many a time I'd hear "Smackhead" shouted from a car at me as I looked so thin and ill with all the meds. This hurt me at the time. I take things personally and that was personal. I think people understand drug addicts more nowadays. They get more help, not as much as they should be maybe, but help is out there. Back in 91/92 it was a dirty thing, and to be called it constantly by people who knew nothing of what I'd been through, did hurt.

1) My Grandad in Africa during WW2 looking after a Zulu!

2) Grange Hill on the canals - 1986

3) The heyday in 1988 with Jay and John in the Lakes

4) 1991 – In a psychiatric hospital with Alf and Mandy, the finest nurse I ever met.

5) With my surrogate father Geoff and Drummond in 1995

6) With John Alford and a young Kirk

7) Headshot in 1993, 2 years after 6 months in a psychiatric ward.

1994 – Me and Steve, in our prime

8) 2013 – With Steve, and my Dad in Spain. 2 weeks later I would relapse

9) With my Mam and sister Zoe at my 40th in 2010

10) Passing out day in Plymouth with my son Kirk, and Mel.

11) My little cutie niece, Lana, at the Grange Hill exhibition in Liverpool, 2018.

12) A little Grange Hill reunion in London, 2016.

13) With Phil Redmond, Todd Carty and Mel in London, 2018

14) With some of my closest pals in
Spain, 2018.

14) Paradise in the Caribbean with
Mel, 2019

Chapter 14
Spain

'A true friend is someone who sees the pain in your eyes while everyone else believes the smile on your face'

So Brookside was done and gone. Enter Steve, my old red coat friend who let me and the lads in at weekends. He had finished his Butlins days and was home. For the next 20 years we would become inseparable. The adventures with this character are endless. He had the same outlook on life as me.

I was strong now in 94, had my sense of humour back, and looked much better like my old self. We would live and work in many places including Warrington, Turkey, Spain, London, Devon, Scotland, Great Yarmouth, Boro and finally South Wales. These are just places we worked, there were many other adventures with this fellow adventurer; money making schemes, Glastonbury '99, trips to Belfast to visit my friend Franco and Alex Higgins (who I got to know in his final years) and many concerts including Stereophonics and UB40 where we did the George Christopher's in town trick on both.

We also spent time on Dartmoor writing our film script 'Spain' which almost got made, down to a combination of an agent called Frank, Gangster Charlie, a top lawyer Kevin and a producer in London called Richard. It went into post production but needed changes, which we didn't want to make, so it never got made. We both look back in despair as we should have made the sacrifice but we were young and moved on.

I've spent more nights in hotels with him than anyone. He was good looking; he knew it and had a confidence and charisma women fell for. The perfect partner in crime for me! When I say every man has one pal he confides in the most, Pape was my Dads and Steve was mine. Steve is the first I ring if shit hits fans. The simple reason is he knows me better than I know myself.

I could write a whole book just on our capers but over the next few chapters I'll just include the best and important parts; it's not all rosy. Steve was to face a few terrible tragedies in his life later on. I was with him throughout these events, and tried the best I could to console him. He needed me like I've needed him. Most importantly in 1999, when I was to break down again, (on a mountain in South Wales) Steve was there before, during and after the event. It was the scariest night of my life. Possibly worse than the night I flipped in the loft but that was gradual, this was more or less instant.

But to begin our story, our 4 months living in Spain is a great starting point as that's where the close friendship began and the problems we have later are a long way away.

Just before Callella in Spain, we spent a month in Warrington helping to run a pub whilst the landlord was on holiday for a week. Steve's sister Pat was his partner and she invited us up for a weekend but it lasted a month. Francisco the owner was going away on some business and Steve told him we'd had some experience working in the pub game. We hadn't of course. So Francisco trusted us while he went away. Great for us, but not great for him. Once he'd gone we ordered tonnes of sand to be delivered. We spread it all over the floor and turned the place into a Hawaiian night weekend, with this written on the boards outside. It brought them in as me and Steve greeted them with Hawaiian shirts on and did Hawaiian raffles where they could win a surfboard we found in the cellar of Fran's pub. All kinds went on that week, many stay behinds were held but only with females. Fran came back and his stocks and takings were down and he wasn't happy!

We had bigger problems a few weeks later when, in a club called Mr Smith's, we noticed 5 or 6 heavy looking guys standing not far from us, looking over. Wherever we moved, they did, so it was obvious they were after us. A plan was set. We knew we couldn't fight these guys; they'd kill us and probably knew the doormen as they were locals. So, we asked the burger seller in there if there was a door leading behind his counter to a way out. Thankfully he said yes. But it was too soon to go yet as they were watching us. We walked towards the exit. There was a huge partition in the middle where if you went one way and followed your way round you would lead back in the club again, but it would look like we left the club. We walked straight ahead and did the U turn back round into the club. They followed as hoped and went into the street to do whatever they planned. Meanwhile our Italian burger flipping friend let us through his kitchen, out the back door and over a wall to safety! Who those guys were and why they wanted to get us, is a question we never found out the answer to. I guess one of us entertained the wrong girl.

Steve went to Spain to become an entertainer in a fairly big hotel. He'd been there a few weeks singing, telling jokes, and doing his usual raffles that he'd do wherever we'd go. Then after 2 weeks he rang me to ask me to join him as he'd found me a job nearby in a Spanish bar. I was bored with no work back home, claiming sickness benefit, so thought why not? I embarked on a coach trip that took 2 days. It was the cheapest way, but it drained me; the heat, babies crying and it just seemed to take an eternity, but soon enough I arrived on the Costa Brava and joined my pal.

My job was outside the Spanish bar at first, 'propping' they called it - getting people in. I felt a bit nervous at first but got into it. After a few weeks, I was behind the bar. Things were great; we sat on the beach all day or found a luxury hotel poolside. There were endless tourists to make friends with. We worked at night but finished at midnight so would party until the sun came up. The laughter was constant.

I remember in the first week, we hired a jet ski, the first time I'd ever been on one. We jumped the waves with the sun on our backs without a care in the world. I remember him saying as he jumped a huge wave together "Just think son, this time last week you were walking up Green Lane." Green Lane was where I had to claim my sickness benefit.

A few bad things happened over there. Every few days I'd call home to speak to either my mam, Dad or sister. Then after a while, either my mam was out shopping, at the pub, work etc. and never in. I suspected something wasn't right after a while and demanded my sister tell. She said "Mum's left Dad, they've split up and gonna get divorced" This hit me like a train. Talking in this phone box in a Spanish square, I felt so many miles away and so helpless in it all. They didn't want to tell me as they knew I was having a good time in Spain and this would ruin it. After the call, I smashed the receiver against the dialler in anger. I just kept wondering if I was the cause of it after being in hospital, when I was saying things out of my mind against my Dad. Steve comforted me and we got very drunk that night.

One night we had an argument, and being young and drunk, decided to have a one on one on the beach. We were close but when we argued it was ferocious. We got to the beach and I took my shirt off. We squared up but then, in the corner of my eye, I saw two or three Moroccans behind Steve. Now we both knew if there was any crime on the island like a tourist being raped or mugged or beaten up it was 99% down to these Moroccans that had come over, all mainly criminals causing trouble on the Costa. "Steve, Moroccans 12.00" I told him. He didn't believe me, thinking he'd turn and I'd throw one on him. Then I assured him "I swear to god there's a few behind if we fight, the loser is gonna get had off." He walked beside me and we faced them together. Now we weren't as easy pickings as they thought; we were now 'one' so to speak. "Just walk slowly the way we came. If they follow we gotta do our best" I told Steve as we walked up the beach and up a path back to the town. They never followed.

The second thing that was bad was I was set up whilst working in the bar I enjoyed. Only twice have I been set up in a job and this was the first. The owner of the bar, Jessie, accused me of robbing his watch. It must have been an expensive or very personal watch as he went ballistic on me. "Where's my fuckin watch?" he kept screaming. But I had no idea what he was talking about. This went on for a while. I even had tears in my eyes as I pleaded with him. I knew nothing of his watch. I was many things, but not a thief, and certainly wouldn't rob the hand that feeds. He said I had been seen by his other barman taking it. The other barman was English; one of my own! I couldn't believe he'd said this. He must have taken it and set me up to get away with it. I somehow convinced him in the end, but he was angry to the point of wanting to kill me. I lost my job and not for the first time, for nothing.

I somehow worked in a Norwegian bar and became DJ Wilson for a while. They constantly asked for the song 'Life Is Life' by Opus. All I had to do was play that over and over and everyone was happy. That was enough to get a man sectioned; hearing that over and over as dozens of Vikings sang and bear hugged me.

One evening, after we both finished work, we headed for the nightlife, but must have took a dodgy back street. Out of nowhere, a wild dog ran at us. I stood still, but Steve ran and it jumped up and bit him on his buttocks. Luckily it let go after the initial bite, but his arse had blood coming through his jeans. We had to get to a toilet to check it, so walked into a posh hotel nearby. Steve dropped his jeans and bent over the toilet in the cubicle as I checked. I'd seen a bite mark and he said "You gotta wash it pal." This was not something I really wanted to do, possibly the last thing I wanted to do, but I had to. I got a soaked pile of tissues and from behind began to dam his buttocks.

Suddenly, the door opened and the night porter of the hotel shouted "Hey! There's a fucking time and a place for this!"

I turned with a soaked tissue and replied "I'm just bathing his wound!" Our plans were cut short that night as we spent the rest of it in the local Spanish hospital whilst he got a tetanus. The look on that night-porter's face I will never forget though. Horrified is not the word.

One of the funniest things I ever saw (and still laugh about to myself), was when on my break, I decided to go and see Steve in his hotel. As I turned the corner he was dressed as a chicken whilst dancing to the 'Birdy Song' in the street surrounded by kids. I stood and took this in for a while with uncontrollable laughter, until I made my presence known to him. What I wouldn't give for mobile phones to have been invented then!

Spain came to an end as Steve got sick. He said he had to get home and see his own doctor. I was gutted as I'd just started dating a blonde Dutch girl who had a look of Marilyn Monroe. What I liked about her was that she never had a clue who I was; no Grange Hill in Holland. Steve couldn't have timed it worse as I was starting to like this Norma Jeane looking Dutch bombshell. Next thing I know, I'm stuck with him on a coach for 24 hours with him coughing and spluttering like

so at the end of Midnight Cowboy. Our adventure had ended, and I never had a chance to say goodbye to my Dutch friend.

After Grange Hill, this was the second time I'd live away from home, Guernsey being the first, this was 10 times better as I had a pal with me he looked out for me over there. He was always that bit wiser than me, although I'd never tell him at the time. It was Pure freedom after all the torment, pain and suffering during my breakdown. To be free, living life to the full with my pal was something no doctor could ever prescribe me. No medication beats freedom.

Chapter 15
Money

'Money, so they say is the root of all evil today'
Pink Floyd

I've always been quite lucky in regards to making money. I've never had it on a plate and was never born into it. I always had to make it myself, one way or another. From milk rounds to Celebrity Pointless, it doesn't bother me how I earn. I just have to earn one way or another as I can't bear being skint and not being able to buy anything. Even if I've just got a tenner in the bank, it's better than nothing.

Sometimes luck comes my way though. In my favourite year (1988), I was in a private cab in London, taking me to Mitcham. It was after work. I probably couldn't be bothered to get a bus. I was doing a sweep for the Epsom Derby the next day. The cabbie was watching me as I worked out who owed what and he said "Put your mortgage on Khayasi." I'd never heard of this horse so asked why. "I have a brother who works for William Hill and he's given every Derby winner for the past 15 years. He's never wrong. It's 16-1 now but in the morning it will go in, so back it early." he confidently told me.
I thanked him, thought about it and the next morning, on the way to work, threw £50 to win on it. I told the lads, Alford and Drummond, Condo and Josh but they laughed saying it will never win ('A Wilson tip etc.'). It romped home that day. £600 I won as I'd got 12-1 for it. The lads were

gutted they never listened, but I treated them to a few drinks in Woods restaurant in Elstree on the way home. I never got to see that cabbie again, to thank him, or to give him my number for next year's Derby!

In 1982 my Grandfather Jeepers happened to be in a pub in town and noticed Prince Charles was greeting a crowd near by. He wandered over, not often Royalty is on your doorstep. The crowd were asking questions like "How's Diana?" or "What's the baby gonna be called?" etc. He got near my Grandad, until he was close enough for my Grandad to ask him : "Who do you fancy in the Grand National tomorrow Charles?" The Prince spoke quietly and confidently looking him in the eye. "Grittar" was his reply. Later that day he rang all the Wilson family to give the royal tip. We all backed it. It romped home in the 1982 Grand National at 7-1. Old Charlie knew....

I had less glamorous jobs. For example, in about 1990 I somehow got involved in dressing up as a lion in Chester Zoo, handing out ice creams to kids. I foolishly told one of the lads before I set off. It was the middle of summer and it must have been 80 degrees and I was sweating. I had kids coming up and pulling my tail, then running off. I put up with this for most of the day, then I spotted about 5 of my pals on a hill, on the floor in laughter. It was the funniest thing they ever saw they said afterwards. Especially when I patted a little boy on the head and give him an ice cream. I went home with them not long after they tumbled me. It was too hot and for £40 it wasn't worth suffering anymore I thought. I never got paid for this awful job as I never finished, but I didn't care.

The day got worse later on as I put the stupid lion's outfit on to amuse my Nan when she came around. She laughed in the garden with me, Zoe and my Mam for ages. Then I said I'd walk her home in the costume. She lived at the top of my road. Halfway up the road there was a man, out with his two golden retrievers off the lead. Suddenly the dogs began to chase me. I ran as fast as I could in a lion's outfit and had to hurdle a wall to safety, with the dogs barking furiously beneath the safety of the wall. The owner soon got them away. Me and the family had a good laugh afterwards and that's the main thing.

Not long after I got out of hospital in 91, I sold clothes for a while, for a man known as Jurassic Jerv. Mainly men's designer shirts or jackets. Not blag like you get in Manchester these days. He had really nice dress shirts and I usually sold everything he laid on me. Our little enterprise went on throughout the 90's, as well as my money making schemes with Steve.

The money making schemes with Steve were usually great ideas, but went wrong somehow. During one Xmas he had the idea of renting a van, buying a load of Xmas trees off a dodgy farmer we knew called Fat Harold and selling them to all the pubs in the city. So the van was piled with over 50 huge pine trees, plus about 100 little Santa teddies we were to give away as gifts to any kids in the pubs. We weren't even halfway up the motorway when the back doors of the van burst open with the pressure of those trees. I looked in the rear view mirror to see dozens of trees rolling down the motorway, and teddies bouncing everywhere! We stopped and jumped out to sort this mess. People were shouting and beeping as we piled everything back in. Chants of "Sort it out Ziggy lad"

Mobiles were out by then, so we had business cards made up called 'Greenland Trees' with the mobile number. The trees were stored in my Dads back yard. It looked like Delamere Forest. Before long, we were selling to many pubs in the area. We went through the phone book ringing every pub A-Z. All was going well until we arrived at one pub in Gateacre, the manageress asked us to put it up outside on a veranda and put outdoor lights on it. Steve being Steve assured her this would be no problem, so sent me to buy some gaffer tape. We put it up and insulated the lights with the gaffer tape. Later that evening, we were counting our money when the phone went, "Hello Greenland Trees" I said.
The reply was not what we wanted. "Bloody Greenland trees, my tree is on fire outside, it's a bloody blizzard out there!"
I looked out the window and it was snowing heavily. "Ok we're on our way" I assured her. We got there to see the fire brigade, all the pub emptied out and the landlady waiting to kill us. "There's nothing we can do here, Sod this" I told Steve so we went home. Nobody got hurt as the tree was outside. It was just an inconvenience for the pub, regulars and staff that night. That was the

end of Greenland Trees.

We sold toys, clothes, barbecues, paintings and countless other useless things we got our hands on. We worked the Ideal Home Exhibition for a few weeks on a stand. A guy called Freddie the Fly gave us a stall on Camden Market for a time. We had market stalls, boot sale stalls.

We sold Titanic paintings outside the Titanic film exhibition in London. We had a 1000 of these fantastic paintings, only because two crooked welsh businessmen tried to have us over! We used a room to create an acting agency, it never worked but as Spandau ballet once said to cut a long story short, they were crooked and tried to stiff us, but we had evidence of their trail of fraud. So we gave them the ultimatum; either print us a 1000 of these Titanic pictures or we blow you up! They had no choice. Our plan was frame them up and sell them outside the Titanic film exhibition whilst the Titanic soundtrack played on a ghetto blaster out of view. They sold well, but this lead to our biggest project yet. We wrote and produced a play about two Welsh boxers, who perished on the Titanic. A great idea which went down well, but it took it out of me and that's what lead to my 2nd relapse in 1999. My mind and body had simply overdone it.

All the running round making money was fun. The chase was great. Nobody ever gave us money we earned every penny of it.

In-between our capers, I had a few acting jobs. I

lived in London for another 6 weeks, to do a radio play for Radio 4 called 'The Mall' with Denzil (Paul Barber) out of Only Fools and Horses. I did another radio play with local actor Ian Hart called 'Goose'. He was amazing to work with the second they'd shout action, and not before. So there was the odd acting job but not many until the Spring of 96. Suddenly I was given a chance to do something I'd yearned for, but had so far proved elusive. I was given a chance to be in Brookside.

As it had been four years since I last played the part of Little Jimmy, I had to re audition again. This time I was to be Little Jimmy the drug addict and therefore it would be so much more difficult. I would have to delve deep to pull this off. My mate John Alford was flying in London's Burning, so now was my chance to have fame and money again.

Chapter 16
Another Chance

'Count your age by friends, not years. Count your life by smiles, not tears.'
John Lennon

I had an agent in London at the time and she got me the audition for Brookside. I knew I was up against some stiff competition as I was playing a heroin addict. I knew if I got this, it would -for want of a better word - get me out the shit.

I never had long to prepare as, within days, I was sitting outside Phil Redmond's office at Brookside, like I was 11 years earlier for Grange Hill. I read some of the script, then he asked me a series of questions again, like he did in 85. The last one is all I remember "Why should we give you the part?" This had to be answered carefully. There was a million reasons I could have given him, but the one I gave him was the greatest lie I ever told. I wanted this so bad, I wasn't gonna let it slip now. So I said "A few years ago, I had a friend who was on Heroin. I watched it destroy him and eventually kill him. I could play this part better than any man you will ever find, because I've seen what it's like with my own eyes" I was almost crying as I believed it myself. I never planned on saying this, I don't know where it came from. All I knew was I needed to convince this man I was right for the job. He knew I could act but just needed assurance I could handle this tricky role. In that moment it seemed the best answer.

I waited over 2 weeks until I heard, I even had a holiday in Benidorm with Fozz, Hagan and co. I couldn't quite relax during this holiday and kept ringing our Zoe every night to see if the agent had rung but each night it was a no.

The only thing I can remember about this holiday. was that all hell broke loose one night at the hotel bar. These 3 big Geordie lads mistook us for these Welsh lads who'd been throwing water balloons at them earlier whilst they lay by the pool. Because we were sitting with a gang of beautiful Welsh girls the error was made. The biggest one, on a similar scale to big Brummie the doorman (but not quite as big), came over shouting and calling us this and that. Before I knew it Hagan was fighting with him one on one. Big Al was fighting the 2nd biggest whilst I got left with the oldest, probably the father of them. Kojack threw plastic chairs at them when he could get a shot in. Because he'd spilt a drink Fozz was changing his shirt and was luckily upstairs in the hotel room. He heard the commotion but never dreamed it was us. There must have been over 100 people sitting around this massive hotel bar and all scattered. A Spanish manager came over to try and intervene but the big Geordie knocked him down. I carried the manager to safety and got a waiter to help him. It went on for ages. We held our ground and when we heard the Guardia Civil arriving, made haste away from the scene.

The following day we heard the 3 Geordies got deported as the manager picked them out. Nobody said nothing to us; they started it, plus we got the manager out of danger so I guess they thought leave them be. Thank God as it wouldn't have looked good getting deported on the fringe of getting on Brookside!

Some people boast after a big scrap saying I done this and I done that, well I don't. I shake and feel physically sick inside afterwards. Give Hagan his due for standing toe to toe with this big bruiser though. It doesn't surprise me, as I remember Big Al telling me when they went to a new senior school in Norris Green as kids, 5 schools joined up. With 5 different top boys of each School. Hagan couldn't be bothered with all the fuss of fighting each one, Being top boy already, he took the other 4 all at once and beat them all. He wasn't scared of anyone all his life.

Once home from holiday, the phone went one afternoon. My Grandad George answered it as we all lived in the big house then in Darley Drive. It used to take a while to work out which George was wanted, as 3 George's lived in the house; me, my dad, and my Grandad. He eventually told me my agent was on the phone, so I rushed to hear if it was good or bad news. For weeks it had been at the back of my mind. "Yes George you got the part and the first 4 days are in Marseille, you fly out in 2 weeks" she happily informs me. The sheer joy, the relief, the gratitude all hit me at once. I ran round the house informing the whole family. Everyone was thrilled again for me. I was just as happy hearing this as I was getting Grange Hill, 11 years earlier.

I had to fly from Stansted Airport, alone. So I decided to stay in London the week before and spend some time with John Alford. He was releasing records at the time, as well as doing London's Burning. We went to the Top of the Pops studios which were at Elstree. He was getting ready to go on, so I went for a walk and Shaun Ryder spotted me walking past his dressing room "Fookin hell its Ziggy from Grange Hill man, come in" This was nice being recognised by a man who was in a band I loved; 'The Happy Mondays' I spent a while in that dressing room with Shaun and co, the banter was good. Everyone was on their guard when Scousers and Mancunians are in a room together!

One person that did intrigue me that day was the singer Donovan's daughter, Oriole. She was going out with Shaun, but we went for a walk round the BBC together. He didn't mind, they had trust. I just thought she was mysterious, strange in a nice way and very friendly. She was hippy looking and stunningly beautiful. I took her into the back bar and we played the £250 jackpot fruit machines. We talked as we played and she couldn't believe I'd heard of her dad Donovan. I said "Of course I've heard of him, I love his music! Hurdy Gurdy Man, Catch the Wind, Season Of the Witch" I kept reeling songs off and she was so pleased. "He's a fucking legend", I told her. She smiled. I remember we won big too!

So I spent most of the day with the band. It was Black Grape then, rather than the Happy Mondays. Bez was around and so was Kermit the other singer. In fact I ended up going on the tour bus back to Manchester with them and spent 2 days staying in Shaun's house. I also danced beside Bez in a video they were making for the 1996 Euros finals. Bez had great skills using a football. He could keep it up longer than anyone I'd seen and balance the ball on his head, flip it back down etc. It was magical to watch. I had a few days with these nutters, then back to London, to the hotel at Stanstead airport.

On the opposite sides of the scale, I met a few members of the band, The Farm that week in a pub by The Angel in Islington. I was doing Brando and Pacino and Quint from Jaws impressions for them and they loved it. They invited me to a party in Suggs' house so I was over the moon. Along with a girl I met that night, we all got in a taxi. Also with us was the drummer out of Madness, his name evades me. After about 20 minutes of Godfather & On the waterfront impressions, the drummer says out of the blue "Suggs don't know him, he can't come"

There was nothing I could do. Nobody argued my corner, so I had to get out in the middle of nowhere, I asked the girl if she was coming with me, but she decided to stay for the big party which made it worse! I was in the back of beyond and somehow bopped my way back. I was cursing the Madness drummer who obviously hated people who outshone him, or the Godfather film. I have never listened to a song by them since, and I liked them too!

A day or so later, I was in the top hotel in Stanstead. I flew in the morning. Two pals, Harry and Dr Boyd came to join me but I took it easy as didn't want to arrive in France looking like Boris Karloff. Even so a few were still knocked back. The boys left, but I sat on my own for a while listening to the pianist, then hit the beautiful double bed in this luxurious hotel Channel 4 were paying for, and slept like a baby.

It was a private plane. I had my own personal hostess, free drinks and food. I remember thinking to myself I feel like James Bond here. It was kind of surreal, suddenly being treated like a king after years of ducking and diving and mental hospitals etc. Life was good again and I prayed I wouldn't wake up and it was all a dream.

I soon arrived and settled into another plush French hotel. Nicer than the one in Stanstead mainly because of the views. Before I unpack my stuff I always head for the balcony to see the view. It was incredible I could see the port of Marseille, small boats sailing up and down, all the hustle and bustle you'd expect from a busy port. Most spectacular was the mountains above with a golden monument in the middle. I wasn't filming until the morning so I had a stroll and a few French light ales in various bars.

The basic storyline was that Big Jimmy comes over to France to bring Little Jimmy back as he's in trouble with the foreign legion, and needs to get out. However, he also smuggles heroin through, strapped around his waist. I met Dean for the first time and Sue who played my mum and Dad. We got on fine. The scenes went well but the heat was unbearable.

The hardest day was the last because me and a couple of the riggers went out round the back streets of Marseille. It was cheaper than paying the ridiculous hotel prices I made the mistake of once. It had that edge about it too with a few shady characters knocking about. Prostitution was rife, but we stuck to ourselves. The following morning I was hungover to hell and had to film high up on mountain side ridge in the blistering sun. At one point I nearly keeled over and went all faint.

Luckily the rigger who I was out with the night before, Graham, got me to one side and told them to give me a few minutes. He poured water down me and dabbed my face with water till I felt better and functioned better. He knew exactly how I was feeling, and knew how to sort me out. So I got through the day and flew back the following morning.

One thing I did notice was on the last day, Steven, who played Max, instead of drinking with the rest of them in the hotel, took the time to take one of the cast, a young handicapped girl and the nanny on a boat, and rowed up the Marseille river. He never told anyone. He just took them, but I saw it and respected him ever since.

They were very important days. I had to know the lines, be the part and conduct myself sensibly. It was very dark stuff, the closest I got to playing a Joker type character. The only light relief was having Mickey Starke who played Sinbad around some days. He would have everyone in stitches with his capers. That helped take my mind off going too deep into my own world.

A few weeks in, the cheques start coming in so I've got money again. I used to think money was everything. 'Without it, what can you do?' was my philosophy. Aged 49, I don't believe that anymore. Money is important, yes, but I've seen too many good people die of illnesses out of their control and all the money in the world couldn't save them (or me in my months of madness.) Many said it before me and I agree with them; health is more important than money. Closely followed by family and the love that comes with it. What good would money be without family and friends around you? You'd die a lonely rich man, and I wouldn't want that. But I made good money doing Brookie.

Some Scenes later on were very intense, I had to cold turkey, overdose, cry in one scene, be drugged up, throw my mother down the stairs and die. All heavy duty stuff that mentally took it out of me. Playing this sad, pathetic character with no hope was draining, especially doing the crying scenes. They offered me a stick that you rub under your eyes, like lip balm. 99% of soap actors use them, but I didn't. I wanted to cry for real. I wanted real tears not fake. I spoke about this to a drama teacher I knew from London called Ernie Brando. He took classes called dangerous acting. He took you into places most drama classes wouldn't tread, very clever he was.

During breaks in London, prior to Brookside, I'd attend Ernie's classes. It kept me trim. He said "You can do two things here, one is think about something sad from your past, or two, think of something that could happen that would make you sad" I thought about what I seen in April 89. That was the saddest thing I'd ever seen – Hillsborough. I got the tears alright, but again it took me to a dark place. Later that night I struggled to sleep as things came coming back to me. Memories I'd moved on from were tantalising me once again.

A girl who did help me during it all, was Claire Sweeney, who played my sister Lindsey. She was always a great person to have around and very friendly. Fame never went to her head even afterwards when she went on to do all kinds, she kept her feet on the ground. I bump into her from time to time and enjoy a coffee in the town. She is a very good hearted person, with a wicked sense of humour.

Chris Evans and Danny Baker turned up on the set once. I saw them sitting on someone's lawn drinking a can of beer. One of the crew asked me to tell them to move. So I walked over and Chris offered me a can of beer saying "Bloody hell It's Ziggy come and join us!" So I obliged, and for about half an hour, I had such a laugh with them I forgot to ask them to move! I would have stayed chatting and laughing all day, only I got called back on set.

Strange that some people in showbiz I take to instantly, and others I take an instant dislike to. The first person I ever met who was famous, and I didn't know it at the time, was Bill Shankly, kicking a ball on Barn Field (now called The Bill Shankly Fields), with my Dad. The ball went past me and towards this old man walking his dog. He kicked it back, saying "Here you go son" Afterwards my dad told me who he was. I was only about 7 at the time. Not bad looking back that the first celeb I met was Shanks.

So Brookside was over and a few years later, the show would end itself sadly. But I look back fondly on the memories of my 4 months or so playing my part in it. Phil again gave me another chance and for that I will be eternally grateful despite the white lie I gave him. I'm sure he'd understand. I wonder if he fully knows the impact and the destiny he's given me?

In fact I saw him last year, in 2018, at a Grange Hill reunion in London. We chatted and laughed over things. The main laugh was my girl Mel asked me to book the hotel so I booked one online for the first time 4 miles from white city. What I didn't realise was once we got to London, the hotel room I'd booked was in White City, Oregon, USA. I had to re book another quickly......well, Mel did, as I wasn't to be trusted. Phil and his wife found this very amusing. But Mel never!

Chapter 17
Theatre

'Movies will make you famous, Television will make you rich, but theatre will make you good'
Terrence Mann

After Brookside I seemed to ride a rollercoaster of plays. They never ended until my second relapse in South Wales 1999.

The first was a pantomime at the Royal court; 'Dick Whittington' were I was to play the 'King Rat' alongside the bubbly singer Sonia, playing Dick. Many Sword fights and scares for the kids. My Auntie Brenda always says that was the best thing she saw me do. The secret to finding this character was not easy. I did a few rehearsals and it wasn't quite working, I just couldn't grasp the villainous character it needed. So an old Shakespearean actor who played the Captain had a quiet word with me one morning. He suggested I watch the old Disney cartoons, find a villain in one of them and I'd get the character by basing it on him.

Fortunately, I had all the Disney videos as I'd been selling them on a market stall a few years earlier for the local Del Boy called Liam, who later became a man of God. I went through as many as I could, then Jungle Book and Shere Khan the tiger, played by George Sanders just sprung at me, I watched it over and over all night, repeating his lines till I had it. I've always been a good mimic. For many years I've done the Godfather

Marlon Brando as my main party piece. I've done all over the world, even to the mob in little Italy in New York. I thought if they buy it, I got it. And they did.

So, the following day I walked into rehearsals and did my lines but had Shere Khan's voice in my head as I delivered them. It worked wonders. The directors and producers knew now they'd got the right guy. The old guy was right!

Everything went smoothly, but the last night I got some tragic news. It was the interval, so I rang my mam to see how my Nan was. She thought I'd come off stage. My Nan had cancer, not for long, or at least didn't know for long. She'd nursed my Grandad Albert for years who had Alzheimer's disease and had gone blind. It was a very sad ending to his life though both my mum and Nan did their best to look after him. He had died earlier that year. When I rang, my mum told me my Nan had just died. It hit me like a train again. I cried on the stairs of the theatre as the costume lady tried to console me. I had to go on stage shortly. I did go back out there and luckily it was an angry scene where I sink the ship and shout and curse. I would have got an Oscar that night because the cries and curses were of real pain. I was angry and must have frightened every kid in the audience that night.

One of the biggest regrets I have was not going home to my mother that night. I should have been with her, but Steve turned up that night and all I wanted to do was get drunk. So we sat in a Greek restaurant we knew, owned by a guy called Fatso, which had a bar downstairs and we hit Mr Jack Daniels. Steve was to console me as I was to console him a few years down the line.

One night during the panto, my old mate Danny who initially helped get me in Brookside for a few episodes in 92, appeared outside my dressing room door with a man I didn't at first recognise. He had glasses and was a bit older than me. I let them both in and a glass of JD was given to all.
"This is Paul," said Danny. We spoke, laughed and hugged goodbye. I thought what a nice guy Paul was, all the time thinking I know that voice. It was only afterwards, word got round Lily Savage was in the Audience. It dawned on me that it was Paul O'Grady who was the man behind Lily Savage. Hardly anybody knew what he looked like back then as he hid behind the Lily persona. Still, it was nice meeting him and not knowing. You don't make a fool of yourself as you sometimes do if conscious of who the person is. Danny would often do this in my life; just turn up out of nowhere alone or with a celeb of some type. He keeps me on my toes I guess.

After the panto I needed a holiday. I had plenty of money in the bank now from Brookside. In fact I lived off this for nearly 3 years and that included renting 3 houses, one of which was on a mountain in South Wales. The holiday was to be in Turkey and with Steve. It was only a week but a few things happened of note and one of a paranormal nature.

Before I went, I'd heard horror stories about the Turks, about how they hindered English girls on holiday or didn't like the English etc. I was a bit wary to say the least, but throughout my life I take people as I find them (i.e. cockneys, gypsies, Mancunians and Irish - who a few I know were wary of) but I never had a problem with any of these people. Only through football is a hatred of Manchester, but the times I've gone up there for shopping I've found them most pleasant. The same in Belfast, people would say dodgy going down the Falls Road or Sandy Row, but again they made most welcome. The gypsies they say will rob you, not one robbed me. The Turks hate us, well we were fine. We had a great holiday, even playing football with the Turks.

However, what we saw towards the end of the holiday I cannot explain. I couldn't then and I can't now. We'd been out, but were taking it easy this night as the night beforehand had been a mad one. We were sitting by the hotel poolside with a Turkish barman, chatting and laughing away. I grew tired and decided to lay on a sun lounger and stare at the stars. It was a perfect night for this. I'd never seen so many stars in the sky, anywhere in the world as much as this night. Wow I thought. So I stared for maybe 20 minutes, then I noticed something the same size as a star, moving in between the stars, like an ant crawling amongst the cosmos.

It took a few moments to register, then I called Steve over. It took him a few moments to spot it and then he was mesmerised too. We watched it move around at some speed, going back and forth and up and down. The strangest thing it did at one point was split in two; one went one way and the other the opposite. It was at this point, the Turkish bartender ran in the hotel to get on the roof to take photographs of it with his camera. It was so far away that the finest camera in the world would struggle to capture this. It was not of this world I'm convinced, to be able to travel so far across the stars, light years from home and at that speed. It was a good 30 minute spectacle, I don't believe man has invented something that can do this so far away; too advanced for mankind. I rarely mention it nowadays as it has caused a few arguments and laughter so I keep it to myself. But I know what I saw that night, so did Steve and so did the Turkish barman.

After the panto came Fredonia. This was a play written by a curly haired eccentric fellow from over the water. It told the story of two Scousers hitchhiking across the New York State in 1980. A comedy with me and big Marty who was twice the size of me, so we looked a great double act. We would get different lifts from whacky characters, then the ending would blow people away. They'd get to their destination, Fredonia, only find out from a barmaid that John Lennon had been killed. Being Beatles fans they then sit on their cases with a tear in their eyes, clink bottles and 'In my life' comes on. Lights down. Winning formula every time. We had a tear every night. On one night in the Everyman, Marty went on having just heard his Grandad had just died. How he got through 2 hours of comedy I don't know but I respect him highly for this bravery, and his tears flowed without hesitation that night.

The play toured and somehow Fredonia became a treble act now. Steve was written in. I never drove due to nearly causing a bus to crash into me during a lesson. It had to slam on the brakes, putting me off for life, but Ste did, so I put it to the writer it would be easier to get to all these places with Steve on board.

It was a lovely hot day when we arrived in Salisbury. First port of call was Stonehenge. Me, Steve, Big Marty, a Welshman named Joff who sadly became a recluse afterwards, plus the band, as we had live music throughout. We all sat off on the grass enjoying a bottle of beer staring at these historical stones that no-one could fully explain being there. One of the seven wonders of the medieval world, each one standing 13ft high. These are moments I look back on most fondly. Freedom and doing what I loved doing, acting, and with friends.

Me and Marty were to reunite 25 years later to perform this play again at the Adelphi hotel. It still got great acclaim from those who came, The curly writer Marc was still at the helm too. I worried that I might not get the tears when hearing of Lennon's death, but by 2018 I had enough sad things to think about sitting on that case, I hardly tried. The tears just came, for both of us every night.

I remember the day he really died. I was 10 in 1980 and my mother shouted up the stairs to me and my Dad, that John Lennon had been killed, as it was all over the radio. I felt instantly gutted as I was just getting into the Beatles and his solo albums then. Only a few big stars hit me when they died. The first was Lennon, then Rik Mayall, Robin Williams, Muhammad Ali and Bowie. When I left the house to go to school that day, I remember seeing former Beatle Pete Best get into his car. He lived opposite most of my life, he looked like he'd seen a ghost. He was white with grief, haunted with sadness as he went to work. The whole city mourned that day and still does, such talent taken in the blink of an eye by a madman, or is there more to it?

Another play I got involved in and did 5 times in total from 98 to 2016 was 'The Alehouse' a comedy set in a working class pub written by Furlong and Power. The cast would change every time except for me and an Irish actor Les, who played the priest Father Flaherty. It was great to have a different cast every time as I worked with some great local actors from the fantastic Micky Finn, Jake Abraham, Phil 'Tin head' Olivier, Bernie Foley, Lyndsey Germaine, Jimmy Gallagher (who was at the Grange Hill audition with me in 85) and Chrissy Rock to name a few. Years later Donna Furlong would take the helm and get the band back together in 2016 as sadly Tony Furlong passed away.

A funny thing me and Les from Dublin who played the priest would do was dress Les as the priest and walk around the town, talking to people, or go in the churches to watch priests look on confused. We had endless fun with this caper, and doing the play.

I also compered bands for a girl named Sue; all for charity as she has Dystonia so raises money for their charity. A brave lady; I'm very fond of. We also made money for Winnie Bennett who lost her son Keith at the hands of those bastards the Moors Murderers. The owner of the club wasn't so generous, he took most of Sue's money she raised. I was fuming but had to stay quiet. I witnessed some great bands such as the Sums, Inbyones from Huyton and The Crescent, so it was a great number this job as I love live music.

The Hillsborough play which I've talked about, was done, difficult as it was. Then Steve moved to South Wales with his wife Tina and their two young children. Soon I was to follow!

Chapter 18
The Titanic

'God himself could not sink this ship'
Unknown crew member

I was renting a flat that overlooked the Bill Shankly Fields. I had it exactly how I wanted it, like an Aladdin's cave of all my interests and things I'd collected on my travels. Many parties were held there after nights out with my pals. The neighbours hated me; I was their worst nightmare. At 3am, all of a sudden rave music would blare out with raised voices and people talking on the balcony. The occasional argument would break out but nothing serious. When I left, they must have had a party themselves.

One night in the Cabin nightclub, a girl came over for a light. I said to her "Did you know you glide when you walk into a room? Most girls merely plod along but you glide." Little did I know, after flicking my zippo, that I was to spend the rest of my life with her, have a baby, and go through four breakdowns with her at my side. We'd travel the world and live together.

Enter Mel into my life. Very pretty, long darkish blonde hair, petite little thing, but not knowing then loyal and strong. She found me in a bookies after we'd dated for a while, to tell me she was pregnant. I was happy and sad at the same time. Happy because for years I'd wanted a son, although I never knew at this point it would be a boy. On many long car journeys, me and Steve talked of wanting sons to carry on our family name and do the things our fathers done with us. I was sad because I was 28 and enjoying my life and had arranged already with Steve to put a big play on in Wales about the Titanic, so knew I wouldn't be around for most of the pregnancy. I promised on visits home I'd visit her, but it turned out she'd end up visiting South Wales more. I assured her I'd be there at the birth. It was not until Kirk was born and I looked into his eyes moments after, he stared at me and I stared at him and said to myself 'I will never leave you, or your Mum, ever.'

He was called Kirk after Kirk Douglas as the first film I ever remembered was 'The Vikings'. I must have been about four years old and watched it with my mother. He didn't take long to be born, couldn't wait to get into this world. But 9 months earlier, I couldn't wait to get to Wales.

With the money I still had from Brookside, I rented a lovely little house high up in a little close, on a mountain in Cwmbran, South Wales. Steve was at the bottom of the mountain in a more working class rougher estate. I liked my little house with a garden where I could feed the birds and watch them in the mornings, before running round madly for the rest of the day.

We had the idea to write the play when selling our paintings of the Titanic, in London. We stumbled on the fact whilst reading a Titanic book that two professional Welsh boxers died on the Titanic called Davey Bowen and Leslie Williams. They were supposed to go to America and prize fight in

Pittsburgh. It was only a small chapter in the book but played a huge chapter in our lives.

The first thing we did was go to Cardiff library to see if we could find any information on these men. You had no Google on your phone in 99! We looked through many books and found nothing; it was like they never existed. Then, one of us stumbled on a newspaper article that the librarian put us on to, which was an interview with one of the boxer's relatives. She was still alive and her name was Gwyneth Coombes. It didn't have any details of how to contact her and the paper wouldn't give us any info, so we got the local Cardiff phone book. That was where Davey the boxer once lived and this relation now lived. We rang every Coombes in the book, asking the same question "Sorry to bother you but did you have a relation on the Titanic?" Maybe a 100 people hung up, instantly thinking it was a crank call. Some were polite and said no, some told us to piss off, but one said "Yes I did. He was my Great Uncle what do you want?" All those hours and perseverance paid off, we knew she was out there just took a bit of time. We arranged to meet at her home in Cardiff, to tell her our plans to write a play based around the story of these two boxers. It was 50/50 she'd entertain us but when we briefly told her over the phone, she loved the idea instantly, as it had never been told. Hence we called it 'Titanic! An Untold Story.'

We could never have written it without this lovely lady's help. She then informed us that the other boxer Leslie Williams' relation called Jean was still alive and she helped tell us Leslie's story. It was ultimately a tragic tale for these two men as they had families; Davey or Dai as he was known in Cardiff, and Leslie in Swansea. That's where Mrs Williams lived. They were only planning to go to America to prize fight in Pittsburgh for a while, make their money and come back to their families in Wales. They were due to sale on the Lusitania on 9th April but Davey's suit wasn't ready, so they set off on the Titanic on the 12th April instead, which tragically sank on the 15th. They didn't stand a chance as they were in the steerage section, which is 3rd class. Leslie took ill, so he would have been in bed during the worst disaster at sea.

We listened and took notes of everything they said. We would meet in little Welsh pubs in the hills of Cardiff or the edge of the Gower in Swansea. They were two of the friendliest, kind hearted old ladies we ever met. Gwyneth showed us a ring she had kept that Welsh flyweight champion, Jimmy Wilde, had given Davey. It was recovered when they found his body before being put in a sack to be buried at sea. It was a beautiful ring and its value I can't imagine, but she never dreamed of selling it. We kept in touch for many years after but after I moved house so much it eventually ended.

Now we had to write it and bring in all the other characters such as the Captain, officers, chefs, workers down below, the boxers' families, sailors, Irish bands, dancers, passengers etc. etc. There were so many characters we didn't think about how big this cast was going to be. For nights on end, we went through different Titanic books, watched documentary after documentary (including the old classic film 'A Night To Remember') squeezing every fact and info we could, to combine with the boxers' story. All we ever talked about was the Titanic. I even dreamt I was on it on more than one occasion. We were instant experts on the subject and even travelled to Southampton to do research there where it set off. We talked to people and attended a function in a hotel where we met a lady called Millvina Dean, who was the last remaining survivor of the Titanic. She was an infant on the ship that fateful night and lost her father. His body was never found, but she was put into a lifeboat and survived. Another lovely lady who chatted to us for some time when we told her of our play.

Once written we wanted to produce it, didn't want some idiot to come in and take over. Together we figured we could handle it, but to direct it as well we decided would be too much. Write, produce *and* direct would be madness. We put word out that we wanted a director. We'd already booked the theatre in Cwmbran (a little trick Marc 'Fredonia' Gee taught us - book it and you gotta do it.) Various people came forward but none appealed to us as they never had the enthusiasm we had about it. Then, the only other Scouser on the mountain found us. Enter Gricey. He moved to Wales as a kid, had a family and lived happily there. Within minutes we both knew this was the man to direct our play. He'd directed a few local plays and a short film about a confused man who jerked off on top of a mountain. He knew how to help cast, get everyone prepared and deal with everything else a director does. When you're laughing and joking with someone after 5 or 10 minutes and the Scouse wit is in the air, we knew Gricey was bound to be our man. Although later that day he may have been in two minds. After we all had a few light ales, me and Steve had a ferocious disagreement but Gricey stayed on board, so to speak. He must have thought "what the hell am I getting into?" I think he'll agree his life was never the same after he met us. He was barred from most of the pubs on the mountain, left his wife, moved back to Liverpool and spent all his inheritance money he'd attained from his father.

On one occasion, Gricey came with me and Steve to do a bit more research in Southampton. We booked into a hotel and hit the town. Gricey left early as he wasn't as big a drinker as us two. When we got back later, around 3am, we were making a terrible noise, shouting down corridors and singing. Gricey said he put his head under a pillow. Then a while later, Steve knocked on his door asking for tomatoes. Gricey was confused telling him he had none, but Steve burst in and began rooting through Gricey's belongings looking for these non-existent tomatoes. After 5 minutes he gave up and slumped off to bed. When questioned about his actions the next day, he remembered nothing.

We did what we did every morning whilst living in Spain, and stood on the balcony and yelled "Good Morning Vietnam." This confuses anyone below whilst amusing us. Around the breakfast table, people were talking of the noisy Scousers from the night before. Gricey was agreeing with them until me and Steve walked in and said "Alright Gricey lad" He put his head down in shame!

Years later, Gricey brought his young autistic son to Liverpool for the weekend. We drove round in Gricey's big car. I was in the front and if I see a woman with a decent arse I put the window down slightly and comment "Interesting cheeks". I've done it for years and thought nothing of it. The girl never hears, it's just for the amusement of the company I'm in and to alert everyone fine buttocks are nearby. Years earlier with Steve, some would be marked out of 10 but that stopped. Many interesting cheeks were spotted over the weekend and Gricey's son went back to his mother in Wales at the end of it. Two days later, Gricey's ex wife rang him and said " I took Sean to school today and all the way there he kept popping his head out the window and shouted 'interesting cheeks' at every girl, woman and even old pensioners. Can you tell me why he's suddenly doing this? " Gricey tried not to laugh, especially the bit about the old people. Young Sean hadn't quite grasped it was only young women this applies too. Almost 20 years on, Gricey tells me his son who's nearly 28 years old now, still opens car windows and says "Interesting cheeks" whenever the opportunity arises!

Although I didn't know it back then, and he didn't know it about me (because we never disclosed it back then) Gricey also suffered anxiety and depression. We never spoke of it, not until nine months or so later, when I had my second relapse. Gricey confided in me then, whilst visiting me in a Welsh hospital in the middle of a beautiful valley. That's when me and Gricey became good friends. When he visited, you know someone is a good friend then. If they take the time out to sit with you for hours and they've only known you less than a year, you can almost guarantee you'll become closer.

So Griceburger, as he was known, began organising the auditions at the theatre. We all were there but we let Gricey do all the work. Me and Steve just watched carefully as the different actors and non-actors did their piece. The hardest thing was everyone was good, there wasn't anybody we thought couldn't handle a part. I'd say forty auditioned that day; I'm not sure if it's been done before, but we cast them all! We thought even if there's not a part for them, they can be in a dance scene or crowd scenes and a few we wrote into the script too. Everyone was happy. Nobody got the 'Sorry you never got the part' Phone call or 'we'll be in touch' and never do.

One person that did interest me was a guy known as Billy Boy. He was a tough looking, ex-navy, ex con, who had never acted but always wanted to. We gave him the role of Officer Lightoller, an important part and with Billy being ex-Navy, he took to it like a duck to water. He was handy to have around, and like most of the tough guys I'd known, never talked about it.

Rehearsals took place and tickets were selling, but the main question people asked was 'how are they going to build the Titanic on stage?' Good question! One of the girls in the show told us her Dad was a carpenter. He came and looked at the stage and said he could build the ship made from balsa wood but you'd only see the bow (Front) coming at you, with clever blue lighting you wouldn't see the sides or stern (back). This sounded good and we put him to work. He was told like everyone else, whatever we make on the box office we all split, so everybody gets something. He built it and it looked amazing!

Another guy turned up who wasn't an actor and had no intentions of being one, but he knew every fact and figure on the Titanic. He was an expert in this field and his name was Nick, soon to be called Titan-Nick. He just wanted to help out, advise etc. This man had every book and documentary imaginable. When we went into his house weeks later he had paintings on the wall, books everywhere, models of the ship on his mantelpiece, Titanic rugs, Titanic wallpaper and a rubber blow up Titanic in his bath. His help was most welcome.

Meanwhile bad things were happening to my close mate Alford. He'd been set up by the News of the World in a drugs sting, set up by the fake sheik. He fell into a clever trap set up in a hotel, where they got him tipsy, offered him vast amount of money to go to Dubai to open a nightclub and then asked him to get drugs. He called a pal not wanting to ruin the Dubai deal, not knowing there were hidden cameras in the tellies. He was all over the papers the next day. His life would never be the same again, and it broke my heart to watch him go through it. He even got sent down for 9 months. Although I was in Wales and he was in London we were still in contact, but there was nothing I, or anyone could do for him, he had to serve his time. Looking back 1999 turned out to be a year of Hell for him and soon for me.

So Alford's in prison and I'm in the middle of producing the biggest thing I'd ever taken on and Mel's getting close to giving birth. She came up a few times. The first time she came she met Steve's wife Tina who is very attractive with dark curlyish hair, almost Gypsy looking. They hit it off instantly. I always remember the first night she came up, me and Ste went out on a massive pub crawl round pubs in the back and beyond the mountain. We returned at 9am with a stone statue of Achilles as a gift for her. Her face wasn't happy as she stood at the door with Tina. Tina told her straight "You better get used to this girl!"

So we kept on trucking along producing the play but without realising it I was getting slowly more stressed. Although things were running smoothly, it was still taking it out of me, gradually building up to the climax to come. We had to deal with the building of the set, keep an eye on Gricey, make sure the show looked right and deal with publicity with local newspapers and TV. HTV took an interest; I told them Gricey was like the Francis Ford Coppola of Wales. The local Argus paper loved the story. We contacted sponsors to get funding, and had to push ticket sales and so on.

We decided for the last night to hire a room in a hotel and throw a party for everyone. Our families and friends would come up, including Terry Burkett the chairman of the HJC group, his lovely wife Anne and daughter Jennie, who had the voice of an Angel we found out that night. They lost their son Peter at Hillsborough, so we decided to hold an auction that night for the Hillsborough families.

We needed prizes and one of the journalists involved with the play was friends with Joe Calzaghe, the future super middleweight champion of the world. She told us roughly where his gym was in Newbridge. So me and Steve decided to visit the Italian Dragon and get some signed pics off him. It took a bit of time looking round the Welsh countryside of Newbridge, amongst hills and forests until we came across a shack. Surely this can't be it we thought, as we expected some plush gym. We knocked on the battered down door and a little Italian guy opened it. This turned out to be his father and trainer Enzo Calzaghe. We were polite and told him briefly of the play and that we were doing an auction for the Hillsborough families etc. so he let us in.

It was a typical gritty, dusty, old fashioned no holds barred gym, cobwebs on the ceilings, posters of Manchester United on the walls. Joe looked down from the ring where he'd been sparring with his Dad. He looked good, Italian and Welsh in him, dark and handsome, not like your average boxer. He looked at us and said "Bloody hell it's Ziggy!" Great start I thought, he knows me. We spoke a bit of Grange Hill and Brookside and an instant banter between me, Joe, Steve and Enzo erupted. Football naturally came up too. Then we told him of the play and the auction for the Hillsborough families. He couldn't do enough when he heard this. He rooted round the gym for decent gloves and signed them all. He must have signed 50 publicity photos of him holding a belt he'd won in 95. The man that had 46 professional fights and 46 wins in his career, in both super middleweight and light heavyweight. He couldn't do enough for us that day. I liked and respected him and his Dad that day, they were very kind to us. Steve was later to attend a few of his fights as he said if he ever fights get in touch. Sadly I never did as I was to be in hospital. If I hadn't been I would have loved to attend to watch the Italian Welsh gentleman.

Then one day in March, I got a call off Mel's family saying her waters had broken. Usually Steve would drive me up, but we were deep in rehearsals and things had to be done, so I had to get the train up, whilst he held the fort with Gricey. I got home and got a cab to Whiston Hospital. I'd heard horror stories of women spending days in labour; many said I'd faint. He never took long to arrive, she was in labour for no more than 4 hours.

As I've said, the bond was instant. That one glance had me. He hooked me in instantly. Young Kirk Michael George Wilson was here. I spent a few days there until all my family had seen him and everything had settled, then back to the valleys. This was a high of the greatest magnitude; I had a son!

For a few years I'd talked of wanting a son and my wish was granted, or prayer was answered, depending on which side of the fence you sit. I wasn't to know on that train back to the Valleys of the laughs, tears and adventures I was to have with this little child in the future. Or how I would watch him grow and go through all his trials and tribulations with him. Now he's 20 and as close to me as I am to my father. The Wilson bond continues.

When you're living on a mountain above a small town, everyone knows your business. Most people knew who I was. The Grange Hill thing and Brookside refreshed the memories of what I looked like. The local pub by the theatre was rough and ready. Most of the cast wouldn't have dreamed of going in there until we came along and used it to plan things or all have a drink after rehearsals. One particular guy in there, scruffy with long hair and older than us, always passed comment every time he saw me and Steve; things like "Fucking Scousers" or "English fuck off home." I let his comments go over my head. He always had a few people with him and Steve would always say ignore him.

One particular night, just before the play opened up he got to me. The whole cast were in there sitting quietly, talking downstairs while I played pool with a local. Billy was near me, he always stayed close and became like my bodyguard for a while. I think this night was the first night signs were showing of a relapse coming. Every time I took a shot, the local guy who'd been making comments, who was sitting behind with his girl and a few mates, kept shouting "Foul" meaning I was cheating.

I ignored him the first few times then about the third I said "It wasn't a foul and you know it so keep your mouth shut" but the next shot he shouted it again and I warned him again. "If you shout that again you'll be kissing the carpet." Now if it was 2019 and someone did this I'd just put the cue down and sit with the others thinking he's not worth it. But being 29 and on the edge of another breakdown in a room full of people, I wasn't going to back down.

"Fuckin do it!" he yelled. Without hesitation I turned and hit him to the floor with one punch and he couldn't get up. His mates stood up and Billy intervened saying it's a one on one. Then the bouncer ran over (incidentally called Tiny, but he wasn't). He was about to grab me when the guy's girlfriend jumped up and said "No Tiny, it wasn't his fault it was my feller's"

I couldn't believe it, she got me off the hook with the doorman. Maybe he treated her badly; knocked her about or bullied her somehow, as what girl would defend the man who's laid your man on the deck? My adrenaline was pumping. I kept waiting for him to get up but he didn't fancy another go. I do hate fighting as I've said but at the time I didn't know another way out. I'm not proud of what I did, I would have been a braver man to have walked. Built up anger mixed with stress comes out in different ways and that night it came out in violence. The only good that may have come out of it, is he wouldn't insult Scousers minding their own business again.

The manager soon came down and threw us all out and barred us all. The next day Gricey, who wasn't even there that night, walked in there to read the papers and he got told to leave. Steve and I had to find a new local so we walked into one round the corner that was supposed to be equally as rough, called the Moonraker. I approached the landlord and told him what had happened in the other pub and that we were doing a play and needed somewhere to go afterwards. He said he'd heard the incident but didn't care, we were welcome there no problem. It worked out better because we had stay-behinds till dawn and all the locals befriended us. Everyone was happy as his pub had 50 new regulars and they were to bring people after the show.

Once we had all the costumes, me and Steve one night decided to turn up at Jah's Fetish Club dressed as officers off the Titanic. His regular fetish goers were not happy about this saying "That's not fetish" etc. Our reply was "Who gives a shit?" Jah was running round somewhere in a latex dress, whilst me and Steve sat at a table watching a pretty black woman in a red leather catsuit whipping a naked man on a rack. It was entertaining to say the least.

Then Steve went to the toilet as I sat watching the various capers around me. Next the catsuit lady approached me and said "I would love to put you on that rack and whip your ass."

I thought about this experience for a few seconds, knowing the wrong reply could be catastrophic so i replied "As much as I'd love you to do that, my pal has just gone the loo and if he comes back and sees me strapped naked to that thing he will tell the world about it for the rest of our lives, but thank you all the same," She looked disappointed and walked away. I told Steve when he returned and he was devastated I never took the offer up, as he knew the mileage he would have got out of it would have been phenomenal. To have things on each other was vital back then.

Years earlier, I went to audition for a play in London. I knocked at the director's house and he answered in a baby's nappy. In the background others were in rubber gimp masks and latex outfits and leather keks etc. I should have walked there and then but needed the money. I went in and before long, I'm in a pair of black leather keks and whisked off to a fetish club by Kings Cross to discuss the play.

Before long I'm dancing to rave music, sweating in these leather trousers with all kinds of men coming over asking me stuff. I noticed men being strung up in cages around me. It was a sea of leather. I had to get out. I sneaked out while these guys chatted. But it got worse.

As I stood outside Kings Cross, I was mistaken for a rent boy for the next hour by guys asking me to get in their cars. Then the police came and asked me to move along and told me if they saw me again they'd arrest me. I tried to explain I was auditioning for a part and they said they'd heard it all before. I got home in the end. I love leather on women but not on me! What scared me more that night was not the gays or the fetish crowds, it was the people looking at me thinking I was gay. I was about 25 and it scared me, the looks.

Another night all hell broke loose in an Indian restaurant in Newport. Earlier that day on 15th April 1999, it was the 10 year anniversary of the Hillsborough disaster. We'd driven to Anfield to pay our respects. It was an emotional day, talking to some of the families and survivors. I'd go every year without fail, but it was never easy and I always came away angry, upset, numb and emotional etc.

So sitting in this restaurant are myself, Steve and Jah. Steve had a red Liverpool shirt on this night. We were relaxing and talking, as I enjoyed my chicken tikka (my usual dish in these places). Out of the blue, a voice shouted "Fuckin Scousers go home." It was Steve that began this confrontation by asking him to be quiet etc. It was a fat Welshman about our age, 29, sitting with his girlfriend. I remember Jah kept saying ignore him but he continued by shouting things like 'you're not welcome here', 'everyone watch your wallets', 'you're all fucking robbers' etc. We took all this, but then he shouted something I'll never forget which was so cruel and instantly hurting, it was a race to get to him. He shouted "You two should of died at Hillsborough with the rest of the bastards."

Instinct took over; pure anger and rage came upon me, I never waited another second. I was on him, dragged him from his chair and kicked his arse so bad he was out cold, I even somehow picked this lump up and said to Steve "You hit him now." He did and knocked him down again. Never had anyone angered me as much as him that night in Newport. As he lay on the floor with the Indian guys picking him up, the manager phoned the police and said the police are coming. I told him "You don't know what he said" Then we walked out and got in a cab quick. Even Jah who was a pacifist understood my anger. If someone was to say that to me now in 2019, I'd probably do the same.

That's what we've had to put up with because of what the Sun wrote in 1989. For years we took shit from people all over the country who believed we caused the disaster. He'll never shout that again to two Liverpool fans.

When I got home I was gutted. I'd lost my beautiful Camel watch Alford had given me a few years earlier. He was sponsored by Camel whilst doing London's Burning. He knew I liked it and gave me it. It was worth about £800 pound so I rang the restaurant to see if it was there and they said yes come and get it. I could hear cops in the background telling him what to say so I hung up. I knew I'd never see it again. Alford was in prison at this time, so it made it all the harder. That watch was personal to me and a lovely unusual one. I knew Alford would understand when I told him why it got lost ; coming off my wrist during the mayhem etc. He was always behind the Justice 96, constantly in touch from day one and went to Anfield to pay tribute days after.

The play opened up in the May and on the opening night we made a fuss of the boxer's families; red carpet treatment and front row seats. Everyone was on form. Me, Ste and Gricey even played little cameos; the 3 Slade brothers who were firemen and got on the ship only to be turned away because they were intoxicated. It wasn't a hard part for us because the tradition for the show was to have a couple of beers before, stagger on singing etc. then get hauled off, back to the mixing desk high up at the back of the theatre and watch the show enjoying a beer. It was a success. The two relatives of the families loved it. It was very emotional for them, but they loved seeing their family history brought back to life. All week it played, then the last night came, an array of characters came from back home.

The play went well, the party was a party of all parties afterwards. The Hillsborough family chairman, Terry's daughter, Jennie, got up and sang the Titanic film song 'My heart will go on' which brought the house down. Terry and Anne both stood up for what they believed in. I remember, years later, Anne told me she went to a meeting with some of the Hillsborough families. Some high members of the government looked down on them and said "I know how you all feel." Anne was astonished by this comment. So Anne stood up and looked into the then home secretary's eyes and replied. "No you don't know how it feels, how do you know?" With the gloves Joe Calzaghe gave us we raised a good few hundred for Terry to take back for the Hillsborough families. That felt good.

 The perfect night and probably my proudest moment in show business. It was our baby. We created it, we'd done it and felt on top of the world that night. Both mine and Steve's families came up along with all our pals. I was on as much as high as getting Grange Hill and Brookside that night....

The next night, I took Kirk to the top of the mountain and did a 'Roots' on him; lifting him to the stars saying "Behold Kirk, the only thing greater than yourself." These are the highs. Unfortunately they don't help me further down the line though. I stayed on a high after that play, and without knowing it, never come down.

Chapter 19
The Mountain

'I may go crazy, before that mansion on the hill.' Van Morrison

There had been many highs and lows that year; the birth of my son, the last night of the play, a few brawls, Alford being set up and sent to prison, and the final high was to come before the meltdown.

Me and Steve decided to go to Glastonbury in the summer of 99. We got there the night before it started. We planned to either jump the fences like I did as a kid at the Grand National. Many times me and my pals would climb the walls of Aintree racecourse and watch the National free. When we arrived at Glastonbury it was chaos. Security were throwing people out and some getting beaten up for retaliation. Bunking in may not be the best idea we thought.

By chance, the following morning, we bumped into some local Welsh gangster types who knew Gypsy Dave in London. They'd met me years earlier with him. They had what's known as the stamp to get you in; simply stamp your hand and you're in. They would take money all day doing this and fortunately never charged us. We were in.

Now, I love music as does Steve; especially live music. The atmosphere was amazing and electric with peaceful, characters everywhere, I'd never been before so it was a whole new experience for me, and Steve. 3 days of musical bliss.

We saw REM one night, they brought the house down. Gomez on a small stage with a big crowd. I watched Al Green on a mountain, on my own as Steve met Jah. The Manic Street Preachers, Underworld and on the last night, the one I enjoyed the most, was The Fun Lovin' Criminals. The crowd bounced as the song 'Scooby Snacks' came on, I was in the middle of thousands of people bouncing in the air. My head was touching the clouds that night. I felt on top of the world. It was one of the most feel good moments of my life, I still watch it on YouTube to this day and it sends goose bumps down my spine. How I stood in the middle of that crowd I'll never know, as I couldn't now.

We came home from Glastonbury physical wrecks. Me more because I had hardly slept for 3 days. We shared a small tent but we partied constantly. After the bands finished, there would be something happening. Steve had an audition for Brookside on the Monday after it. He walked in looking like Worzel Gummidge and said the worst opening line he could have given. "Sorry I'm late I just spent 3 days in Glastonbury with George Wilson" He never got the part.

Billy was hanging around a lot. Mel was up with Kirk that June. I got a skinhead after Glastonbury. My appearance looked frightening now. I even put the clippers on Steve's poor son Jack, who was only about 5, and gave him a skinhead. He wasn't happy but I felt he should have one.

A week or so before the episode, I started waking up in my sleep in pure panic. There were realistic visions of somebody above me with a baseball bat, about to hit me over the head. I'd awake sitting up in shock and out of breath. Another time I was asleep in bed, then found myself at the bottom of the stairs panting and couldn't breathe, not knowing what had frightened me in my sleep. I went to a doctor and he gave me Seroxat. Things got worse after I started taking this drug; that I am sure of. Paranoia slowly started creeping in. I began to think about people I'd lost in the past; my Grandparents mainly. I worried about my Dad's mate Phil Pape for some reason. I rang my Dad to see if he was ok and he said yes he's fine etc. It would be years till Phil passed away but something worried me back then. I thought he was in trouble. Only thoughts at this stage nothing major yet.

After a few more nights of waking up in fear and disturbed sleep, I then found I couldn't sleep. It was torture. For days and nights on end, I tossed and turned and got more wound up as I tried. Then out the blue I'd shout aggressively for no reason, Mel was on the phone to her sister Lyndsey one day and I suddenly yelled "And you can stop it too." She thought I was acting and asked what was up. I said "It's happening again, I'm having a breakdown" Now she never knew what I meant as I'd never told her anything of my breakdown 8 years earlier. She was only 22 at the time and never had any experiences with mental illness whatsoever. I never told anyone once I'd got over it. It was my skeleton in the closet, my taboo subject which nobody needed to know. But now she knew, or at least sensed something bad had happened, but it still never prepared her for what was to come.

The following day, I only remember parts. The parts I remember are still very clear so I have had to ask the people involved to fill in the gaps so to speak. The first thing I remember was thinking my life was the same as the film 'The Truman Show' with Jim Carey. I'd watched this film only once but didn't think it had much of an impact on me at the time. This was a film about a man whose whole life had been a reality TV show, without him knowing it, all his family and friends were actors and actresses for the cameras. I believed everyone I knew was not really who they said they were. All set up to make a film about my life. Hidden cameras had been following me all my life to a mass audience watching. I believed the cameras were on me as I imagined it, so I started talking into thin air, thinking the world was watching. I cried looking up saying "Why Mother why?"

This delusion went on for a while. I went upstairs and saw Mel was bathing Kirk. A few months earlier, Billy had told me a story of when he was in prison, a guy came in accused of drowning his baby in the bath, when all along it was his wife. I thought Mel was drowning Kirk and setting me up, so I grabbed her forcefully, to stop her. She was petrified now. She'd never seen me like this. She begged me to hand Kirk over, which I did. This gave her a chance to call Steve, then the police, and Steve ran from the bottom of the mountain to the top to try and help.

I then went downstairs and took all my clothes off. Totally naked, I jumped across all the cars in the close; from one car to the next, screaming nonsense. I screamed at the moon and the moon screamed back that night. During this naked rampage, I then had the vision a UFO was on its way to abduct me so I ran inside and hid in the corner praying it wouldn't get me. Every time the lights of a passing car passed I thought this was it; I thought I was to be taken away by aliens and never seen again.

A film called 'Fire in the Sky' always played on my mind, about a man who was abducted in a spaceship in terrifying circumstances. I thought I was next as I cried naked in the corner of my home. Then the last delusion came to me and it was more frightening than the Truman one and the UFO, as this was a vision of pain to be inflicted. I imagined and believed that every hard man, gangster, or dangerous person I had ever met were on their way to beat me to death. One by one I thought of a new one who was coming up the mountain. I'd turn my head in fear, rolling it around, crying and begging God to save me. I pictured Gypsy Dave, Big Stan, Mad dog, Joey, Nish, Brummie, Charlie, Lenny, Billy & Bobby, in fact every bad ass I'd ever met.

I thought I was going to die. They were all going to kill me because I'd set them up somehow. The papers had maybe done it. All that had gone on with Alford, regarding being set up, was spinning round my mind now. That was the overriding thought, that I'd been set up. Then I thought the whole world was against me; everybody from my mother to the old lady next door. Maybe that's where the saying comes from, having a vision like this.

Steve arrived to me, standing naked in the living room. Mel had locked herself in the bathroom earlier but had come down to try and calm me but it was an impossible task. I thought Steve had set me up too, that he was part of everything, so I shook my penis at him, saying "I was always bigger than you." I then attacked him with the Pink Panther lamp.

We struggled for a bit, but he somehow calmed me. Years later, when I was to have panic attacks, he was one of the few that could calm me. He was now seeing me at my worse. He'd never seen me like this and it frightened him as much as it frightened Mel.

I remember putting Pink Floyd 'Wish You Were Here' on and saying "Listen to this Steve, you gotta listen again, it means everything." I must have been relatively calm at this point, not manic for a few moments as I listened to the words and sang along. God knows what he spoke to me about, but that all changed when the police came through the door. There were about seven of them. I thought they'd come to take baby Kirk away. I was ok until they tried to go upstairs.

To this day, I don't know where I got the strength, but the first one who came towards me went down. Then the next I threw over my shoulder. The third I flicked aside like a fly. Now I'm enraged, my only thought is to stop them harming my son. In all my mixed up confusion I thought they were harming my child. I fought with them for what seemed an eternity, screaming at them as I laid blows until they got me down. Before I knew it I was handcuffed and my feet shackled as I tried to kick, aware my hands were of no use. I still tried to resist these chains and ripped my wrists and feet during the struggle. Wriggling like a coyote in a trap. I fought the law but the law won. Mel had come down now and insisted they don't take me like that. "Let him put his trousers on." So my keks and top were put on, then I was put into a police van.

The journey to Newport hospital was where I had my final delusion. I was Christ himself being taken to be crucified. As the van sped along the Welsh roads, I looked out the window, shackled to a seat, crying as I imagined I was going to arrive to crowds of people including my family. Then I'd be strung up on a cross and nailed to it until I died, like I'd read in the Bible as a child and seen in the movies. I begged the police not to take me, "Please, I don't want to die." It was all so real and I was so helpless.

I soon went into my own world. The fight was gone from me for a time and I drifted like a satellite. Next thing, I'm in a room full of doctors and nurses, plus the cops who brought me. A nurse approached me and I spat in her face telling her to 'fuck off' as I'm held down by the cops on a bed. I can't punch or kick so the only thing left I must have thought was spit. I'm ashamed to this day of doing that, even though I know I didn't know what I was doing. A doctor came in from the other side and rammed a needle in me. I turned and he'd moved. I waited a moment and felt no different, but pretended to fall asleep. A foolish doctor came close to me then I opened my eyes and tried to bite him.

"Give him another shot"

They were injecting me with pure Valium; the next shot was surreal, everything I had been feeling that night was suddenly drained from me. All the anger, confusion, hatred, delusions, visions, fears and thoughts went. I felt calm, relaxed, remorseful, and sad. I sat motionless and could feel the tranquillity within me. I didn't want to harm anybody now. The whole room stared at me, not knowing if it had worked or not.

I spoke to the cops first holding me down. "I'm so sorry guys, I don't know what came over me, please forgive me" I said with tears in my eyes. They all replied saying 'It's ok George' etc. Then I saw the nurse I'd spat at, I apologised profusely to her and she was fine about it. I asked the cops to take the shackles off me as my wrists were killing. A few said no, but the main one who must have overridden them all, agreed and they took them off. I stood up and began to hug the ones I'd been aggressive to earlier, apologised and so forth. Soon Mel and Steve came in and we spoke for a bit. I said to Mel "I bet you're gonna leave me now," but she never. The night was over; probably the scariest night of them all.

There were signs it was coming for months but I never saw them, nor did anyone else as they never knew what to look for. That to me was Hell. Hell in the mind; the devil playing tricks on me on a huge and frightening scale. I could have died that night or worse, someone close to me, because I was out of control. The cruellest of illnesses had caught up with me. It beat me again as it did in 91. I was to awake the next day in a Welsh psychiatric hospital in the middle of a valley. I called it my Cuckoo's Nest on the Hill.

I awoke with the sun in my eyes, unsure at first where I was. I walked out of the room to see a few patients sitting round calmly reading or eating their breakfast. That's when things started flooding back from the horrors of the night before. I felt ashamed. "Oh God, I hope I didn't hurt anyone" was my first thought.

There was a back door that lead to a huge garden overlooking the mountains and valleys beyond. I could see a stream not far away flowing gently through the grassy terrain. I could hear and see many birds close by and I believe this was the first time birds became one of my obsessions. Not a house in sight in this non-urban area. I was in the back of beyond in a stress free environment away from harm's reach. All the stresses I had were lifted for a time.

Not long after I'd checked out my surroundings, a

nurse brought Mel and Steve in. They'd slept on the grass outside all night. They insisted the police take them to the hospital too but weren't allowed in so late, so they slept under the stars on a hill outside until morning when they were let in. I still wasn't well by any means and talked mumbo jumbo, but I was calm that was the main thing. My Mam and Zoe arrived as soon as they could. Seeing my mother's and sister's face was an instant comfort. Thank God they never saw me the night before. Mel did though and how she stayed with me after that is testament to her devotion and loyalty, as many would have run to the hills.

I was harmless now in my own little world. No more manic behaviour for another five years or so. I was just confused, imagining things that weren't real and was still zonked from all the Valium that had been pumped into me. Apparently it was the highest dose they'd had to put in anyone in that Welsh hospital that night. It was like in the film 'Jaws' where they put 3 barrels on him but he still keeps coming up.

As the days passed, I remember looking out over the valley and the thought of escape never crossed my mind during this time. I was too dazed and confused to contemplate or try it. I was happy enough just relaxing and taking life in there at easy pace. Escape was the furthest thing from my mind, although it would have been easy if I wanted. I got visits from Steve, Mel and my Dad. Gricey was to come, and that's when he disclosed he'd suffered over the years so knew exactly how I felt. He was a comfort I will never forget and he ran around for Mel on errands. Him and Steve made sure she and young Kirk were fine. Billy came once or twice and helped me in many ways too, telling me to take things nice and easy now, I was in the best place.

Two eccentric gardeners recognised me one day and invited me to their hut. One had one eye and they both looked quite scary, but were the kindest staff at this hospital to me. We would sit and smoke roll ups whilst listening to music in their little hut for hours. We became good friends whilst I stayed there. Steve said afterwards they were probably ex patients who they let do the gardens and stay on the grounds. It made sense looking back. He called them Bill and Ben, the flowerpot men.

I wasn't there long, maybe a month in total. It was mainly spent sitting on a hill looking out at the valley below, i could see the swifts flying in low gathering the insects from the fields beyond, like jets, the speed was phenomenal. I believe this is were I found my fascination with birds. I would gather what food I could, scraps or wet bread and hang it off the fences. Later on, my friend Gricey would bring proper bird seeds in for me. It wouldn't take long before the usual suspects would come, wood pigeons, ravens and crows, Robins, starlings, blue tits and one day was treated to a woodpecker. I'd sit for hours just watching, strange how such small little creatures we take for granted can give a man so much comfort in his hour of need.

One of the last things I remember was a psychiatrist sitting me down in her office and looking at me all serious and saying "Why are you in here?" There was no compassion or friendliness the way she said it. I remember thinking 'if you can't tell me then no one can' but I just replied lamely "I don't know." I was too weak for confrontation, the fight had gone out of me. Mel told me years later I tricked them all into believing I was well, as if I hadn't a care in the world. I may of fooled them but inside I was crippled. This weakness and insecurity would last a long time; over a year maybe more. Where I had felt strong and invincible living on the mountain for a while, I now became a nervous wreck. The total opposite to how I felt before. I became so bad I was even afraid to bring the milk in from the step. These are the lows. For me to go that high, there has to be a comedown, a period where I am in recovery. These are depressing and awful days. These are part of my life.

Chapter 20
The Comedown

'The loneliest moment in someone's life is when they are watching their whole world fall apart, and all they can do is stare blankly'
F. Scott Fitzgerald

After a relatively short spell on the mountain retreat, I was allowed home. Mel had sorted a house in Huyton for us to rent. I had around a year until I would relapse again, but this time they'd be no massive highs at concerts or putting on plays, or even going out at all. I was on a drug called Olanzapine All I know is this drug never made me feel better. I was as much use as a hedgehog in a greyhound race.

This relapse was caused by doing nothing. No major thrills, it came by going into a shell. I went reclusive, agoraphobic, quiet, and shy. Frightened to leave my home. Nervous all the time with the feeling something bad was going to happen at any moment. I never wanted to go out with my pals, never answered the phone. My family would visit but I wasn't with them. I could hardly string 2 words together for anyone. I couldn't wait for people to leave so I could lay on my bed upstairs alone. My sex drive had totally gone. Many a night Mel would put her arm around me in bed, but I would pretend to be asleep or say I'm not in the mood. This I know hurt her as she thought it was her fault. But I had nothing, no go in me whatsoever. A shadow of my former confident self, that loved to laugh and joke, tell stories and make love like a Greek God. I barely opened the front door. This went on for some months, I started to get a bit better in time but not much.

Steve came back from Wales at some point and took me to NL Amsterdam, saying it would help me. I went but I never enjoyed it one bit, not like I would have if fully fit. I walked around in a daze, paranoid if anyone looked at me twice. There were no problems, he looked after me, but it wasn't what a usual weekend away with him entailed.

I started to venture out a bit step by step. The shop first, then for a coffee here and there with my family.

Then old Charlie came round, he'd heard I was home and living in Huyton. He was the guy who straightened out that mess in 91 when I had the scrap in the village where I went nuts on home leave. He'd spoken to one of the lad's dads who was also a gangster, and asked if I could be left alone now as I was not well. Charlie was also the guy who made me stay by his side after the doorman had locked me in the room and put the fear of God in me.

Charlie was also the guy who in 1998, I stood in the Crown Court as a character witness for, during a gruelling murder trial. A man was shot dead in his kitchen, two had stood trial and been released so Charlie was the last. The night before the trial, I was a bit nervous over one thing; a man named Joey had stood trial and was found not guilty, but I knew the prosecutor would ask me about him. So I went to the village where I knew he'd be and told him I was up the next day. He said "Say what you like about me, I got off with it. I'm innocent, I'm free, help save Charlie now." This was a huge relief as I didn't want him as an enemy. So the next day I went to the Crown Court. It was packed with faces from the underworld and Charlie's family. Steve was beside me as usual. I got introduced to an old gangster called Billy who ran the Southend in his day, Dave the gypsy had told me about him, saying he's the main man in Liverpool and if I was in trouble look him up, but I never needed too. Billy shook my hand and staring at me up and down in my Armani black suit and blue shirt he said "You look the part kid." These were the last words I heard as my name was then called.

Walking into the court I felt a bit better after what Billy had just said. I couldn't believe someone as respected as him said that to me. It gave me a quick confidence boost I had needed until I saw the packed court and a hundred eyes on me. I stood in the dock and could see Charlie looking at me opposite. He looked old and grey, after all he had just spent a year in Strangeways on remand in a cage. I never knew if he done it or not, nobody knew, but his brothers came to see me and said he was innocent and he needed my help. I kind of couldn't refuse. He'd always showed kindness to me and helped me so I thought I'll repay him. A dangerous man was killed in his kitchen. I'm no threat to anyone, just a friend helping a friend. So a character witness I was to be.

The barrister bit was easy. It was when the prosecutor got up it got trickier, but I never let him intimidate me. I had the jury laughing and the gallery. If he leaned on the podium, I leaned too. I mirrored him. When he asked about Joey and a party I attended at Charlie's the night before the shooting, I told him we'd had a kind of argument over a UFO I had seen in Turkey. This brought the house down. The prosecutor couldn't wait to get me off now, I was doing too well for my mate. So it was over and I went back to Wales.

Charlie got 'not guilty' a few days later so he was a free man. If he'd got guilty he would have died in prison. He knew it, I knew it. He told me over a coffee a year or so later "You had a big part in my trial. It was a gruelling case for 2 months, then you came in and broke the jury. You were important" He gave me an expensive Gucci watch for my troubles, and I still have it to this day. All this went on about 6 months before the mountain madness. I got through it, but I must admit before I stepped into that dock, I was more nervous than getting on any stage. It's just I never showed it, simple as that.

So living in Huyton, I'm out of my comfort zone of West Derby. I don't know anyone except some of Charlie's family further down the road. I'm trying to conquer my fears of agoraphobia and nerves. Charlie would call regularly and take me out. I felt safe with him, but he was writing a book and some of the stuff he was writing played on my mind. He'd read it to me, although not intentionally meaning to scare me, he would. It was stuff about him being kidnapped and tortured and this caused nightmares.

All my other mates were either working or were away, Steve had gone to work on the cruise ships so he was out of my life for a while. Mel was looking after Kirk, besides a postman pal Billy, I only had Charlie visiting me in what they call 'two dogs fightin (Huyton) Every time I left the house kids opposite, hanging round the corner, would shout 'Jimmy' constantly, in reference to my Brookside character. Normally I'd go over and say hi and break the ice with kids like this but the way I was feeling at the time, nervous and lacking in confidence, I shied away from them, putting my head down every time it was yelled. I was lethargic round the house and couldn't be left with the baby in case I switched off or went funny again. This was the lowest I had ever felt in my life. Long gone it seemed were the memories of being king on the mountain, living it up with Steve, feeling important and a useful member of society. Meeting nice, important, famous and decent people every day. Now I felt trapped in an area I didn't know, knew nobody and couldn't see a way out. I felt like a canary in a man-made cage instead of flying round an orchid or forest in the Azores. The only good thing about it was it was better than being manic and out of control like I was months earlier.

Unfortunately things began to get worse before they got better. I don't remember any Dr or nurse ever visiting me in 2000, or any help in any way shape or form. It was just me, Mel and baby Kirk having to deal with it. I visited a psychiatrist once every blue moon to talk of how I was, but there was no real help, or anyone to see I was getting bad again.

After months and months of feeling down, low, bored, depressed, uninterested, lethargic and tired, zonked etc. a new symptom hit me, in the form of panic attacks. Similar to the ones in Wales when I'd wake up halfway down the stairs in sheer terror. These began again, sometimes in the day watching TV, or walking to the shop, my bottle would go and I'd run home. They were mainly at night, just before I'd go to sleep. That split moment before I would be asleep I'd jump up frightened out of my skin, petrified and not knowing why. A common one was someone was about to smash a baseball bat over my head. A shark about to grab me, drowning, attacked by a gang, falling from buildings etc. This went on for weeks, whatever medication the doctors gave me did nothing. It got to a point where I didn't want to go to sleep for fear of these night time terrors. It was too unbearable.

I fought my sleep for almost 3 nights. On the 4th day, the black dog that had caught up with me twice before, had reared its ugly head again. Mel was upstairs when I went into the other world again, the twilight zone of deep confusion, the release from reality, the hell in my mind. It was in the hallway mixed thoughts were flying round. I don't remember as clearly as I do on the mountain as to what I was thinking, the main thought was I was going to die. Something hellish was going to happen, someone or something was coming for me. Over-tired and confused, I cried in the hallway as Mel phoned the police and ambulance. I was gone far from reality but not violent or aggressive this time, just frightened to death, like a fox cornered by a bunch of bloodthirsty hounds. I sobbed in fear, in the middle of the hallway.

Then my mobile went off, it was Charlie. At this point Mel slipped 3 Valium's in a glass of water. Before anyone arrived I drank it believing it was just water. Maybe I thought Charlie could save me, so I answered it. He asked if I was alright and hearing me crying he sensed I wasn't. "Get me a priest" I remember saying to him. We laugh at that now. God knows why or what was going through my mind at the time I said it. He rushed from his house in West Derby to see if I was alright. Knowing I was in a house with my girl and baby, he wanted to make sure they were going to be alright too. It was a godsend he did come!

Although no aggression or anger had surfaced yet, it was coming. I could feel it and knew I had to get out the house in case I did any harm to anyone. I tried to open the front door but Mel slammed it shut and locked it. It was a main road outside and she knew if I was to go out anything could happen. I might harm someone, someone might harm me, not understanding what I'm going through. Anything could happen.

Mel told me I picked up a globe and said this is the News of the World, obviously that paper was playing on my mind, the feelings of 'I'm being set up' were creeping in. I also picked up a kitchen knife and held it. I never threatened or tried to use it but kept it close to me until Mel somehow persuaded me to put it down. I believe I was holding it for protection thinking I was being set up again somehow. This form of paranoia took place in all of the five episodes.

After 15 minutes the Valium began to kick in. I was becoming drowsy and more relaxed. Of all the drugs I have taken, Valium (Diazepam) is my favourite. It's the only one that truly calms me when I'm stressed or anxious, or can't sleep or my heart is pounding for no reason, and that still happens to this day. Once known as 'mothers little helper', invented in 1960 and released in 63 it has helped me since 1991. It's very addictive so you can't take it on a regular basis but I have 10 a month and take when really necessary

So now Charlie had arrived. He'd never seen me in this agitated state before. He met me just after the 91 breakdown and was in Liverpool during the 99. Being in and out of prison at different periods of his life, he'd seen a few things, and been through hell himself so when he saw me he showed no fear. The first thing he said when Mel let him in was "You should never lock yourself in like this, love."

During these horrific episodes not many people can handle me. They don't know what to say or do. Some can, for some it comes naturally. The main thing is they stay calm. If they show fear or any sign of weakness, I get worse. My Dad in 91 couldn't handle it, he didn't know what to do or say etc. but over the years he's became calmer now. During the last episode I had in 2014 he dealt with it fine when I erupted into the madness again. My mother could always handle it as she knew no matter what, I'd never purposely harm her. Although I frightened her many times, I never touched her and that goes for all my family, none were physically harmed. Emotionally yes. My sister was only there for one episode and she dealt with it fine too. Mel has become an expert. She's lived with me and knows the signs. The time I'll eventually flip can be pinpointed now. Although tiny in stature her strength during these episodes is gigantic, and she has been there at the height of four manic episodes.

So now Charlie's in my kitchen with me, at one time one of the biggest gangsters in the city. I don't trust anyone in this state, but he remained calm and hugged me telling me everything was going to be alright. He kept me calm long enough for an ambulance to arrive and come with me to the hospital. I remained calm in the ambulance for a time, but then my mind started working overtime again, I was worrying, started to get frightened. I'm not sure what I was worried about it's a blur. I only remember getting to the A&E at Whiston Hospital and a vision came to me. Charlie had told me a story once of a paedophile who was on his wing in prison and as soon as a chance came they put sugar in boiling water and poured it in his face as they passed his cell, inflicting catastrophically horrific burns. When he told me this months earlier, I thought nothing of it; I believe they are the vilest people on earth, but my mind was playing tricks on me again, I imagined I was him, that guy who got burned and was about to face hell in a new jail. I began screaming "I'm not a sicko, help me. They'll kill me, please dont let them take me away, God I dont want to die, i beg you help me lord etc." All over the packed waiting room.

That's when Charlie came in the room and was like Obi Wan Seiga, Yes he's robbed banks, blown safes and been accused of killing other gangsters, but never convicted. So now before I went totally ballistic he turned into the Bipolar Whisperer. I'll never forget the calm and cool way he did it. He enticed me over with his arms "George, George come here come here. It's all in your mind, whatever your thinking is not real. Sit down beside me son." So I sat with him. He continued "Just sit with me. You know nobody will ever harm you when I'm with you. Just relax now, breathe nice and slowly, look into my eyes, look deep, your safe now. Forget about all these people around you." He was like the snake in the Jungle book, hypnotic, calming but firm. He calmed me enough until the Dr came and for the third time in my life I was sectioned. This time to Whiston Hospital. To define sectioned 'having been committed compulsorily to a psychiatric hospital in accordance with a section of a mental health act.' Mel arrived shortly after, followed by my family but at this point I was on my way to Whiston.

My mother had never really met Charlie before. She never liked me being in the company of gypsies, gangsters and dangerous men; just wary I guess. But when she learnt how he rushed to the house, stayed with me, went in the ambulance with me and realistically calmed me from going ballistic with paranoia in a waiting room, her views changed. She knew now that he was more than just an acquaintance, he was a valued friend who helped her son in another desperate hour of need.

To briefly sum up the possible reasons for the first three hospitalisations, I believe the first in 91 was due to the disruptions, fame, living the high life, occasional drug taking, witnessing a major disaster, running out of money, feeling a failure, unemployment, being arrested and feeling the shame and working mundane jobs.

The second, in 99, was possibly due to 8 years of living abroad at times, constant partying, occasional drug taking during the rave scene in the mid 90's, divorce of my parents, working non-stop from 96 to 99 in theatres all over the country, writing and producing the Titanic play, sudden commitment of having a child in the world and being on Seroxat.

The third, in 2000, was possibly down to living in an area where I knew nobody, feeling low, feeling isolated, bored, disinterested in anything, no job, barely leaving the house, agoraphobic, sitting about doing nothing, nervous, lethargic, feelings of failure again, not ready for fatherhood or a relationship yet, spiritless and constantly feeling sad, lack of and no sleep in the end and then panic attacks at night.

Another thing that I do physically is reach for old photo albums, pick out certain pictures of mainly loved ones who have passed away and place them round the house. This is like ringing the dinner bell for Mel that I'm about to erupt.

Chapter 21
Obsessions

'Cure for an obsession ~ get another one'
Mason Cooley

Before I talk about the third spell in hospital, which I remember little about as I was drugged up on so much medication, I'm going to break the storyline and talk of all the main interests and obsessions I have had throughout my life. This will give some understanding of some of the things I imagine or obsess over either before, during and after my episodes.

Music
The first big musical interest I can possibly remember, the first band I ever got into was The Beatles. As soon as I heard the Beatles, I had to collect every album. Whether I bought it or borrowed it to tape, it wasn't long before I had every album they ever made. My favourite always being The White Album. Pete Best, the ex-drummer before Ringo, always lived opposite to me. His daughter Bonnie was a good friend, we were inseparable for many years. So he was a great source to ask questions to and probably annoy, but he was always very forthcoming and even borrowed me a few albums. He was a really nice guy who didn't have to do what he did.
Once I conquered every Beatles album, I then went on to John Lennon's solo stuff and Wings. I couldn't get enough of these guys. I read as much as I could about them and had pictures on my walls. Then in 1980 when John Lennon was

assassinated I was heartbroken, I've just found this band and now my favourite Beatle has been cruelly taken away from me. When his album, Double Fantasy, was released at Christmas in 1980, I played it non-stop.

There was a musical play at the Liverpool Everyman called 'Imagine' starring Mark McGann in 1981. It was all about the Beatles and the death of Lennon at the end and it was that which made me want to go into acting. This powerful play and an equally powerful performance by Mark McGann made me think 'I want to do that'. He was Lennon on that stage to me aged 11. I had tears rolling down my face when I heard "Mr Lennon" then the drum bang 5 times, then darkness. What an ending, it summed up everything for me.

Then came David Bowie. At a very early age at some event, the song 'Starman' played over and over and over. It was in a school hall and it must have subconsciously stayed in my mind because around the same time I was getting into the Beatles, I was also exploring the works of Mr Bowie. My cousin Jason was equally obsessed. Every bit of pocket money was spent on a past Bowie album. I even found a gold engagement ring once when I was 11 years old, walking down the road with my Dad. My mother made me hand it in to the police. Nobody claimed it so with the £30 I got from a jeweller, I went straight to Probe Records and bought 5 Bowie albums. Even at the age of 14, I had my hair dyed red like his with henna colouring. I walked into school the next day to be the source of great amusement and was known as Henna head for a while.

I became Ziggy on TV named after Ziggy Stardust as my character loved David Bowie so much, like me. I was Hunky Dory for years, I was Ziggy, I became low, I was Aladdin Sane, I was under pressure and I was the man who sold the world. I had the golden years and fame, I was the man who fell to earth. I always felt I had so many connections. Hence I was gutted I missed him at the BBC that day.

When he died in 2016, I checked my phone texts in the morning to find out the sad news. I instantly cried, he was part of my childhood. I grew up on his music and still play it to this day. Not since Lennon had I shed a tear for a rock star. It sounds bizarre but I felt lost for a few days and am still gutted he's gone.

So it was only really the Beatles and Bowie that I really went over the top about as a young kid. I also liked Roxy Music and the band Japan but never took it to the extreme of the other two. The first concert I ever went to was Japan aged 14 on my own in Liverpool. They were similar to Bowie, the best new wave music I thought. I loved every minute of that gig, on my own with all older teenagers around me, I just sat and took it all in. They had a great bass player called Mick Karn, cool as they come. When he came out and played the opening chords of a song called 'Sons of Pioneers' the hairs on the back of my neck stood up. I'd been introduced to live music and it felt good and this was to be the first of many to come. When I look back, I was on a high for days after and can still feel the excitement I had in me that night.

Four times have I have gone to a gig on my own. The first was Japan in 84, then Oasis in 95 (when their definitive album 'What's The Story Morning Glory' came out). I turned up at Earl's Court as I was staying at Jeff's in London, taking acting lessons in the West End. I bought a ticket off a tout at a fair price and got in with a bunch of Mancunians at the back. We drank and danced on the seats. It was electric. The songs were fresh then, so I was bouncing with my new found Manc friends till the end. I also don't forget what Noel Gallagher said after the truth come out about Hillsborough in 2012. I know he hates the team but this is more important:

"While I'm at it let me say I'm writing this on the day that THE TRUTH has finally been exposed about the Hillsborough disaster. Respect to the families of the 96 for exposing the lies of Thatcher's government. With my hand on my heart I salute you"

Another gig alone was in 2016 when I went to see Echo and the Bunnymen in Liverpool. This turned out, after Pink Floyd, to be my 2nd favourite concert. I was bouncing so high I almost hit the Philharmonic roof. I was seated and most sat, but I was on my feet with a few others singing and dancing all night. I was so high Mel had to calm me down for days after. That's the danger, but if I'm having a good time the last thing on my mind is to stop enjoying myself. Echo and the Bunnymen nearly put me in a mental hospital!

The last time was Sheryl Crow in 2017. I got the train to London to catch her in Shepard's Bush. I got into Sheryl the first time I heard her and every album she released I bought. The ultimate rock chick for me and I vowed I'd see her live one day. I loved every minute. I must say she did look good in her leather outfit!

Aged 14, almost every kid in West Derby Comp loved Genesis. Everyone was swopping tapes, albums and bootlegs. It didn't take me long to catch on, I loved their music too. For a time I played nothing else. I had everything from the Peter Gabriel stuff to Phil Collins.

On my first filming day of Grange Hill, I insisted I wear my Genesis T-shirt (the Genesis by Genesis album one with the yellow shapes on). The character was yet to have a uniform, so this was a great opportunity to slip my favourite band at the time in.

I nearly got to see them at Twickenham in 2007 with my pals Kojack and Scatty, in a mad pub we got something that wasn't what it should of been. I felt terrible and knew it was bad when I seen Kojack bad. We arrived and all collapsed on a grassy verge outside the ground, in a land of confusion. We couldn't move, we felt like we was going to die there and then. The only thing we could do was get a cab back. Ketamine a few said afterward it may have been. So I never got to see one of my favourite bands. Such is life, but I never died on the sidewalk like I thought I would. I can honestly say that was the last time I have ever taken any illegal drugs, twelve years. It made me realise the true danger I was putting myself in. Imagine my son growing up to find out his Dad died of an overdose outside a Genesis concert.

The best concert I took Mel too was Rod Stewart in Manchester for her birthday. Halfway through this great gig he started kicking signed expensive footballs into the crowd, maybe five in total. One came towards us and I felt I could get it, so I waited and waited, then just before a few guys in front caught it, I dived like Ray Clemence in his heyday and grasped it tight. I passed it to Mel and said "Happy birthday!" 50,000 people were in that crowd that night and I got it! I made Mel put it under her jumper walking to the train, as many eyes were watching and it could have been easily taken if the wrong eyes gazed upon it.

One evening Jeff played me a live album by Otis Redding called 'Otis live at Monterey.' I had only heard 'Dock of the Bay' before this, but when I heard this live album, as Jeff predicted, it blew me away. It was quite simply the finest live album I'd ever heard. It was raw, it had soul, and it made the hairs on the back of my neck stand up as he blasted it into my subconscious. Not then, but many years later when I was about 40, I had every Otis CD he ever made. I read up about him and the tragic way he was taken in a plane crash at the height of him becoming world famous. I realised there was much more than just Dock of the Bay. He was the king of soul and I adored his songs. In many hospitals I would blast this album when feeling elated and sing along as if I was the Big O.

Lynyrd Skynyrd became a big one. My Dad used to have an American Anthems album and on it was 'Sweet Home Alabama' which I would love when he played. This is probably my favourite song of all time. It's a feel good rock song about home. The title says Alabama but it could be anywhere. When I learnt the lead singer Ronnie van Zant and another member had been killed in 77 in a plane crash in Mississippi it angered me. Later it would affect me during my 4th breakdown.

In 2015 me and my Dad would travel to Manchester and see them live at the Apollo. I turned up in a Yankee bandana, not realising these are from the Deep South, I wondered why I was getting funny stares from bikers etc. It was only weeks later it dawned on me that my bandana attire was totally wrong. The gig was spectacular, the final song they did was their main anthem 'Free Bird'. I was on cloud 9. I went into another dimension when this kicked in. For just over 10 minutes I forgot everything; where I was, who I was with etc. and just let myself be free and at one with the music. Only music can do this to me, no drink, no drugs just a pure and natural high. Ronnie who had died had been replaced by his brother Johnny van Zant, but you would never have known that night.

In the mid 90's, I got into rave music as me and my pals starting going the State, The Buzz, and The Quadrant Park etc. Many nights and parties after were spent with Buzz Williams, named because of his love of the Buzz. Hagan, Dr Wheels and Big Al loved these nights along with Brian. Fozz went, but only because we all went. He would have rather been in the Cavern listening to The Kinks. There always the element of danger in these places and occasionally it did kick off, but we were never involved in anything during these times. The bouncers knew us and would frequently come over to say hi to us. So for us The Buzz was probably the safest place in town. Years later, before a few hospital admissions, I'd play this music and go into my own little world, reminiscing of the great nights dancing till all hours to this music, with all my pals around me feeling on top of the world. When Mel sees me playing this music and getting excited she worries and alarm bells go. In going back in time, I have to be careful.

Sam Cooke was another huge musical hero. Reading what happened to him, after listening to his music and watching docs on him, didn't add up. His death didn't ring true, being killed in a seedy motel by an old lady whilst he was with a two bid hooker. At the height of his fame? Do me a favour. This was to also play on my mind before breakdowns.

As my Mother played Bob Dylan to me since I lay in my cot as a baby, it was a only natural that one day I'd get into him. The album 'Desire' was always and still is my fav. The story of the boxer the 'Hurricane', the gangster 'Joey' etc. Street Legal closely followed, then once I hit London, Jeff and Dot would introduce me to more Dylan stuff that had eluded me. I finally got to see Bob with my mum and Mal and her mate Sue in 1996 in Liverpool. It was a cool gig but it was also the night England played Germany in the semi-final of the Euros. When my mother booked the tickets I wasn't to know this was going to take place. I couldn't let my mother down, and I couldn't not know what was happening, so I took a little transistor radio and some headphones. I kept checking every 20 mins or so.

My mother and co weren't too happy but it didn't disrupt the concert, yet. Then it got to penalties, a few lads standing in front of me asked what was happening so I said it's pens. Word got around as I commentated the goals as they come in. Now half the Royal court in front of me are hanging on my words, 2-2 etc. Even Bob looked down and saw the disturbance; half the audience with their backs turned on him, he spoke to the crowd "What's going on down there?"

My mother and her mate at this stage were fuming with me and the chaos I'd caused, but soon England were out of the World Cup on pens. I put the radio away and enjoyed the rest of the concert.

'One good thing about music, when it hits you feel no pain' Bob Marley.

Movies

The first film I became obsessed with aged 10 and probably the first film I watched over and over and knew every line, was 'The Warriors.' It was dark, violent, it was all about the night. Me and Zoe watched this over and over, but I think she watched mainly because she fancied Swan!

The Godfather had an instant impact. This was my introduction to Brando, Pacino, James Caan, and Robert Duval etc. I would have been about 14 when I first saw this and watched it over and over.

I began to watch the Brando scenes over and over and start to take him off. It took years of practice, but years later it became a party piece for me to do at weddings or for gangsters all over the globe.

It's hard to pinpoint one all-time favourite, but when I discovered 'It's A Wonderful Life' in Wales, not long before I went berserk, I instantly said this is my fav film. I watch it every Xmas now and always feel grateful afterwards. Every time I cry at the end too when he stands on the bridge with nothing. I have felt like that, more than once. The thought that the world would be better without me. My family would have suffered or people who met me would have to suffer, but like the film says 'No man is a failure who has friends.' So this film is very, very important to me, not just at Xmas but if I feel low or something bad has happened, the old Frank Capra classic comes on.

'One flew east, one flew west one flew over the cuckoo's nest'
I first saw this aged about 12. I enjoyed it but didn't really understand it. I remember being sad at the end, but it never made a huge impact on me and I never watched it over and over like The Warriors or Jaws etc. Then about the age of 17, I watched it again and I totally got it. I understood everything about it after watching it maybe 10 times. I could take Nicholson off too. Many times at parties I'd do a few Cuckoo's Nest impressions for lovers of the film. I threw his lines in Grange Hill. I wore woolly hats like he wore in the film. I read the book by Ken Kesey. When I escaped from hospital in 91 I got the idea of throwing the

chair through the window from The Chief. I've sat in psychiatrist's offices banging the table like Jack or saying "where do you suppose she lives?" It's the ultimate bipolar, schizophrenia or any mental health sufferer's film anthem. It makes you laugh at the madness of it all and ultimately cry. There will never be another film with so much heart and truth about mental illness as Cuckoo's Nest, period. *"You're no crazier than the average asshole walking around on the street."* That sums the whole thing up for me in one line. No wonder Nicholson got the Oscar for best actor.

'Jaws' hands down is the best film I ever saw at the cinema. Aged just nine, my Dad took me and Fozz to the ABC on Tuebrook. From the opening scene, where the girl is treading water and harrowingly taken, during the scariest music I'd ever heard since my Dad played Tubular bells as a kid, I couldn't take my eyes off the screen. I'd just never seen anything like it. It blew me away is the only way I can describe it. It's had its affect on me since. I won't swim in the sea! I might for a few minutes then I think of that film and head back quick. People laugh at me but I couldn't care less. Once that fear goes in my mind it's the flight mode. Those few moments when me and Kirk come off the jet ski in the Caribbean were horrendous, I froze in time knowing we were miles out, I don't know what's beneath me. Jaws had a massive impact on my recreational activities!
Even though I fear them I learnt as much as I could about sharks. I read books, watched documentaries (including about the Indianapolis, where a naval ship was sunk during WW2 and

many were taken by sharks). I even, and I don't know how or why to this day I did this, but whilst on holiday in Turkey with Mel and Kirk, I got into a cage at a Turkish sea world and got lowered into a cave with sharks swimming around us. It was just me and Mel as Kirk was only 10. They weren't huge great whites or anything but 3 to 4ft at least. One thing I'll never forget is the fins flapping on the surface. It was eerie as I imagined treading water without the cage and these things flapping around me.

'Papillion' was also a big interest. I loved it as a kid and thought Steve McQueen was the coolest of cool. I always admired the butterfly tattoo on his chest. Over the years I had 3 tattoos. Many years later in hospital, in 2014, I was doing paintings with wood, black and white. They looked incredible and I put them on Facebook. A mate from school was a tattooist, Big Simon Mac. He looked fearsome with his Maori tattoo on his face but he was a gentle giant. He sadly passed away from cancer a few years ago. Si got in touch and wanted me to do Brandon Lee from 'The Crow' film which I did. He said I owe you a favour. When I got out of hospital a few months later when I felt confident, I went to his house, laid out on the kitchen table and he did the Papillion Butterfly tattoo on my chest. I loved it and still do. My nod to Steve McQueen.

'Back To The Future' I enjoyed immensely. The prospect of time travel and changing your past would appeal to anyone surely. However during my 4th breakdown I began having delusions that

Dr Emmett Brown was real. I kept saying to Mel that the Doc was coming for me, to take me away and back in time. I had visions he was going to help me and that he was my friend like he was to Marty McFly in the film. I never saw him as, like I say, I don't see things, only imagine. But I waffled on about the Doc for hours in the hope he was coming in his DeLorean, to meet my old mate Jeff in the 80's again. Going back in time is a constant symptom before an episode, looking at old photos or wishing I was young again with no problems. Then during a manic episode I can go back in my mind too, imagining I'm somewhere in the past. On one horrific occasion during a later breakdown I have imagined I'm in one of the twin towers, and all hell is breaking loose around me. During the same breakdown, I thought the world was about to end, a nuclear bomb was about to go off whilst I was in the hospital awaiting a doctor. So I go back in time constantly during my episodes; time is a huge factor.

Animals

I've always loved animals as far as I can remember. The first pet I ever had was a black cat called Humphrey. I adored it. It was only about 6 months old when it went missing one night. I must have been about six, but I remember for a few days being upset and praying he'd come home. Then on the way to school, I saw a black cat lying dead on the roadside round the corner to where we lived. I pointed him out to my mum who told me it wasn't him. I knew it was him. It was a black dead cat; mine had gone missing, and it had to be. I never saw it again. Maybe my mother got it moved, but this was my first experience of loss, death and grief.

Not long after, we got another cat; a lovely brown tabby type. I called him Miffy after a rabbit book I had. Miffy went missing one night for 3 days. I waited by the window looking out. Then one night, me and my mum were watching our usual Friday night movie and heard crying outside. She opened the door and Miffy ran in. I was overjoyed, Miffy came home!

I also found a ginger kitten when I was about 12 in a field once. Ironically I called him Ziggy after the Bowie album and he lived to a good age.

Mel's mum Lil has a Bengal cat now, beautiful animal, very clever, can drag its food out of the cupboard with its teeth. I have never seen a cat like it. Worth best part of £800 too.

The greatest cat tale I ever heard was from my father. Whilst he worked on Seaforth docks in Bootle, a docker stumbled on some precious cargo containing a very rare Persian cat. In 1980 these were almost unheard of in Liverpool. Everyone just had your average ginger toms or tabby or black cats. This particular very expensive Persian was being shipped to a millionaires in Boston. The docker who spotted it told my dad and a few others to keep it there. Don't put it on the ship until he comes back. He went missing and returned with a scruffy ginger alley cat he picked up in a back alley in Bootle. He took the Persian cat out the container and put the alley cat inside. He sealed it, then they loaded it onto the ship. He then took the beautiful Persian cat home to his family in Bootle, whilst the rich lady in Boston would have opened her container to find a horrific flea-ridden alley cat. That's dockers for you.

Dogs are my favourite of all. As a kid I would find them and bring them home. One summer me and Bonnie (Pete Best's daughter) were playing in the old railway and a mongrel half Alsatian half Doberman we thought, came over to play. He had no collar and looked hungry so we took him home. I begged my mam and dad to keep him and they did. Being about 11 at the time I took him everywhere. Wherever me and Bonnie went, Rebel came too - named after the Bowie song Rebel Rebel. He was so loyal. Anyone came near me he didn't know, he'd growl at them. Rebel was my best mate for about a year, then he got sick. We took him to the vets and he had distemper. There was nothing any vet in the world could do to save him. It broke my heart at the time. I remember sitting on the step with Bonnie and our Zoe in tears, all of us. The most loyal and protective dog I've ever had, and a mongrel. I've also had Jack Russell's, whippets, Staffs, and now a German Shepard Husky called Sonny.

I always liked horses. My cousin Helen has horses and is a keen show jumper. But one day in North Wales me, Fozz, Brian and Jay booked a ride across the mountains on four horses. I remember my butt was killing me after a while. It was very hilly terrain most of it. Four Welsh girls came with us. I had seen Jay using all his best lines on one, telling stories etc. The horse Brian was on in front of me, kept breaking wind all the time. We joked saying we couldn't tell if it was him or the horse, as Brian was in the Pape category in this department.

Anyway I got bored and I'd always wanted to ride a horse at least once in my life at full speed. So I edged out when we got onto flatlands and whipped him hard. He flew! I could feel the wind in my hair and face as it galloped as fast as it could across the Welsh fields. It felt exhilarating, that few minutes of riding and controlling this magnificent animal in the wild. That was until the Welsh instructor caught up on her horse and grabbed the reigns to slow me. I knew they wouldn't be happy, but I had to do it. I had to have a Crazy Horse moment. Years later in Great Yarmouth, Alford did a similar thing on a beach, only he came off and knocked himself unconscious. It was a scary few moments till he awoke dazed. Weeks later we spotted Jay with the instructor in a quiet bar, he did get her number after all.

Birds I think started when I was in the Welsh hospital. I had a canary called Jeff in 88 who got gassed when our boiler went on fire. He was in my loft so smoke rises and Jeff perished. Luckily nobody got hurt as our Zoe calmly turned the electrics off and got Pete Best over to help, or dishy Pete as my Mum called him. That's the solution during a fire in our house, get Pete Best out.

My favourite bird is the peregrine falcon. Fastest Animal on the planet and I fortunately talked a Brookside fan, a birds of prey member of staff, into letting me hold one. My greatest bird moment.

My obsessions are many : from Yankee candles, Mobsters, The Twilight Zone, the Zulu wars, Crazy Horse, Vikings, the band SWV (after watching the brilliant, but disturbing 'The Way They See Us' I heard them during a scene- that's all it takes to spark an obsession).

Monroe, Bardot, Brando, Sharon Tate, (Years before the fantastic movie 'Once Upon A Time in Hollywood' came out. I just found it so sad what happened to her. If only it happened like in the Tarantino version.)

Raquel Welch. Scarlett Johansson and last but no means least, Muhammad Ali. (I must have watched every fight, doc, read many books on his extraordinary life. The day he died hit me hard too. There will never be another like him. As Ali once said :

'The man who has no imagination has no wings')

Chapter 22
The Day The Sun Forgot To Shine

'It is both a blessing and a curse to feel everything so very deeply'

Everything at first is very vague in this place, Whiston Hospital. I must have been heavily sedated for a while since almost flipping out in the A&E department, but luckily calmed down by Charlie. If he hadn't done what he did, God knows what I could have done in that state, as the manic behaviour was building like the Hulk about to unleash in me. That's a bit what it's like but over time. For a while I'm David Banner then this monster comes out that I have no control over, like the Incredible Hulk. I feel it coming like David, but there's nothing I can do to stop it once it's got past a certain point.

There were no birds in the small yard in Whiston; no trees or places to walk. Just a yard with a huge cage like wall in the middle separating the men from the women. I joked to my pal the Duke that this was "Heaven's Gate" when he came to visit me with 20 ciggies and a ghetto blaster one day. There were no guys I could talk to. They were either so far gone or didn't want to talk.

At first this was the loneliest place on earth for me, until visiting hours. Then the usual close knit family would come; my mother, Dad, sister and Mel, close mates etc. I kept a close circle of visitors in these places. For some it's too much and they don't visit. I understand this. One night, I went out for a cigarette alone. I was sitting on a bench looking at the stars (there was nothing else to view) when I heard a voice call over from the female side saying "You alright?" I looked over to see a dark haired girl around my age, sitting close to the huge fence smoking a cigarette too. Her name was Julie Anne, dark and attractive from Huyton. I wandered over to check her out and after a few pleasantries sat opposite to join her. Through that gap we spoke every night for my 3 months in there. We passed cigarettes to each other if one had run out. We spoke of music a lot as both loved Floyd, Led Zep, Beatles etc. so we'd talk whilst playing 'Dark Side Of The Moon' or 'Wish You Were Here' on a ghetto blaster (not too high as we'd bring attention and maybe be told to separate or go to bed, so we respected the volume).

We talked about movies as she loved her movies too. We talked of her son Conor, who she adored, and was terminally ill in a wheelchair. I can't remember ever really talking much about our illness, it was mainly happy things, things that helped one another stay positive amongst the madness around us. We spoke about the world and everything in it except our own problems. There was a lot of laughter once we got to know each other. Laughing at the whole mess we were in, you had to just to keep sane. Just silly things we may have done in other hospitals like me breaking out or jumping naked across cars, never the serious frightening parts. She had nobody to relate to on the female ward like I never on the male. So to find each other was a godsend to each other. I know for a fact I would have got worse in there if me and Julie Anne never had our nightly chats. I looked forward to them all day. It kept me sane in an insane environment. No doctor in there could help me, with meds maybe but not talk to me and communicate like my new friend did.

I talk of certain Angels I believe I've met, well add Julie Anne to the list, as she appeared out of nowhere at a time I needed someone. Sadly she passed away a few years back. Her mother Julie informed me, there was a mix up with her meds. She was on so many in the end she didn't know what was going on, and the doctors let her down. Her family are fighting to this day for justice over this. Her young son Conor passed away not long after. Although I only knew her for 3 months, we grew very close in that time so I was absolutely gutted when I heard this news. Way, way too young and shows how cruel this illness can really be when it rears its ugly head like this. The Angel of Whiston was gone. I miss her as do many others who she would have touched too.

Now while I'm in these places, the main aim is to get out, one way or another. Although I'm not fully well I'm still clever enough to pretend I am. I have fooled many psychiatrists over the years into believing I am feeling great and ready for society again. It happened in 91 on home leave which I shouldn't have had towards the end, as I caused chaos. The hospital in Wales was way too early as I relapsed within a year. It's the same every time. I am the world's greatest actor when I want to get out of these places. Only Mel can see through me. She only has to look into my deceptive eyes. I tried and tried and each time she'd say he's not ready. I'd hate her for this, but I know now she was right. I was only going up the hill backwards. I'm safer in there unwell, than in society. Soon enough I was out and spent months again regaining my confidence, getting my weight back and finding work again etc.

Chapter 23
Home

'Home
Home again
I like to be here
When I can'
Pink Floyd

So I'm home, and about 6 months down the line I'm back to my old self.

Me and Steve had a great night in Liverpool with the band the Stereophonics. After their gig we went back to their hotel with them and partied all night. I loved chatting to Kelly about Bob Dylan, and the late drummer Stuart Cable was legendary! The nicest drummer I have ever met. Lived on the edge, I had much in common with him. He didn't give a fuck but sadly he never slowed down like I did and died young.

Another pleasant experience was when Alford came up to join me. Whilst he'd been on holiday in Aya Napa he was staying in the same hotel as the Liverpool team. He made friends with a few of them and when he returned, we both went to Melwood training ground to say hello to Jamie Rednapp. In those days you could watch them train for the last half hour but all that changed a few years later.

This was my second time at Melwood, the first being in 1979 when my uncle Tony won a competition to meet the whole team. I remember I was too small when they took a photograph so Phil Thompson put me on a crate so they could see me. Wow I thought, Phil Thompson's just put me on a crate. Kenny Dalgleish was in front of me but we never spoke. He was my hero back then; he was the Messi of my childhood. It was a memorable day and years later I met Kenny whilst working at LFC during Ronnie Moran's funeral. He walked in with Ian St John towards me and spoke to me for ages. I was so in awe - probably more than anyone I'd ever met, but he was a gentleman.

Anyway Jamie gave us 2 FA cup balls, one for Alford and one for me. Sadly mine was wrecked within 2 years as Kirk thought it was one you could just play in the street with, so that was the end of that, but still it was very kind of Jamie to give us them. I met him again years later in 2018 working at LFC and he ran over and gave me a big hug. I was surprised he remembered but he did and we had a laugh in the short time I walked him to his car.

One night, my dad was away for the weekend and my horrific mate from London, Harry, was up. We got drunk and separated. Harry thought I was in bed so had been knocking and kicking the door down for over an hour, whilst shouting my name, waking up the whole street. I got out the cab and noticed he'd broke the keyhole as my key wouldn't fit. There was an argument which resulted in me telling him he has to go through my Dad's bedroom window, which was open. There was a ladder hanging over the end house wall which we took, and Harry embarked up the ladder; all fine at this point. I looked around and half the road are at their windows watching this saga. Colin lived opposite. He had already lived next door to me and gone through many parties I'd had. He was watching things unfold as had been awoken by Harry's antics. Harry got to the window and started to shuffle his way through. Then he got stuck. He was half in and half out with his legs dangling and kicking, screaming "Help George!" I couldn't do anything as I'm holding the ladder for him. I just kept telling him to keep edging in he'll squeeze through etc. For about 15 minutes, he hung out of my dad's bedroom window wailing and swearing. Now people are on their steps, including the ladder owner who wasn't happy. Finally Harry pushed through, landing on my dad's chest of drawers, smashing a soldier ornament as he hit the floor with a thunderous thud. The next day I had to get the door fixed and fit some new locks before my dad returned. I told him of the antics as I knew he'd hear anyway from someone. He was cool about it, Harry however didn't show his face for many years. Only Colin laughs about it now from that road. The rest still glare at me as it all floods back to them.

I conquered one of my biggest fears shortly, spiders! in Great Yarmouth, when I worked on a holiday camp. Me and Mel had split up for a few years so I lived here. Things were great I worked on the cocktail bar on a holiday camp. Steve was the entertainer, we had the local bars and clubs boxed off by meeting Reece who run the doors and Keegan the owner. Anyway my boss Gary persuaded me to allow his tarantula walk up my arm after he heard I feared spiders. I had a few Aftershock drinks then said let's do this. He told me it's nowhere near as bad as you think, don't be frightened it will just tickle a bit. It won't feel hairy and horrid as you imagine. He was right; it felt nice to be honest. I let it walk up my arm twice to a crowd of nervy fellow workers. That's how I overcame that fear. One weekend Drummond come up and we got drunk with some scouse friends I'd made called Jayne and the Reverend Russ, in their caravan. We left very drunk and decided to make seal noises outside their caravan once they went to bed. It confused them for a while, then we moved around the caravans doing the same underneath random caravan windows. People were looking out their windows at 3am thinking seals had come up from the beach and surrounded the place. It was the talk of the camp the next day! When I come incidentally, me & Mel got back together. It was first thing on my list..

I got a call from Brian Toilet. He had this unfortunate nickname due to the fact he travelled around the country dropping off chemical toilets, at places such as Glastonbury and other festivals and would then pick them up when it was over. I laugh at his name, but give him his due when one afternoon I was having a panic attack on the London underground. I came out and put an SOS on Facebook outside Euston station. He was the first to ring me and calm me right down; he knew the ways, distracted me whilst talking calmly. This I won't forget. Brian Toilet was in Northern Ireland on holiday when he rang me and put me onto a man called Franco from Carrickfergus. He was to be known as Francofergus. I instantly got on with him and he asked would I come over to Ireland to play in a charity golf match, I told him I was useless but he said so was he. I agreed and talked Alford into going as he was supposed to be staying at mine that weekend. It was only supposed to be for 2 days but we stayed 10.

We would spend most of it with Franco and his mate who happened to be Hurricane Higgins. It was his last years before cancer took him. I said to Alford "I'll be safe, but you won't." He replied "How do you work that out you cunt?" So I told him the story. My Dad's pal Dave the Head told me of years ago. The Army caught five IRA men and were about to execute them in a field but a Scouser who held rank said no they must go back to camp and stand trial. The other cockney soldiers couldn't argue so they survived. When the head of the IRA found out he sent word that if they capture any Scousers let them free, kill any others.
The Irish made us most welcome on all corners, The Falls Road, The Shankhill Road and Sandy Row. We never had one problem. It was an eye opener. You're safe when you're with a local!

Steve's older sister Pat who lived and worked in a pub in Warrington in the early days had moved back now. One night I went round to Steve sister to have a go on her sunbed. I stayed a while after for a bottle of beer then headed home. That was the last time I saw her alive. The following day, Steve came round in tears to tell me she died in her sleep that night. He was devastated as was her daughter Sarah and Steve's brothers Jeff, Wally and the Major. This rocked them all as it was unexpected and she was only in her forties, way too young. For weeks Steve and I would drink in mine till he could think. Bad days, very bad days.

Whilst working for Denzil it wasn't all work, work, work. For as soon as Denzil left the building me and Tremmo set about our constant phone call prank to a man who was oblivious to the caller; me. What happened was one day Tremmy tried to get the head of the North Korean tourist board to advertise on taxis. Last thing he wanted! He refused but was quite rude about it. I had a good think about this and invented a character called Barney Hooper, an Australian obsessed with surfing and fishing. So at least once a week we'd ring this man, called Michael Michael oddly enough. We expected him to hang up on the first call when I said "Michael how the devil are you skipper!?"

"Who is this?" he'd reply.

"It's Barney here Barney Hooper, your old surfing mate" He was confused but intrigued as to who I was.

The next call he kept saying things like "Who is this? Is it you Tom?" Trying to work out this mad Australian shouting down the phone to him to come on fishing trips or shark diving off the Great Barrier Reef.

Further down the line Tremmo even got the sounds of a thunderstorm on YouTube on the work pc and I rang him as if in the middle of a storm and needed his help. Thunder & lightning blasting down his ear. It went on for months and he never worked out it was 2 scouse clowns he'd refused business with. Hooper became the stuff of folklore! Especially when I'd ring and he'd have a story himself ready so it became one big laugh in the end, but we never revealed ourselves.

But the pressure of this job was building up despite the luxuries of days out and great commissions. Pressure overrides the capers and signs were showing I was about to break.

Another catastrophic blow was to come Steve's way. He lost his wife Tina. Although they'd split up, he was still very close to her and she was the mother to his two young children, my goddaughter Melissa and Jack. When he rang me from the hospital I couldn't believe it. Mel was distraught too as they were mates. For a long time this was heavy duty. He had to tell the kids she'd died, the hardest thing he's had to do and says nothing can be harder. Whatever he faces won't be as hard as that hell. The funeral was a killer too, watching them and her family who I knew well and respected. Especially her brother Daz who on many a night played chess with me and Steve. He too would sadly pass away just over 10 years later. Tina was only 30 and beautiful. These were sad times for all of us. Many a night with a JD, Steve would look in my eye and ask 'why?' I was damned if I could tell him why. Tina was Kirk's first babysitter. She adored him and was his godmother. I've mentioned Angels have appeared here and there in my life, well she was one too.

Months went by and Steve's niece, was going out with a guy who beat her at least once a week we found out. Steve and his brother The Major wanted to kill him, but she said if you touch him I'll never speak to you again. One night in a busy pub on Dale Street I was out with Steve and the Duke. Also in there was my sister Zoe with her partner and Steve's niece with hers. I had heard from Steve he'd knocked her about bad, I had also heard off one of her neighbours she was covered in blood one night, wandering the close crying as he'd beat her so bad. At some point Steve went to loo and I looked over to see the guy have his niece by the throat in the corner, choking her! She broke free and ran out. He finished his drink and followed, and so did I.

I wasn't family so I didn't care if she didn't speak to me. I'd watched her grow up and I couldn't let him get away with this. As he got outside I tapped him on the shoulder, he turned and said "What the fuck do you want?" but before he finished his sentence he was punched with about 3 or 4 jabs. Somehow, and I don't know how I did it, I threw him over my shoulder causing him to land out of breath and bloodied on the roadside on Dale Street. I went to hit him again as he lay there as I was so angry at this man knowing what he'd done over the years but the Duke, who came outside with me, pulled me back.
"You've done it now" he said and pulled me back. A crowd had gathered watching so I knew this was the right thing to do. The doorman had been watching it unfold and told us to get inside before the cops arrived. He got us inside quick;

apparently the lad had been annoying the doormen all night too so they were glad at what I had done.

I wasn't proud. I was shaking after it but some things you gotta do in life and I knew Steve was over a barrel with it all. He came out the loo to hear of mayhem. I'd also broken my little finger during it all, which I didn't realise till I got inside. It's still bent to this day. I'd caught his skull which is pure bone. The Duke brought me a Brandy over and somehow made a makeshift splint for my finger. It was pointless going to the hospital as they could do nothing.

Not long after, she ended it with this guy. I think what I did helped the cause, and not long after that she met a guy from South Wales, who treated her the way she should be, like a lady. She is still happy with him to this day, with children to show for it. This is not bipolar behaviour it's just what most men's reaction would be, seeing a woman they know being abused. Incidentally that was my last brawl, thankfully.

So over the course of a few years, stress had been building up at work. Losing my friend and Steve's wife Tina affected me. Pat was a friend too. I also had bailiffs knocking at my house over a foolish 15 grand loan I got. Ironically they were called The Vikings (one of my favourite films). The Vikings are finally coming for me I thought. I also had the taxman on my back over my Brookside money. I had to go bankrupt or I would have ended up in real trouble. I sat in court and it took no more than 20 minutes. That was it; no more money worries. I never owned a house or car so I lost nothing.

The final straw before my 4th visit to a cuckoo's nest was Steve's stag holiday in Fuengirola in Spain in 2011.This was to be one of the funniest holidays ever, only 3 days but I overdid it. It had an array of colourful characters including my mates and my Dad's mates. With all these people it was just laughter from the airport till I got to my front door home. I was on a natural high and combined with drinking in the sun, then later at night, I didn't see the effects it was having on me. I turned into the Jim Carey character again, making them all laugh, I could have happily laughed for the rest of my life on that holiday. Everywhere I turned there was someone else to laugh with. Denzil who had become my boss over the years, was chilled and laughing too. No work talk just fun in the sun. Nobody could see I was slowly heading for a fall. I couldn't see it, only my Dads mate Lord Bassie noticed on the plane home when my hands were shaking badly, that something may not be right. I wasn't on any meds so I could drink as much as I liked then. The Duke sensed something too, I remember all the way home he kept ordering bottles of water for me to try and dehydrate me, but sadly it was more than dehydration. It was the beginning of more chaos and sadness. So Spain was my bow out drinking holiday. If I go away now I don't drink.

I can do it, as I went to Benidorm in 2018 with 10 other close pals for Big Al's stag weekend. I never touched a drop. For 3 days I drank non-alcoholic San Miguel. It felt like drinking as it tasted like San Miguel but I never got drunk like all the others did. There was no problem on the holiday but on the plane going I had a panic attack. I almost ran off in a terrible state, but controlled it, but I was a millimetre from getting off that flight as I panicked. I will explain in more detail later in the bipolar summary chapter. I controlled it alone though, none of my pals were beside me. We were all split up.

All the boys looked out for me on that holiday. They didn't think I knew but I was aware they were keeping a close eye on me after the potential Mr T on the plane. Even Junior was making me cups of tea when I awoke and Kojack made sure I wasn't drinking alcohol, checking my bottles constantly. Hagan and Big Al never stayed out my sight. If anyone came over and bugged me too much Hagan would diplomatically get rid of them. A funny holiday without a drop of alcohol! In the end I have to control my illness. I've captured the devil now so I control him. I've learnt that much.

Chapter 24
The Cell

'Depression is a painfully slow, crashing death. Mania is the other extreme, a wild roller coaster run off its tracks, an eight ball of coke cut with speed. It's fun and it's frightening as hell'
Dave Lovelace

I got home and I was still on a high, telling the stories to Mel and Kirk and others on the phone. I was still on cloud 9 but on my way to ground zero. That night I never slept, I was too up there on a high too sleep.

The next day, I went into work and couldn't function. I was tired, emotional and my heart was pounding. I tried to explain to the manager but because he'd been on the holiday he thought I was just hungover and was trying it on. Things were said I won't go into, but it resulted in me being told to go. I knew I wasn't right but just how serious I didn't know yet.

As I walked down the long road to try and flank a cab, Ad-van fitter Davey Cumbo pulled up beside me. He was a Godsend at this moment. "Get in son." I got in and he took me home. I was so relieved as I didn't know the area and could have been ages getting a cab, and feeling vulnerable, he saved all this. He was young and never understood what I was really going through, but never the less seen his pal in distress. He took me back and I went to bed to try and sleep.

Unfortunately sleep never came. Another day and night of staying awake. This becomes torture for me, it attacks the core of my mental and physical health. The CIA used sleep deprivation on suspected terrorists after 911. That's how horrific it is, when people like that know they can obtain information through lack of sleep. After so many days and nights to get a good night's sleep I bet they'd tell the CIA where their mothers lived.

The problem at the time is until I do something, like hurt myself or someone else, they won't admit me to a hospital. Everyone has to wait for the eruption. Mersey Care came round but they try to heal you from home, to avoid hospitalisation. I was given Zopiclones to help sleep and probably diazepam or temazepam but it's too late. At any point I'm going to go into that other world and lose another year of my life.

Denzil knocked the morning before the madness and said "Don't worry George, get yourself well and come back to work when you're ready, no rush." He was really nice and I appreciated it, knowing my job was there later down the line. To keep young Kirk away from it all, I went to my mother's. It's the best place; quiet and no distractions. I was fighting it as best I could; to sleep, remain calm and utmost remain in this world.

At one point my Mam thought it best to get me out of the house for a bit; a little drive to a supermarket in Belle Vale. I was relatively calm on the way, just in a world of my own I guess. Then as I got out of the car in the car park, out of nowhere I went into this other world again. An uncontrollable panic where I didn't know what I was doing; a mixture of total fear and anger. I was shouting things I cannot recall. I can't even recall what was going through my mind, only that it was mixed up, but whatever it was, it was frightening me. Gone is Dr Jekyll and enter Mr Hyde. I then did something that to this day plays on my mind; I punched my mother's car windscreen. Thank God it never shattered as she sat behind it in total shock. This is how out of control I get and don't know what I'm doing; I could have harmed my own mother. It scares me just thinking about it. Then I ran towards a taxi rank where a few taxis sat waiting. The first one I came to I punched his windscreen so hard I broke my hand. He drove off as fast as he could. I approached another to do the same. Despite the pain, I couldn't feel it. He fled and I don't blame him. I turned to cause more mayhem but then saw about 8 cops standing there. My mam had called them and luckily they must have been nearby as they arrived in no time. I screamed at them to come and try it, I'll take every one of ya etc.

Fortunately my mother had spoken to them moments before and quickly told them I was sick, maybe bipolar. One spoke calmly to me, I don't remember the exact words but something like "George it's ok, take it easy, we're not going to harm you" etc.
He spoke calm words but firmly. Then the strangest thing happened, I just came out of it, just like that. I was calm, as if I'd just been on a picnic

in the countryside. Maybe the prospect of grappling with 8 cops brought me out of it. Who knows? I said to the cops "I don't know what came over me, it's passed now." They totally understood and told me to get my hand checked out. Soon I was in the Royal Hospital for the first time that day to get my hand tended to.

Later that day I went up the stairs to the toilet, and Mal was standing at the top of them. He has long hair and a beard. I said to him "Help me Jesus, help me!" Then I looked into his eyes and saw Jesus looking at me and continued "Are you Jesus?" He laughed and said "No George" That's the last thing I remember before the ambulance came and took me away, and a night of hell was to follow.

As I've said before, it's strange how you remember certain things and some are gone from your memory forever. I remember sitting anxiously in the waiting room in the Royal Hospital. It was a Friday night, so it's quite busy. Within an hour, some of my closest family are with me; my Mam and Mal her husband, my Dad and Verna his partner, (who's never seen me like this) and Mel. They were all trying to keep me calm as they can sense I'm getting more anxious and frightened by the minute.

I don't know how long I waited until a Portuguese doctor came out, called Dr Fernando. He told me it shouldn't be that long. I told him I need help quick as I'm going to flip. I begged him to hurry. But another hour passed and I was no further down the line. I called him over again but he repeated the same. Time was pressing and at some point between his last conversation and the next, I had changed dramatically. When he told me it won't be long this time, I punched him to the ground. Within moments security were on me. The police were called and I was dragged into a police van, agitated, frightened and not knowing why I'd done what I'd done. I look back and feel absolutely awful about hitting this man doing his job. I can't explain what made me do it. It wasn't planned or calculated, just a spur of the moment frightened reaction in a confused and vulnerable, anxious state. In a normal frame of mind I would never do that. My past violence has always had good reason, never hit anybody for nothing. As far as the police were concerned I'd assaulted a doctor, so a night in the cells for yours truly. I'll never forget looking out of the police van window and seeing my mum and Verna's face sobbing as it drove away. My night hadn't even started yet.

Before I knew it, I was locked in a prison cell for the second time in my life, only the first time I was in control and just slept on the bed regretting my stupidity. This time was totally different. I'm going manic and I'm alone, not knowing what is happening to me, and out of control. Many things went through my mind that night; the reality TV delusion was one. I thought there was a hidden camera watching me. As a result of thinking the world was watching me I played to it by doing my greatest impressions. I did my Godfathers, On The Waterfront and Cuckoo's Nests. I danced like Ali by doing constant Ali shuffles and dancing round the cell imitating his fights. I screamed his quotes; "I shook up the world" and "I am the greatest" etc. I laughed, then cried to myself. I thought I was Papillon for a while, stuck in a prison in French Guiana and paced up and down as he did in solitary confinement. Then I thought I was Steve McQueen again in 'The Great Escape', imagining I'm throwing a baseball at the wall, and outside the cops are Nazis. The cop sitting outside the cell I freaked out so much, he had to walk away and swop. I don't know what I said, but I had the devil in my eyes and spooked him enough to stand down.

I was like a man possessed for many hours, then around 8 in the morning, after a good 9 hours of delusions, fear and rage, 3 doctors came in to evaluate me. It was 2 men and a woman. All foreign. They were psychiatrists. They came too close. I remember saying "Please I beg you to move back, I don't want to hurt you, move back, I warn you!" They could see in my eyes this was a warning to heed as I must have looked like a cornered animal at the end of its tether. Even though I was delusional and dangerous, I still in my heart of hearts didn't want to hurt anyone. The cops were beside them as they asked a few questions I do not remember. All 3 had to agree on me being sectioned and they did. Soon they were gone and I waited to see what was next. Through all of this, what I didn't know was my mum was outside but wasn't allowed to see me. Again this woman's loyalty to her son was unprecedented.

Soon some new police arrived, not from wherever I was being held. These were like riot police and had protective clothes and helmets on. They told me they were coming in to take me somewhere else. I stood still and calm. In my mind, I thought I was being taken to be executed, electric chair or hung; one of the two but definitely taken to be killed. If you believe this is real you will do anything to stay alive or save yourself. I waited until they came in and came close and, like in Wales on that mountain, the first few (despite the riot gear clothing) went down and were tossed over my shoulder. It took about 6 to pin me, handcuff both hands and feet and escort me into a cage in the back of a police van. It was my Hannibal Lecter moment!

I don't remember what I did or said in this cage, only that I was chained in it. I couldn't move for many hours. The next thing I know, I'm in a psychiatric hospital in Bradford. They had no beds in Liverpool and this was the nearest.

Looking back on the night before, I couldn't help but feel bad about what I'd done; hitting the doctor doing his job, upsetting all my family again, saying God knows what to that cop - who was only making sure I was alright- then tackling with police just doing their job. I can't control what's happening, that's the scariest part, and that's why I fear these relapses. Thankfully Dr Fernando didn't press charges. I guess he knew I was sick but that doesn't make me feel better. I did get word to him once I came around months later, that I was very sorry for what I did. That made me feel a bit better.

However suddenly standing in a huge yard full of about 50 to 70 patients in Bradford didn't make me feel better. I looked around and I was the only white man in the place; everybody was Asian, Black or Indian. Bear in mind, at some point before this, I must have been taken to a room and injected with some kind of drug (maybe Valium) to calm me down or sedate me. By the time I was in this yard, I was dazed, I was calm and luckily not manic. I had to ask someone where I was and they told me Bradford. My immediate thoughts were 'oh my God I'm going to get beaten up here' or 'I'm not going to survive in here.' The same if an Asian guy suddenly walked into a large confined space with dozens and dozens of white guys, he'd feel uneasy.

I looked around to see guys playing football, basketball, lifting weights, playing cards or just chatting on the floors with their backs against walls. Some walking around confused or lost. There was so much going on, I'd never seen a place like this in my life. It was like one of those American prison movies when someone gets murdered in the yard by a street gang. I stood and watched about 15 Asian guys play football. It was all men this place, no women to be seen. I watched for a few minutes, then one approached me and asked if I wanted to play. His name was Khan if I recall. I thought yes, I wouldn't mind a game and get some exercise, so joined in. Things were fine for about 20 minutes and then I got the ball near the edge of what you would call the box, and fired a rocket even Robbie Fowler would have been proud of. It flew towards the keeper and broke his finger as he tried to save it before going in. The poor guy is standing there holding his broken middle finger. I felt terrible. We all crowded around him until the doctors came and took him away. I couldn't apologise to him enough but he was fine about it, he knew it was an accident. The ball just caught him wrong. The next time I saw him, his poor finger was bandaged up but we were cool and spent a fair bit of time together in the week or so I was there.

Khan was my closest companion in there. He looked scary as he had only had one eye, but was harmless and very friendly to me. I learnt he lost his eye in a racist attack. A few of the guys had suffered racist attacks, maybe that's why they were in there; the stress of persistent racism.

The only other time I'd been around so many Asians was in 97 when me and Steve did a movie called 'Dirty British Boys' in Leicester. It was funded by the Asian mafia, we got paid in curries for this film as they ran out of money. Every night Frazzle, the producer, treated us both to a curry; the best in town. Me and Steve got to know many Asians and their culture in the short two or three weeks spent there. Even Lee Macdonald came on board, and Paul Usher from Brookside. Shame it ended as it was a decent film, first time I got shot in a production, the device of fake blood exploding when the guy fired, bit nervy but an experience.

The short stay in this out of town cuckoo's nest,

for me, was mainly spent in the yard playing football with my new found Asian friends. I was more careful when I had sight of goal not to break any more fingers. I got to play basketball too. It was my perfect chance to do official 'One Flew Over The Cuckoo's Nest' impressions on a grand scale. There was a guy who was like the Chief in there. This wasn't a delusion as I'd been through that shit. Now was cooling down time, and this guy looked like, but maybe not as big, as the great Chief in Cuckoo's Nest. I told him this and he laughed. I remember long conversations with the Chief sitting outside, both still in worlds of our own, but making sense to one another. I'd love to remember what we spoke about but it's gone from my memory, I just know we spoke deeply, alone. Maybe I thought he really was the Chief, but whatever I thought I know, he was deep, and I went deep with him.

Soon I was saying goodbye to Khan, the Chief, and whoever else I associated with in there. It would be the last time I would see my Bradford patient mates again. Same as most hospitals I go in, you rarely see the guys again. Except Julianne, I saw her a few times - thankfully.

Nobody came to visit me in this Bradford hospital, so for the first time my mother or anyone else couldn't step foot in there. The section they put on me prevented visits because I'd assaulted someone and fought the cops. It was the strictest section type they could impose. I was on my own for the time spent in there. With whatever happy pills they were giving me I never let this get me down. I just thought this is it, this is my life from now on; in this Asian kingdom. Although I had the Chief and Khan by my side all the time, there is always an element of danger in these places. I remember at least one fight broke out between 2 guys. It got broken up not before long, but that's the thing in this type of environment, anything can happen at any given moment. From peace and tranquillity to madness and mayhem in the blink of an eye.

I've sat in day rooms playing chess when all of a sudden a table or chair has been launched across the room and a guy wants to kill everyone. Nurses run in and pin them down. I've laid in bed and heard screaming from a patient who's found a guy hanging from his ceiling a young person with his whole life ahead of him but couldn't take any more. I've witnessed a guy as big as the guy in the 'Green Mile' film, suddenly go ballistic in the room I'm with him in; throwing tables and chairs and screaming and shouting in Zulu tongue. South African he was. I prayed he wouldn't come near me as he could have killed me with his bare huge hands. A giant of a man that made Anthony Joshua look like Arnold in 'Different Strokes'. I just stayed in the corner and kept quiet until it took its course. It took at least 7 big male nurses to control him. They took him out the room and I never saw him again.

The trip back to Liverpool was a lot easier than the one to Bradford. No police or handcuffs and cages, just a straight forward back of an ambulance trip, heavily sedated, I have been told recently. So back to Broad Oak I go and I am soon laying on my new bed, and still not allowed visitors for another week.

The monotony begins again; get up, same breakfast, dinner, tea and supper then bed, but no visits. Earlier on, in my mind I would imagine something was happening to one of my family or friends, maybe kidnapped for instance. I would scream all over the place something like "Get Big Al, get him here!" I wouldn't calm down or relax and Mel would have to call them. Big Al said he'd been relaxing eating his tea, then suddenly he'd have to get the hospital so I could see him. Once I knew he was ok, I would relax again.

Hagan was in Sayers once getting a few sausage rolls when he got the call. I believed he was being tortured by the Illuminati, so he had to rush in too. It was all paranoia, but to me it was all so real. Not once did my friends let me down during these frightening visions, and again I am forever grateful. Luckily this all ceased and my mind calmed.

What gets to you in the end is the boredom of it all once you realise where the hell you are. But after a few days, again, I planned to escape. I walked around checking things out, but again like in 91, I'm being followed. When you're sectioned, a nurse is never more than a few yards away, but this makes it more fun for me; to outwit a big nurse. There was no way out of Bradford. I walked the grounds many times and saw no loop hole. It must have been a high security psychiatric hospital. There had to be one I figured. I worked out the doors that lead from corridor to corridor, if forced hard enough, would open. Everybody thought they were locked but they weren't. My cunning plan was to simply barge into all the corridor doors and make it to the exit stairs and out the main doors at the bottom. After that God knows what I planned, I just had to get out.

I waited till night time. Everyone was in bed. I packed what little I had; cigarettes, lighter and my wallet that consisted of just a picture of my son, no money. I had no phone; the family had that and I hadn't seen them for over 2 weeks. I crept out and ran down the corridor like Usain Bolt. I slammed into the doors and they burst open. Nurses were shouting and running after me instantly. I ran along another corridor and burst through another set of doors. I ran through another ward full of women patients; most in bed, but one or two screamed as I sprinted down their corridor, hoping to find the stairs as I slammed into the next set of doors. I got through but ended up on another ward. There were nurses behind me and nurses now in front of me. I was trapped. I looked to see what I thought was an empty bed in a four man room. I leapt into it, pulling the covers over my head only to find an old man curled up in it. He jumped up screaming "Help! Help! Help! There's a man in my bed" etc. The nurses ran in so I held my hands up and said "Ok you got me." I knew there was no way out of this one.

I continued "Just take me back to my ward I'll go to sleep now". But it turned out I was on my ward. I'd run round in a complete circle, putting myself back where I started. It was the worst hospital escape probably ever attempted. That was the last time I tried to escape from one of these places. Even the nurses laughed when I realised I'd got nowhere.

I was resigned now, and soon enough the family were let back in. I loved seeing all of them. All except Kirk as he wasn't allowed, Mel kept him well away, not wanting to see things a child may see unexpected. Although most were harmless, just chilled on their meds, as I've said previously, it only takes a second to light the fuse. Calm to chaos is a fine line in those places.

At least the grounds to chill outside were bigger now and had more greenery and a few trees. Normally I prefer garden birds or birds of prey but here it was mainly the wood pigeons that became my friends. Putting damp bread under the trees they would gather, letting me watch from a safe distance. Get too close to a wood pigeon, he flaps his noisy wings and is gone. They may not have the angelic sounds of a Nightingale but they were better than nothing! The birds obsession was back, but I'm harming no one.

After this spell in hospital, I recovered pretty quickly. The doctors warned me to be careful of going too high at first, so me and my Dad drew a list of characters who would make me laugh too much or make me too excited. We called it Wilson's List. I had to stay away from anyone who could potentially send me hyper. The lithium was to be taken twice a day for at least the next two years. See how I get on, I may be able to come off it. One of the biggest medical mistakes I made was coming off it two years later. If I'd stayed on it I would never have had the 5th and final spell in 2013.

The line in 'The Usual Suspects' says '"The greatest trick the Devil ever pulled was making the world believe he never existed." Well I go one better; "The cruellest trick the devil ever pulled was letting some know he does exist."

When I was to come out, it was decided amongst myself and Denzil, that working in the sales environment was too stressful for me. The acting I'd given up when Kirk was about six in 2005. It was too unreliable waiting on auditions every blue moon, getting my hopes up only to hear nothing.

The last time I acted on TV was a series called 'Nice Guy Eddie' in 2001 produced by Colin McEwan, one of the biggest producers in the city and still is. He told me back then to write my story but I knew there was more, much more. Anyway I was to play a welterweight boxer. A guy called Chris was called in to get me in shape, he was from a big family in Anfield and was running the doors the night I got slashed. Twice in my life he was to help me.

Everyday for a good few months we'd jog through the town and up the Everton Hills, a bit further every time. We would spar in his gym the Salsbury and spend an hour here and there on the punch bags and speedballs. I'd done this years earlier with Jay and Brian in Franny's Gym in town aged 17 to about 21, but I was in nowhere near the shape I was then. Chris got me in shape and on the first day of filming I had to spar with well-known local actor Andrew Schofield who played my brother. During the first scene, he cracked 2 ribs as I wore no padding. The scene was basically him beating me up as I'd deceived him. I had to carry on as it was the first day and I didn't want to ruin the shoot then maybe be replaced.

The following day at the Adelphi Hotel, I had to fight a proper welterweight from Ireland. He was a lovely guy but the pain I endured with my ribs was starting to show after 3 or 4 takes of a proper fight, 3 minutes a round. Chris was there to guide me; he played the referee. I got through it but it took 12 takes to get the right one. I was exhausted and in excruciating pain with my ribs. Only Chris knew how I was feeling. Luckily I won this fight! It would have been worse if I was to hit the canvas 12 times.

Me and Andrew Schofield shared a trailer. I met him years earlier in a toilet when I was 14 whilst at the Everyman. He'd just finished Skully. I was chuffed as he was the first famous actor I'd met. Other famous people I was to meet in toilets were Gazza in a snooker hall when he played for Everton, the lead singer out the Animals, Eric Burden, an Elvis impersonator who recognised me from Brookside which was surreal, and almost Bowie!

Me and Schofield played the White Album before

we'd do our scenes. What he didn't know about every Beatles song was nobody's business. I learnt more about John Lennon off him than anyone. I always thought the song 'Happiness is a warm gun' was a lovely ballad by Lennon but it's about his penis. Slow it down 'A penis is a warm gun' followed by 'Bang Bang shoot shoot. When I hold you in my arms, And I feel my finger on your trigger.' Doesn't take a genius. I also discovered 'Norwegian Wood' was about Lennon meeting a Norwegian girl, going back to her place in a Norwegian wood and not getting what he wanted. So when she left, he set fire to her house. It was all hushed up at the time as The Beatles were the most popular band on the planet. 'So I lit a fire isn't it good Norwegian wood.

So after Nice Guy Eddie, I hung my acting boots up. I waited a year maybe without one audition, soon I had a sit down with Denzil and his brother Penders, I was to become an estate agent! I'd never done it before, but I was to just answer phones and put people through but it never worked out like that. Before I knew it I was selling houses, getting offers, renting houses, closing deals, showing people round houses etc. I learnt the trade pretty well.

There was a gap between leaving hospital and starting there; maybe 6 weeks to recuperate. I recovered much quicker than in 91 and 99. Just took life in the slow lane for a while. The lithium balances me, stops me going to high or too low.

I've never really read up about it. Some do, they

want to know the ins and outs of what they are taking. Before you know it, you're stressed out worrying about side effects that 99% won't happen. It got me back to reality. The biggest mistake I made was to come off them after 2 years. This was catastrophic as caused my 5th and final hospitalisation, in 2013.

When a Dr said I can come off them after 2 years I had to. I didn't want to be on meds for the rest of my life. That was just one reason, the others being I wanted to drink with my pals again, and the final one was I thought I wouldn't be able to get as excited or as happy, high as much as I would be on the tablets. Finally, they were big white tablets back then too, I struggled sometimes taking them. Choked a few times. They are much smaller and thinner now, thankfully. To sum them up in one brief sentence, they stop me going too high and stop me going too low, and that's all I want to know. I'm like a tightrope walker 50ft up who has one thing he can rely on; his balance.

One of the best things that happened that year was me and Mel went the Highlands for a long weekend. It was a place I'd always wanted to go as my family date back there. The Wilsons date back to the days of William Wallace and were part of the uprising. It was one of the most beautiful places I'd seen. We climbed the 6th highest mountain, sailed across Loch Ness, looked out over castles where Robert the Bruce once stood, and saw a wild deer walk across the glen, a stone's throw away from us. Heaven.

Just before Halloween 2010 Me and Mel also went to New York, the place I'd wanted to go all my life. To sum up the best bits: I watched Pulp fiction on the plane going over to put me in the mood. We saw Coney Island with the Wonder wheel, which was the setting to one of my obsessions, the film 'The Warriors'. Then we walked along Coney Island beach watching the waves come in, Mel's mum commented I'm the only man who could go to New York and find a beach.

We drank in Jack Dempsey's bar the once Heavyweight champion.

Visited the Dakota buildings where Lennon lived. I got goose bumps by the spot he was assassinated - eerie! Strawberry Fields was a lovely peaceful spot where we sat on a bench. Went round Central Park in a rickshaw pulled by a Chinese chap -not what Mel wanted, she was rather hoping for a horse and cart scenario.

Visited Little Italy, doing Godfather impressions for the Mob. That was when I knew my Godfather impression was good, when I dis it for these wise guys in a clam bar on Mulberry Street, Little Italy. They gave us free wine all night and took me to a location were a scene in Godfather 2 was filmed, where De Niro shoots the black hand guy on the staircase. These guys appreciated my Godfather impression a lot more than the drummer out of Madness, thank God! We saw St Paul's church that survived 9/11. That was emotional seeing the flags sent from all over the world in solidarity, plus firemen uniforms left on benches. It was used as a refuge during the terror attacks that day. I'll never forget the conversation with a lovely old nun in there too. I bought a beautiful silver Celtic cross and Mel got her usual rosary beads for her Nan Lil (a woman who defies medical science).

On Halloween we got engaged on the Rockefeller ice rink to Hotel California. I dropped the ring on the ice. I'd bought it earlier in Macey's with my pal from New Jersey, Jimmy 2 times. It drifted across but luckily a kid retrieved it for me. Mel thought it was one of my jokes and just stood there in shock until I said "I'm bloody serious here!" A special night.

We stood below the Manhattan Bridge from 'Once Upon A Time In America.' That was some view.

We met Jay's brother Gary who' lived there most of his life, he fell in love with the place after winning the Golden gloves boxing there in the early 80's. He took us round the Meat packing district, the East side and West, places we would never of known. To end the night we done the 'On the Waterfront' cab scene in a New York cab. He's the only man who can do it with me, even looks like Brando. "You dont understand, I coulda had class. I coulda been a contender. I coulda been somebody, instead of a bum, which is what I am let's face it." Greatest scene ever and could also sum up my own life. Still, a great end to the night.

I almost had a panic attack on the plane home as I'd done too much. Luckily a steward called Stacey from Roosevelt, New York calmed me; a man I'll be forever be grateful to. He distracted me all the way home by talking to me, as I was going to have a panic attack on that plane without doubt. I told him I didn't feel right so he said stay by him all the way home. Mel was asleep and worn out after running round NY constant for 5 days. It was one of my favourite holidays ever. As far back as I could remember I always wanted to go New York and I'd finally conquered it thanks to Mel getting it for my 40th.

Chapter 25
The Final Breakdown

'One of the things that baffles me is how there can be so much lingering stigma with regards to mental illness, specifically bipolar disorder. In my opinion, living with manic depression takes a tremendous amount of balls.'
Carrie Fisher

The final breakdown was a result of my own foolish doing. At some point, two years earlier, a doctor had said after 2 years I can come off the lithium. Why I decided to do this after it was keeping me well balanced and well, I don't know.

I was still working for Big Neil Penders in Keybanks estate agents, doing well although things were starting to get to me. Not everyone you deal with selling houses can be pleasant; some were complete arseholes. Plastic gangsters trying to throw their weight around, I've been around em all they didn't impress me, but they wound me up. Penders done his best to put me at ease in there, but things were building up; pressure I couldn't handle like the others could in there. Penders' family who worked there were great; his son Christopher Columbus and daughter Sammy Davis Junior, even though both young they were very understanding, as a lot of the younger generation are I've found. Mad Jill was good to have around too as she laughed at everything I said or did, in fact she made me go too high as I'd perform for her knowing she'd laugh. Julie and Dy were also supportive but none of these people can stop a train about to crash. Hence, I still went in and tried to take my mind off it by carrying on. Again these are people who dont know what I've been through or about to go through. If its gonna happen its gonna happen, nobody on earth can stop it.

I'd stopped the lithium now and then made one of the biggest mistakes in my bipolar history. It was Grand National day and I was out with about 20 mad pals. I drank in the sun outside the Hares Pub in the village all day. Laughing like the old days, drinking pints of lager, thinking I'm invincible now I'm off the lithium. Without knowing it at the time, I was going backwards. I was sending myself into another hospital visit.

In less than a week from that day I relapsed. The hangover I thought would never come, came like a tsunami of madness. Again I begged visiting nurses to be taken to hospital but again was told I could be fixed from home. I begged my mate, Big Stan across the road, to knock me out a few times when I felt it coming. He never did but calmed me instead. I knew asking him I couldn't hit back!

At this stage of high anxiety I simply can't be fixed from home. I'm past the point of no return. It built up and whilst at my sister Zoe's, things came to a head. I was staying there out of the way but then began shouting sentences in the kitchen that made no sense. She rang my Dad who came quickly. He took me to hospital followed, unknown to me, by a police car as Mel had rang them explaining I could get out the car in this volatile state. I got to A&E and begged to be handcuffed in case I was to strike a doctor again. This never happened, but fortunately I never struck anyone this time. There was some control I guess. Before long, I was moved into another section of the Royal Hospital, away from all patients and doctors for a while. This is where the paranoia and delusions kicked in. I just had my Dad and Mel with me; my Mam was on holiday. My mind went into overdrive.

I only remember a few as I must have been heavily sedated soon after. The first delusional thoughts were where I had 2 choices. The first; I was to be thrown into the sea to a circling Great White shark and be eaten or I had to choose my closest family instead; my Mam, Dad, Zo, Mel and Kirk. I had to choose to sacrifice myself to the horror of being eaten alive or my loved ones. This was all very real to me as I cried and pleaded no to the horrendous thought. For what seemed ages, I paced up and down fighting the choices, then screaming 'Take me, take me you bastards.'

At some point, being trapped in the Twin Towers came to me. No escape. I imagined the choice people had that day; jump or burn. This was again pure torture in my mind. The footage on the day and documentaries I'd seen had caused this one.

Another strange vision was I imagined thousands of Zulu's were outside chanting and trying to get in to get me, disembowel me like they did at the battle of Isandlwana I'd read. It was almost primeval imagining these warriors were coming for me. Again the movies I've watched played tricks on me as I screamed for mercy from a non existent imaginary foe.

The final vision was equally as frightening as I believed there was a bomb in the corridor. I heard it counting down and held my ears to my head, waiting for it to blast. Like a Supernova, it blasted in my mind and it didn't just wipe out the hospital, it wiped out the universe. The Earth and the cosmos was gone. Everything except me. I believed I was now alone in another dimension, nothing or nobody was around me. Just me, somehow crouched and frightened on the ground; the last survivor of all that ever stood. Tears pouring down my face because I had nobody anymore in the world to love or talk too. Mel and my Dad must have watched and just let me be. They wouldn't have known what was going through my mind during these tormented visions. I'm so glad I never tried to harm them. I was in my own bubble, my own world of delusions on a grand scale.

The end of the world bomb was the last thing I remember before waking up in a hospital for the 5th time. I pray it's the last! I remember some absolute arse of a nurse, so smug, who wound himself up showing me all the different rooms and places. I told him numerous times "I've been here 3 times before, I probably know the place better than you" but he continued like the jobsworth that he was.

Within 24 hours, I got into a fight with another

patient over my music being too loud through my headphones. He moaned and I retaliated causing a scuffle in the dormitory. It was nothing serious; more two men letting go of their frustration and anger at finding themselves confined again. I was warned by the staff nurse that if it happened again the police would be called and I'd be arrested. We steered clear of each other for a while, but before long became friends in there. When the built up anger fades I mellow in these places. As did that chap.

Luckily my family and friends visited every day including my pal Mad dog who kept slipping me £50 notes. I begged him no, but how do you refuse a man named Mad dog if he insists? But it's not about the money I know he cares as much as any of em. Liam the preacher would visit and say a prayer with me, Steve would come and be the one I'd confide in, the Duke as usual with various useful devices and tales of his Everton away days. Hagan and Big Al as of every spell in these places would come and make me laugh, take the piss out of me, and each other which helps me. Laughing about yourself helps, I needed that. My nickname was the Bipolar King, i liked that. Only your pals can do this, if a stranger done it they'd be blue murder. I needed my pals during these dark days, I'd count the minutes to their visits.

Now until this point, I must have smoked 10 to 20 cigarettes a day. The problem I had in here was we had to smoke out on a cage with steps leading to a blocked off courtyard. Patients crammed together while puffing away was not an ideal location for me. I get claustrophobic at the best of times and huddled together in a smoky small space was hell. That's when a young black guy called Curtis came over to let me try his E cig. I instantly took to him a few days earlier. When I awoke feeling nervous and anxious, he came over and introduced himself saying if I needed anything let him know. This small act of courtesy goes a long way in these places. So I tried the e-cig and the strawberry flavour he had in it and loved it. The next day the Duke came in with an e cig and various flavours for me. From that day on in 2013, I have used an e-cig. My personal flavour being Vanilla Custard and nothing else.

I wasn't as manic during my last stay, my recovery was much quicker than all prior to this 4 month stay.

I remember finding a book on Marilyn Monroe whilst I was in there. I always found her beautiful and talented, but this book gave me insights into her I never knew. This was to become a new obsession of how she struggled most of her life with it. I related to so many things including the putting on a smile throughout her career.
I love these words reclusive novelist Thomas Pynchon wrote about Monroe:
'If the world offered nothing,
nowhere to support or make bearable whatever her private grief was,
then it is that world, and not she, that is at fault.'

My stay would have been pretty comfortable except for one thing I had to battle; sleeping without a sleeping tablet, and that being Zopiclone. I tried and tried and at some point, during the early hours, I'd have to get a doctor to prescribe one as I couldn't sleep. It was catch 22 as I couldn't be allowed out without sleeping of my own accord. This battle went on for weeks.

There was a point I said to myself enough is enough I have to do this or I'll be in here forever. I got my sister Zoe to bring a small bedside fan in for me. Being the middle of summer, it was sweltering on those wards. Funny how I always seem to be in these places during summer, never winter. I downloaded an app on my phone that played calming Indian type music. I drank no teas or coffees that day, only water. Then when I went to bed around 11pm, I had a hot chocolate. I put the soothing music on and positioned the fan so it blew gently on my face as I lay calmly. I blocked out any thoughts of negativity including 'will I fall asleep or will I ever get out'; the main two factors that had swirled around my mind the previous nights. Listening to the music I shut my eyes. The next thing I know, I opened my eyes and thought 'Dam it hasn't worked' but then I checked the time on my phone and it was 10am in the morning! I had done it; no pills. I was so happy with myself I woke the rest of the ward cheering to myself! This was a massive leap of progression for me, a simple thing as sleeping had become a massive hurdle. It was keeping me in there, it was torturing my nights. It had become an obstacle I had to get over, and thankfully that night I did and the following few nights too.

My last night i sat alone on the corridor, thinking to myself. I was then joined by the top doctor in the hospital, I'd seen him around but never spoke, but heard he was the main man. He was waiting to see a patient so sat beside me until he was needed. After a few pleasantries I looked him in the eyes and said "Doc, I been in these places 5 times now. I can't take another one. I don't know why I keep coming back. The next one's gonna kill me I know it, what's the secret?"

He looked me in the eyes and replied " All I can tell you is this, see that guy over there (points) he's going to come out of here and put so much cocaine up his nose for the next 6 months he'll return here. That guy over there is going to smoke so much weed over 2 years he'll end up back. That lady over there will drink so much vodka in...you get my drift? I see them every year, they leave and make the same mistakes" It was like he'd hit the nail on the head for me. I thanked him for his time as he had to go. That night laying in bed I decided I wasn't going to drink anymore. The drugs I'd given up so i knew it wasn't that, so from that moment on I decided never to get drunk again. It was very hard as I loved a drink but i couldn't keep putting myself and family through this turmoil anymore. His tip has worked so far...

The next day I was discharged back into society.
I took it easy for a while then decided I didn't want to work in the estate agents anymore. Nothing to do with my colleagues, but the general public were sometimes stressful to deal with. My time had come there I felt, so I worked from home for Steve doing sales. It wasn't stressful, just a case of

ringing football clubs or councils to get advertisements done in their stadiums or on the streets for the councils. There were no targets. I made my bedroom into a kind of office; a desk in the corner with all my paperwork and used my mobile as I had free calls. I made some good money doing this, but not as good as working for Denzil. Steve has a box at Middlesbrough as we'd done a lot of work there, so that was nice, getting to watch some big games just before they got promoted in 2015. Then again the following season, once promoted. I got some good deals but it wasn't enough to keep me there, so yet again in my life I moved on.

It took a few months of searching with a guy called Jimmy the Jobs, who's employed to help people with mental illness find a job. The next job was to be at Liverpool FC, the team I idolised since I could remember. I worked in hospitality for nearly three years. They paid for many holidays!

Chapter 26
Once Upon A Time In America

'Our land is everything to us. I will tell you one of the things we remember on our land. We remember that our grandfathers paid for it – with their lives'
John Wooden Leg (Cheyenne Indian)

Not long after Kirk passed out in the Royal Navy, one of the family's proudest moments in Plymouth. (Myself, Mel, my Dad and Mel's sister Lyndsey all had a tear in our eye that day) It Was Kirk's 18th and my 47th when we flew to New York. Kirk had never got over us going to NY in 2010 without him, so it was decided we'd all go this time. The departure and flight was pretty straight forward and soon we arrived at an amazing hotel overlooking the whole of Time Square. It was a Novotel hotel and I have to say it was one of the finest hotels I've ever stayed in.

Seeing New York through Kirks eyes was special. That first morning taking in the hustle and bustle of Times Square, standing on the steps in the middle, getting our photographs taken with half naked Indian braves. Kirk couldn't resist spanking her ass as the photo was taken. I could only look on. There was a guy outside the Hard Rock Cafe dressed as De Niro in Taxi Driver, tourists from all parts of the globe all excited in one spot. Huge billboards advertising anything you can think of, lit up signs above theatres for shows such as Wicked and School of Rock and Jersey Boys etc.

There was another visit to Dempsey's Bar after enjoying the first in 2010. As Kirk was only 18 he couldn't get served over there, but on the last night we found a way in Greenwich Village. We had done the Staten Island Ferry to see the Statue of Liberty and been up the Empire State again. A new thing was to go up the Rockefeller this time and at night. It was a better view than the Empire State.

The first time I was up the Empire State I was fine, but the 2nd time after 10 minutes, I started to get a bit panicky. I started to imagine a plane coming at it, my imagination was getting the better of me. I never told Mel or Kirk, I just said I feel dizzy and headed down trying my upmost to remain calm and not panic. Once down I was fine again, but for a moment up there it could have got messy. That's the thing with panic attacks, they come at you from nowhere. A nice day out with my family then boom, it's on you like a torpedo. The best I can do is to get out of the situation as calmly as I can, without looking stupid. Imagine how scary it would have been up there? Breathe slowly and think I'm elsewhere was my tactic that day.

It happened a few years earlier on the London Eye with Mel and Kirk. As soon as it got high up I felt one coming on. I couldn't look out of the window. I had to sit down. The only thing that distracted me without saying anything was Liverpool were playing Arsenal and kept scoring and won 5-0, so I had the commentary coming from the phone. This took me away from the horrific possibility of having a panic attack in a small glass pod over 100ft up.

We walked through Hell's Kitchen, as after me and Kirk watched 'Daredevil' and the movie 'Sleepers', it was discussed we'd like to venture there. It was great looking at the huge tenement blocks with fire escape ladders halfway up like in the movies.

We walked across the Brooklyn Bridge at night to see the lit up skyscrapers. All around was an awesome sight. It seemed to take forever but we didn't mind. You could see the Manhattan Bridge from it, also lit up, which was cool.

Central Park in the day was much different than our rushed Chinese guy on a bike journey the first time. This time I paid a man to ride his horse and carriage around the park, which was what Mel wanted the first time. It was a lovely way to see the park and outskirts. Then we found some huge rocks that you could climb up and could gaze at the magnificent skyscrapers surrounding the park, with the ice rink below.

The last night we arranged to meet our friend who we met the first time; Melissa in Greenwich Village, with her husband Michael. But before this Mel and Kirk wanted to shop in Macey's. I however didn't, as shopping bores me to death. There was something I'd always wanted to do and that was walk around the Bronx on my own. I'd seen the Bronx in so many movies and figured it's daytime I'll be safe. I got the subway to the Bronx and walked alone; Yankee's cap on to blend in etc. Had a coffee in an Irish cafe. Noticed many pawn shops around, the type you pawn your jewellery. This spelt poverty to me. I spoke to a few black homeless guys who were friendly enough and said I was wise coming at this time and not after dark. Subway trains came overhead like in the movies, sprayed in graffiti like in 'The Warriors'. I enjoyed my day in the Bronx. It was something I'd always wanted to see. I had no problems. If anything it was sad as you could see nobody had much money. I'm glad I did it all the same, as I'd never seen such huge tenement blocks in all my life. The Sheil Road flats in Kensington where my Auntie lived seemed minute in comparison. How so many are crammed in in those places is scary.

Later that day, I head back to meet our American friends. We had a bite to eat in an Italian first then tried to get in to the Cafe Wah (a very famous live music joint). The doormen wouldn't let Kirk in due to his age. Melissa said 'The Bitter End' shouldn't be a problem and it's the next best thing. It was fabulous, the live bands blew us away. There were paintings on the walls of some of the greats who had played there including Bob Dylan, Johnny Cash, Joni Mitchell and Amy Winehouse etc., I had a couple of light Buds that night. I thought 'fuck it' as Kirk was drinking and everyone else; two won't harm me on the last night of a special holiday. I also had a couple of cigarettes outside with them. Again I figured 'what the hell', it will be a while till I have another.

On the way home we walked to Time Square and saw the Peace Tower lit up majestically, between one of the avenues. I stared at it for a good few minutes, thinking yes it's beautiful but it should never have had to have been built.

The next day we flew home to Liverpool. Kirk said it was the best place he's ever been to, exactly the same thing I said when I got back from there in 2010. You'd think New York would be too much for someone who can have panic attacks at any given moment, but it's not. I managed to control them luckily. I love it. The hustle and bustle doesn't bother me, nor does the noise, the shouting, or the tourists everywhere etc. Maybe because I lived in London so long all these things don't bother me. It's hard to explain as you'd think they'd be a nightmare to me. I guess I just adapt to my surroundings and accept them.

Chapter 27
Chaos in the Caribbean

'The sea once it casts its spell, holds one in its net of wonder forever.'
Jacques Yves Cousteau

For over 8 months, me and Mel saved for our Caribbean cruise. I worked 16 hour shifts many times at LFC, and was back in the next morning at 8am for another shift, just to pay this off. Mel worked hard too, working long 5 hour days to contribute to it. It cost just over £6,000 for a 1 week cruise, with a balcony, around 7 different islands and 1 week in Barbados. I couldn't wait, some of those days bored or cold at work I suffered, thinking about sitting on that balcony, looking out to sea with the sun going down drinking a nice cold shandy.

We paid it off and our bags were packed. Sunday morning, my pal Mumbles picked us up. I was in charge of putting the luggage in the car. Mel hopped in last and we were off to Manchester Airport. Once arrived, we started getting the luggage out and Mel said "Where's my hand luggage?" We all looked but it wasn't there.
"I put it in. I'm sure of it." I replied. But it wasn't - it was outside our house in Huyton with her stuff for the flight, plus all our passports and $2000 in cash.
The look I was given for this major fuck up was not good as Mel and poor Mumbles had to race back to Huyton (hoping to God it was still there - bearing in mind it's been there about 45 mins

already). She rang her uncle Kenny over and over as he was staying in our house looking after Sonny the dog. Eventually he heard his phone and wandered down to find the case just outside the front gate, where I foolishly left it. He took it in.

Meanwhile Kirk and I are having problems checking in because his case was overloaded so we had to transfer stuff to the other cases whilst other tourists looked on. Mel's case wasn't tagged so we weren't sure if it was even on the plane. Just chaos before we'd stepped on the plane.

When all was settled a bit later, I took 2 Valium's to make sure I'd be chilled and drowsy for the flight, as I felt a little edgy, not like New York the first time coming home, but just nervous, especially after the last flight going to Benidorm, when I nearly ran off the plane. This was on my mind for weeks before the holiday in case I did the same. The minute I took the two 5mg Valium's, the flight was delayed by an hour. Within 30 or 40 minutes I was asleep in the departure lounge. When the flight finally got called I could hardly walk. I was so drowsy Kirk had to help me up the steps of the plane. Ten years earlier, I had to carry him up the steps going to Rome because his shorts blew down on the runway, so he was all embarrassed showing his butt to a line of holiday makers. Now he's helping me. I got on and slumped in my chair. No nerves, no fear of a panic attack or thoughts of crashing. Just relaxed; put my headphones on to listen to bands like Zero 7, Kinobe, London Grammar, Mike Oldfield etc ; all in my playlist for this epic flight to Barbados where we'd meet the ship.

Once arrived, we checked in and settled in our lovely room on the 12th deck with a balcony looking out to sea. I felt so excited, knowing 7 new and different islands were to be explored. There would be new people to meet, animals and nature to find. It wasn't as carefully planned as New York, but we had a few plans. I was told the best thing to do with the Islands was just get off and find a little Caribbean tour guide in a mini bus, pay him $10 each, then he'll take you to different places for the day, instead of paying the cruise $100 each and not being as exciting. This turned out to be true, these guys were great and very friendly.

Arriving at Grenada, our first port was something else; looking out to vast forests and huge mountains above. The thrill was immediate and immense. Our first guide was called Lollypop an ex cop in Grenada. This was a special country; our Kirk said it reminded him of the island in King Kong and when I looked up he was right. We visited a beautiful waterfall, sat on the rocks beneath, taking it all in. A guy every 5 minutes would leap from the top after some tourist would pay him 5 to 10 dollars for the privilege. Out of nowhere a guy came out of the trees on the path back and serenaded us with a song. He looked like an old Billy Ocean.

We had a drive through a rain forest; up and up. Then stopped to look down over the island below where we could see our ship docked. We would drink the juice from a straw straight from a coconut to cool us down. Never had I done this before and it was very refreshing to say the least, as my guide Lollipop told me it would be. I asked him if was there much crime on this island of Grenada and he said only domestic, hardly any other type. It made me feel better that I wouldn't have a load of bandits pull us over by the side of the road and rob my wallet, as I'd heard happens in Jamaica.

That first night on the ship, me and Kirk hit the casino. We won at first but eventually lost. Mel went back to the room as felt a bit seasick, while me and Kirk drank. Being on holiday I had a few shandies and the odd Baileys. I find Baileys doesn't affect me like drinking beer or a JD; they would wipe me out for the rest of the holiday. A few little ones in moderation on special occasions is my limit. I left young Kirmo around midnight as I get tired after so long, especially after all the travelling.

I left him with two young gay chaps from Newcastle. They were funny, loud and brash and didn't care what anyone thought around them. I find a lot of young gays are like now. Years ago they'd keep their sexuality pretty close to their chests, now it's like the closet has been burnt down. At 4am Kirmo rolled in, singing the fair Spanish ladies song from 'Jaws', all happy telling us what a great night he'd had. Within half an hour he was sleeping in our bed with the bin beside him throwing up till the early hours. I got kicked out into his smaller bed, listening to him complain, throw up and moan all night.

St Vincent was next on the menu, but not for Kirk as he was too hungover to get out of bed. He wanted to sleep it off so we let him be. No point in all of us losing a day. I haggled a good price out of a guide, Scooter. This is the island certain parts of Pirates of the Caribbean were filmed. Scooter knew every nook and cranny of the island.

After visiting a fort high up in the mountains we were to visit a place that I look back on as paradise. It is without doubt the most beautiful place I have ever stood foot on. It was the location for some scenes of the Pirates of the Caribbean movie and there was a hut with pictures of Depp, Orlando etc. with props and clothing from the movie. Mel spent much time looking at the Depp pictures, while I stood on the dock of a bay looking out to a few local fishermen in small wooden boats, but not many so you could still appreciate the sea beyond.

I walked along and found a desolate bay with not a soul on it except me. I sat alone on a wooden deck chair that looked out over the tranquil sea of St Vincent. This is the place you'd go in a meditation as your quiet place, a retreat of peace, tranquillity, calm, bliss and beauty. Under a palm tree, I thought about how beautiful the world can be. No thoughts of panic attacks, hospitals, manic episodes or stress. No one coming over to ask if I was on Grange Hill. No selfies, no tourists taking pics of everything in sight, No politicians on tv, nobody trying to sell me useless gifts, nobody at all.

These things were far from my mind as I watched the turquoise clear warm waters lap gently onto the golden sands. Never in my life had I felt so relaxed. I could have sat there forever, no medication can give you this feeling. No Dr can prescribe this view and feeling. After about 20 minutes of pure blissful solitude, I walked over to Mel and sat on another part of the bay, where a few friendly little dogs sat by us. It was like being marooned, sitting on a log looking out to sea watching the fisherman catch their supper. If I was a rich man, this is where I'd settle I told young Mel.

After an hour or so, our guide Scooter came over and we were back on the mini bus, leaving heaven's bay behind. Looking back on all the 7 places, that was the best. I have been to many places, beaches and bays etc. but that was the Dom Pérignon of the lot.

I was gutted Kirk missed it as I know he would have loved it too. His antics the night before put him out of action; he was like me at his age now, casinos, drinking till all hours on the lookout for women, without a thought for the next day. I risked 1 or 2 baileys that night to keep him happy, I knew beer is no good. That's my little tipple now on special occasions.

Martinique was next; a French Island. Our new guide was BA, as cool as they come, and our Kirk's favourite. He got on with him the most. When we'd stop he'd enjoy a cigarette with us. The day started great; new waterfalls were visited, then a rum distillery in the mountains. Then a moment of magic, he stopped the bus to let us off to watch at least 20 to 30 hummingbirds feeding from some hedgerow on a country lane. It was a sight to behold, black ones, red and orange all hovering in mid-air feeding off the flowers in the hedgerow. They were so elusively fast it was hard to get a photo. I wasted too much time trying to, instead of just admiring this once in a lifetime scene. That was one of my special wildlife moments.

Before long, we were on a banana plantation even higher in the hills. This was surprisingly very interesting. We picked fresh bananas and ate them. I have to say they were the best banana I have ever eaten. So full of taste. They hadn't lost any from being imported ; just ripe and pure. In the background behind the banana trees you could see the famous Martinique volcano, Mount Pelée. The story goes that it erupted in 1902 killing over 30,000 people. Only one man, who was in the island's prison, survived. He got out and swam to safety when things calmed and was pardoned. The only survivor of the 1902 eruption. His name was Ludger Sylbaris; he was Afro-Caribbean.

Taking in these amazing views all this way up and admiring my immediate surroundings, I noticed something that I knew was instantly special. Sitting on a signpost not far from a lovely stream flowing under a large wheel, I noticed a very colourful kingfisher sitting quietly. I walked as quietly as humanly possible to get a better look, Mel close behind. He stayed a few minutes, let me get a good 7 or 8 pics of him. Then, like lightning, swooped above the stream and was gone. This was the climax of wildlife for the day; nothing was gonna beat this. There are many species of kingfishers so I'm unsure of this type, only it was the most colourful bird I have ever seen. Just to have watched the greatest fish catcher in the bird kingdom was all I needed to know. Who cares what type he was!

After all the earlier joys it was soon to turn to disaster for me. We got to a lovely white sands beach and Kirk asked me to take a pic of him standing in the sea. As I edged close to the shore I got a few pics, put my phone in my pocket, then foolishly stepped forward to bathe my feet. Unknowingly it dipped about 3ft, instantly wiping my phone out. It was soaked, I was gutted. The next 24 hours was spent trying to save it, in the room, then the next day at our new destination.

In Dominica I was running round like a headless chicken in the rain forests searching for a man called Caesar from the Caribbean Car Phone Warehouse. I found a cab driver called Trooper to take me to this man in the pouring rain, to the top of the rainforest to his place. Nothing like the Car Phone Warehouse in the UK. This was one man in a shack in the middle of a fucking jungle with a screwdriver.

"I'll pay you whatever you want if you can fix this phone" I told Caesar after just paying $30 in a cab to Trooper to this isolated shack. The tour guys at the port told me he was the best man on the island. He had a quick look at it and said he'd need at least 3 hours. So I headed back to the ship to get Mel and Kirk who were waiting for me. The plan was to go whale watching today but because of the heavy rain we decided against it. Being in the middle of the sea in torrential rain in a small boat with no guarantee of seeing a whale didn't seem a fabulous day out. I was gutted as it's on my bucket list. So we paid another local tour guide to take us to another waterfall and mud baths in the hills that smelt like a river of shit. We had to wear green plastic raincoats as it still rained heavily and in a rainforest you feel every drop. We looked like we were in a Vietnam film, walking in green macs through a dense forest.

On the way back to our ship, I asked the driver how far to Caesar's Car Phone Warehouse. He said it was a 15 minute detour. I asked the rest of our coach party if they wouldn't mind me jumping off to retrieve my phone. They weren't ecstatic but agreed. My hopes were high that this man had fixed it. I was wrong; he said it's useless and to just give him $30 for his time. So no phone for the rest of my holiday. It wasn't the phone I missed, it was the camera I wanted. Plus I lost the pics of the hummingbirds, the beautiful kingfisher and the volcano behind us in the banana plantation. Such is life as my old mate Fozz used to say.

Later that night, Kirk nearly set the ship on fire. We were on our balcony enjoying a cigarette during a stormy night when a heavy gush of wind blew it out of his mouth. It spiralled down and down 12 decks below towards the sea then vanished. He thought it blew into the ship and quietly told me as his mum slept, but with panic in his eyes. He believed he knew where it went; in the gym, so set off to put it out. I waited anxiously praying no alarm would go off. He returned 10 minutes later saying it was nowhere. We agreed it must have gone into the sea. He was foolish and lucky.

When Mel awoke hearing the discussion on the balcony, we were both in for the wrath. I don't know who got it worse, Kirk for smoking on the balcony or me for letting him. Whoever it was. it was understood no more smoking on the balcony. That night I spent mainly on the lavatory, it was a case of the Attila the Huns or throwing up. I'd caught some horrific 24 hour bug.

Around 4am when it was still dark I decided to venture out onto the balcony to get some air. The sight that bestowed me was an awesome spectacle. At first I thought the sky was on fire as it was lit up with fire type colours, but as I got closer I saw it was millions of fireflies falling from the dark skies into the sea below. I'd never seen anything like it, I mean how often I would look out of my Huyton window to witness something like this going on. Kirk has never forgiven me for not waking him as I just stood and watched as they lit up the skies and faded below. Another for my list of amazing wildlife moments on this trip.

Guadalupe I missed totally as I was still wiped out with this awful bug. I slept it off with the curtains drawn and starved myself. We had booked the one tour with the cruise line beforehand to see 3 spectacular waterfalls; the biggest on the island and one of the biggest in the Caribbean itself. Mel said she hated it, the tour guide Aggie waffled on all the way there and back and the view was miles from the actual falls. It cost more than the local guys would have charged too. So yet again my name was dirt. "Why do I listen to you?" were the words I was to hear when she got back.

Another mishap on the boat the following morning happened whilst Mel was searching through a computer at the photo store on the boat surrounded by about 15 people plus staff. Me and Kirk stood aimlessly nearby until a loud explosion erupted. Everyone jumped out of their skin. I could see by Kirk's face he was responsible somehow. As he came to me I asked "what was that?"
He said "I think my lighter has exploded in my pocket".
Then Mel ran over. "What the hell has happened now?" I took Kirk to the toilet quick, where we discovered his plastic lighter had in fact exploded in his pocket and was in bits. He said he thought he'd been shot at first.

The rest of the day was spent in the beautiful island of St Lucia, the island with the 2 gigantic pitons towering over the island. Probably the most fun had for Kirk so far, as we got a boat over to the beach. Then the jet-ski incident mentioned earlier when everything was fine as I carefully rode the waves, then let Kirk take over and in seconds I'm floating in the middle of what I was later to find out shark infested waters. Bull shark warnings had been given a few months earlier and a great white spotted numerous times, all added to the shock afterwards. Those moments treading water until we tipped it back over, I will never forget. Time almost stood still. Most people may be fine but a man who has a feared obsession with sharks is not good. As in an earlier breakdown it surfaced! But I got through it. Luckily with Kirk's navy training he was calm and took control. He went back out on it and became very skilled on it, riding the waves and turning at speed like the Eddie Kidd of the seas. As he razzed round I was getting my feet massaged in mud by a young Caribbean woman, trying not to show too much joy as Mel was not far away. Life was good!

The next week was to be spent in Barbados. Luckily we paid extra for the spa on the ship as we had 6 hours of sitting round, so as Mel sat in the sun, me and Kirk took advantage of the chill out room in the spa. We had a double bed each overlooking the ocean. Chinese type music played as about 10 people laid out relaxing..... until we came in and made cups of tea, making noise and disturbing everyone. We eventually settled and after a week of havoc, slept till the coach was ready to take us to our hotel. The view from the hotel wasn't what we expected, instead of a sea view as promised, we got Huggys Drug Store. I tried to change it but I was fighting an uphill battle with the stubborn receptionist. "We're only gonna sleep here" we decided and wouldn't let this ruin our holiday.
The first day we visited Holetown which is the home of Rihanna. We found a beautiful beach side bar where we chatted to a Scottish couple

then watched Liverpool play West Ham inside. We watched the sun go down over the ocean and the Scots told us if you watch carefully you can catch a green flash for a split second as the sun goes down over the horizon. There was something happening, but I never saw the green. Still amazing as everyone cheered as it went down.

There wasn't as many calamities in Barbados as there had been on the ship, except after visiting a wildlife park. It was one where you walk around and the animals are all around you ;such as monkeys above you in the trees, deer walking about, hundreds of massive tortoises, Cayman crocodiles in river pits etc. This was a special place, especially at feeding time when it was a frenzy of all the animals gathering in the middle of this sheltered forest like in a Disney film almost.

On the way home we ended up in a kind of shanty town awaiting our bus. The buses were manic over there; crammed to the rafters, people would be sitting on each other's laps. I'd say sometimes 60 people would be crammed in on a 25 seater bus. The bus stop was quite busy. I just finished drinking a bottle of water and threw it into a nearby bin. Then I got the fright of my life as a huge chicken jumped out of the bin towards me. It was unexpected, it was scavenging for food in the bin, but I did not know as couldn't see it. Everybody at the bus stop, as well as Mel and Kirk, thought it was hilarious. I didn't however. It was quite ironic that when we got near home after the bus ride, we discovered a bar and grill called Chicken Georges! He was to become our local for the rest of the holiday. He was a great guy, Chicken George. A big Caribbean guy who had lived there all his life and worked hard to build a little shack near the beach, overlooking the sea. Every night we would enjoy a bite to eat and a little drink in Chicken Georges and share many tales with this man.

One night, me and Kirk met another Caribbean character with the name of Duck. He was a taxi driver and he ran the rank. He was one of the biggest guys I've ever seen, as big as Brummie. He was called Duck simply because if he came at you, you had to duck! He became our driver for the rest of the holiday. Anywhere we needed to go - call Duck. We wanted to be picked up from somewhere - call Duck, Got lost anywhere - call Duck! He was our main guide; he looked after us and we looked after him with tips. A few cab drivers had tried to rip us off before meeting him but Big Duck never did. I checked his prices with the hotel and they said he's cheaper than their drivers and they were cheap. I even sent some Champions League pens over to him once home which I'd been given by LFC. Another person I've met on the road and kept in touch with.

There were a lot of Canadians and Americans staying in our hotel. We found that the Canadians were very friendly and we chatted to them quite often. Mel keeps in touch with one old Canadian called Dave. Another Dave! He reminded me of Jimmy Cagney. Lovely guy, had a hard life but never moaned once. Lost all his family in a car accident at a young age to a drunk driver. How he was so happy go lucky, I couldn't understand, but as he explained, he would never have met his wife had it not happened. He came to England to retrieve his father's naval items and met his wife in London. Fate led to happiness.

We also visited the Harrisons caves; underground limestone caverns accessed by tram, with streams, pools, stalagmites and stalactites. It is 700 feet above sea level. I must admit before getting on the tram which took forever to go down, my heart began to pound slightly. I had no Valium's on me; they were in my hotel drawer, otherwise I would have taken one.
'You can do this' I told myself. I did do it and I'm glad I did as I've never seen huge lakes underground like this with waterfalls flowing into them, with awesome caverns. One of the seven wonders of the Caribbean.

The one thing I didn't enjoy was when they turned out the lights when we were deep inside the bottom of a cave (the furthest point down) just to prove how dark total darkness is. Those 10 seconds seemed like an eternity as I kept saying to myself "Stay calm George, everything's ok, it's only a cave nobody is going to harm you" etc. I wasn't beside Mel or Kirk for any of this as there was no room on the tram, so I sat beside the driver in a different section. Despite this I never hyperventilated or had a panic attack, which if I thought too deeply about my situation I could have easily. That was the one moment like the Empire State for me, except I couldn't run; I had to sit it out. As I've said, I control the illness now; sometimes you gotta reassure yourself when no one else can.

One day we made a trip to the boatyard beach. Paradise for young Kirmo as it had jet skis, huge slides and rope swings on the boardwalk you could swing into the sea from. After he'd done all this, Mel had her first go on a jet ski and loved it - especially posing for pictures on it! Afterwards, it was decided to go out on a boat and swim with the green turtles 🐢

I got on the boat with them and about 7 others, unsure whether I'd do it. When I saw how far out the skipper went I began to feel nervous about it. The usual thought of sharks was spinning around in my head. Then the tour guide began to give out the snorkels and masks. I declined and he asked why. I said "I'd rather just watch"
He replied "Sharks?" So I agreed. The whole boat is looking at me now, I feel stupid but the last person to make me want to jump in the middle of the ocean is some middle class tour guide. He insisted there was no sharks in Barbados, but I figured if there in St Lucia and Martinique surely they could swim a bit further to here, plus I'd read a great white was spotted in Cornwall, so why dodge Barbados? As I contemplated the situation, it was soon made up for me by some comedian in the water yelling "Shark, there's a huge shark out there" as he climbed up a boat after he'd been swimming with the turtles. That was that, I wasn't going anywhere now.

Mel and Kirk got in with the others and fully

enjoyed it, although Mel struggled to catch her breath towards the end. They saw one turtle but it wasn't that close; they kept their distance that day. I kept my distance catching rays laid out on the boat. I would have loved to have got in and swam in the open water seeing the beautiful turtles below, but my fear got the better of me again.

The last night was spent in Oistens Bay with friends we met from my old stomping ground Mitcham; a guy called Graham (one of the few black guys who hung around Mitcham in the 80's). He knew everyone I knew there. Oistens was a huge party type gathering of live music, dancers, craft stalls and wooden food outlets consisting of fish caught that day. I tried flying fish for the first time and it was delicious. Mel and Kirk had swordfish but weren't so keen. We danced and partied till me and Graham both agreed it was getting a bit like the Warriors. Many local unsavoury characters were on the edge of the dance floor watching everybody. Graham pointed out "These guys have got nothing, they think we have everything". So it was a good time to call Duck one last time.

The next day the holiday was over, but I look back on that holiday with very fond memories; of nature at its best, the animals, the birds, the people. That's one of the important things for me going to a foreign place; meeting people from there, hearing their stories, learning their culture and ways. This helps make a holiday very special for me, and all of us. I'm lucky to have Kirk & Mel on board with me on these trips.

Kirk has the same outlook on life as me. He laughs at the same silly things and sees the funny side to everything and everyone. He even knows how to calm me during a possible panic attack now he's witnessed the experience that much. Even down to our love of Basil Fawlty; together we say his quotes throughout life, like me and my Dad did and still do. Mel keeps us in line. If she wasn't around it would have been utter chaos in the Caribbean.

Chapter 28
Where Are They Now?

'Make new friends, but don't forget the old, One is silver, the other is gold'

The best way to find out what the ex-cast are doing are Grange Hill reunions, as the papers and stuff online are well out of date.

Besides constant meet ups with Drummond and Alford I hadn't seen anyone else from Grange Hill for a good six or seven years. The first reunion was around 1997 on This Morning. Slightly embarrassing as we all had to sit behind desks as Richard Madeley interviewed us one by one. This was the first time I got to see Ian who played Ted and he was madder than he was as a kid and Sean McGuire who played Tegs, who was to go on and conquer Hollywood. It was also the first time I'd ever met Terry Sue-Patt who opened the gates of Grange Hill, and was to sadly pass away in 2015. Lee Mac who played Zammo, Erk who played Ro-land, George who played Tucker's mate Alan who did Kung-Fu!, Michelle who played Trisha Yates and Michael Sheard who played the notorious Mr Bronson.

This was the first time for most of us to all meet in one place. Some meeting for the first time and for me meeting the older ones for the first time ever. Richard Madeley was cool, he must have watched the show in his younger years as I could hear the excitement in his voice as he got to each member. We dis the show early in the morning and by noon me, Terry, Ian, Lee, Erk and Sean and (no connection to Grange Hill) my mate Steve, were in the BBC bar and had a good drink afterwards. In those days you could smoke and drink in a bar without going outside to puff away. This was a nice get together.

Later that night I ended up going back with Sean and hitting the town where he lived then crashing at his in the early hours. He was in the middle of his pop career at the time so was getting attention wherever we went. He took it all in his stride, never let it go to his head. He was a good kid. He'd been the only one, when I was late once, to come over to walk with me as I had to do the walk of shame across the shooting location. I said to him after I'd just been yelled at "Don't worry Sean, I'll be ok" But he insisted on walking with me. He was only about 12, bless him.

Sadly, it was to be the first and last time I was to see Michael Sheard again, as he was to sadly pass away on his beloved Isle of Wight in 2005. When I think, he was in some of my favourite movies and shows such as 'The Empire Strikes Back' and 'Indiana Jones' plus 'Auf Wiedersehen Pet' (which I loved as a teen -especially the character Oz). Michael was in all these and now and then, the more geeky of the cast would quiz him on his Star Wars saga part where Darth Vader strangles him. He loved talking of these things. I wish I would have talked to him more, but since my telling off, I kept my distance. I'm just glad I got to thank him a few years before his death and make amends. He appreciated it I got told years later.

The next was a documentary called 'From Grange Hill to Albert Square and Beyond'. This was all about what some of the cast were up too after they left. The best thing about this reunion was that it was the first time I got to meet Todd Carty as he was doing EastEnders at the time. So, when me and Drummond went in the traditional BBC bar for a light ale, Todd was there. We played a game of snooker and got on like a house on fire. We had many similarities especially regarding our characters. Tucker and Ziggy were very alike. Many times people have thought I was Tucker, maybe he's had Ziggy too? He was the first heartthrob, every teenage girl in the country idolised him and the boys liked him as he was a rebel. So he couldn't go wrong. My character was similar as he messed about like him. So Todd was everything I wanted him to be when we met. Before I started the show, aged 8 or 9, I looked up to him. I thought he was the coolest guy on TV. So if he hadn't lived up to my expectations he would have ruined my childhood memory. Thankfully he didn't and he was as cool as I hoped. We also met up with Patsy Palmer who was in Grange Hill with us. She was doing EastEnders at the time and it was great to catch up with her. Plus she introduced us to Martine McCutcheon who was a great laugh, and both looked stunning I must say.

There was a big reunion in a bar that was arranged without a circus; just cast. It was in the Warwick Bar in London. Here I was to meet my old mate Ricky who played Ant for the first time since leaving the show. He formed a band called 'The Space Brothers' who had a massive following in Ricky's head! Plus Simon Vaughn (Freddie) who went on to produce War and Peace, and the award winning movie Goodbye Christopher Robin etc. He was glad to say goodbye to me in 87! Jonathan Lambeth (Danny) had founded a Public Relations company called Fides Media. Also present was Simone Hyams who was Calley. She worked as a corporate events manager for Richard Branson's Virgin Group for a while. Lisa York (Julie), Fleur (Imelda) and Ruth (Helen) I had lost contact with, but we've kept in touch since. Ruthy lives in New Zealand now and she still can't escape me. Fleur runs her estate agents and Suzy radio where her very talented son Josh is no1 DJ. John 'Oakla' Holmes (Gonch) was involved; ironically Holmes is currently the manager of a casino. Lee (Zammo) runs his own key cutting shop and recently starred in Eastenders which was great to see him getting back in again. Also there was Sara (Julia) and the 2 Alison's (Fay and Louise). So was, Erkan (Ro-land) who has recently found work for entertainment site ME1TV, conducting interviews for their YouTube channel.

It was a fab night and we were even joined by a Kaiser Chief; the drummer Nick who happened to be a big fan of the show. He stood outside with me and Lee and Johnny Alford who I dragged along to enjoy a cigarette. I remember the Kaiser saying "None of you have changed, you all look the same man" Funnily enough, he's not the only one to say this, as over the years I'd hear this comment about myself and most of the others. But he was the first to say it. I asked the DJ to play 'I Predict A Riot' and in the Warwick that night we all hit the dance floor and sang along with the drummer. Finally a drummer I got on with!

I remember this particular night everybody drifted one by one until it was just me and Alford. We ended up in a pub on the Caledonian Road, on our own drinking cold bottles of Sol till the sun came up. As usual we out drank them all, but like we did back then, we paced ourselves. I can never see the point in going in a bar and downing dozens of shots then collapsing in the toilet a few hours and vodkas later. I'd sooner sip a few cold beers and last the night. As would John.

The next reunion was more high profile ;in the form of Justin lee Collins 'Bring back Grange Hill' program. This was a surprise ambush for me at Euston station by Collins running up with a microphone asking me if I would be part of a reunion to bring back 'Just say no'. Now I knew something wasn't right as Fleur had text me and said he burst into her estate agents but she didn't want to be part of it. I figured they'd been speaking to me on the phone and arranged a meeting at the BBC, so I never expected a Cook Report type ambush from Collins and co. But he did - in the middle of Euston and I looked a tramp in a woolly hat and cardigan. I looked like Steptoe. It was all good fun and me and Collins sat outside and got on well. Football was the main topic as he supported Bristol City, and loved his football, so naturally we got on.

The reunion was a few days later in a club in London, in the winter of 2005. The usual array of characters were there Erk, Lee, Tim Polley (Banksie) who was nice to see because he lived in Tenerife and flew over especially He runs a disability scooter and wheelchair hire company over there. Also Joann Kenny who played Jane Bishop looked amazing that night, but sadly that was the last time I'd see her; she died in 2010, way too young. It was also the first time I met Mark Savage who played the notorious 'Gripper'. You know how someone's a good actor when the audience hate them. And everyone despised his racist character Gripper, showing the country what goes on in the playground, that we like to think doesn't go on. He is currently touring a play called 'Human Issue' which is him in a one man show dealing with mental health and suicide. From what I hear, Mark is outstanding in this highly important production. I hope it gets bigger, the more publicity it gets and he gets his message across.

Ricky was there and Ruth, Lisa York - who was the first I fancied when joined the show- and Alison, who played the popular Fay, now worked for Sylvia Young's - my old school! Also Melissa who played Jackie was reeled in too. We had to mime on stage to the song in front of hundreds of club goers in the middle of their night out. It would possibly be the last thing I would want whilst dancing to Bobby Brown one minute then the cast of Grange Hill come on and sing 'Just Say No' the next.

We did it and couldn't wait to get the bar

afterwards and forget about it. I remember they put me up in an amazing hotel that night. I went back and sat at the bar on my own and had a few JD and cokes alone. I looked up at one point and could have sworn Liam Neeson was on his way to bed but stopped and stared at me for a few seconds. I caught his eye trying to think where do I know him, but it looked like he was doing the same. Then after he went, I realised it was Liam Neeson. Wow I thought, I've just been recognised by Oscar Schindler! Nice end to the night.

One person I never saw at any of these reunions was Mark Farmer who played Gary Hargreaves during the Tucker era. He was also in a wonderful TV drama series called 'Johnny Jarvis' in 1983. I watched this 6 part series with my Dad which we both enjoyed it. One night in 1989, me and Jay were in a pub called Peter Kavanagh's pub in Toxteth which was owned by actor Jake Abraham at the time. I met Mark that night as he was doing a play with Jake. He was a really nice guy and we connected because of the Grange Hill thing. Jake locked the doors at midnight and we stayed in there till dawn, chatting, laughing and listening to De La Soul on the jukebox who had just burst onto the scene with their new album '3 Feet High and Rising'. Mark sadly died in 2016 after a short battle with cancer; another Grange Hill legend departs.

After the Justin Lee Collins circus, I decided I would step back from the Grange Hill reunions now. Alford never did that show as he didn't want to and said to me "You're holding yourself back

Scouse, keep doing these silly Grange Hill shows. Lay low for a while or you're gonna be remembered forever as a school kid". It made sense, so anything that came up Grange Hill related I refused. For a few glimpsing moments of Grange Hill glory on the TV again I thought what's the point? I'd done about 3 and that was enough I decided. Drummond stopped before me; he ended with the 'From Grange Hill to Albert Square' show.

A few people who never got involved since leaving the show were Steve West who played Vince Savage. I have never seen or heard of him since the day I left, though I did hear through the grapevine he went into nursing. So now he's known as Sister Savage. I feel a bit sorry for him looking back; me and a few others used to wind him up. Out of so many kids, one had to get it, and he was the one.

Josh who played the daft bully Mauler, I have never seen again or spotted on TV since. I thought his character was hilarious, the funniest bully the show ever had, along with Trevor.

Tina Mahon who played Ronnie kept herself quiet too. Also Sam Lewis who played the lovely Georgina, I keep in touch with via the stalkers paradise that is Facebook. Johnathan Lambeth who played the young rebel Danny Kendall has kept himself to himself too although he was at the Warwick pub reunion and it was great to see him. He runs his own business now. I have never seen Michael Cronin who played Mr Baxter. He was a popular character with an old school way about him. He was in Fawlty Towers as a builder and I recently saw him in the Benito Del Toro version of

'Wolfman'.

Some people may think the people they don't see again on screen have failed in some way because they haven't continued, but I believe there are two possibilities to consider. One is they had enough of child stardom and didn't like what it brought, so found another career. Or two, they may have tried but struggled, as it is hard to follow up. It took me 7 years till Brookside and I could have easily given up in between. Susan Tully has done exceptionally well, as she got into EastEnders right after and has directed such shows as Tin Star, Silent Witness and Line of Duty to name a few. Also lets not forget Michelle Gayle who also followed Susan's Tully's footsteps into EastEnders and then had 7 top 20 hits in the 90's as a successful R and B singer. John Alford also had 3 top 10 singles in the charts, as well as going into London's Burning and the movie The Hatton Garden Heist. He could have been one of the most successful had the News of the World not intervened in his life. Amma Asante who was a year above me directs 'The Handmaid's Tale'. People sometimes say to me, has anyone done anything after leaving the show? Daft question really!

One of the saddest stories of an ex-Grange Hill star is that of Laura Sadler. She played Judi Jeffries, and nurse Sandy Harper in Holby City for three years from 2000 until her death in 2003 where she sadly fell from a balcony to her death. I never met Laura as she was after my time in the show, but everyone I've met who knew her, has said she was a beautiful girl with a beautiful heart. Another sad loss. She was 23.

Another great who is no longer with us is George A Cooper (Mr Griffiths) or Cooperman as I called him. The man that turned down 'Zulu' to be with his pregnant wife. He also appeared in 'Z Cars' and 'Coronation Street' not to mention the classic 'Steptoe and Son' George passed away in the November of 2018 aged 93. One of the nicest guys I ever worked with.

It was quiet for a few years regarding reunions of such. I continued working in my various jobs but also doing short films such as 'My Family' for an Irish director called Tom Begley, where I co-starred alongside Terri Dwyer, from Hollyoaks (and, funny enough, Grange Hill in its last years as a teacher). She was cool. I was also in a local short film 'Our Eddie' by Johnny Hirst about the decline in certain areas. I'd like to add that working with Stan Boardman was special. He had a presence I hadn't been around in a while.

I also ventured to Plymouth to do a short film called 'Sphere of Fear 2' about a possessed football who kills priests, starring local legends Chris Ball Hero and Kung Fu Tony. I got £500 for this Ed Wood type classic. I became like a mercenary actor, come in, film it, get out and get paid. Suited me!

The next get together of Hiller's was to be in 2013, in a bar on Brick lane in the East end of London. This had a slightly different slant. It was arranged by the late Terry Sue-Patt and would feature Grange Hill art by local artist Kranksy (no relation to Banksy). A few hours before I turned up I do what I normally do, whistle beneath Johnny Alford's flat on the Caledonian Road, or the Cally as he always called it. It's the same whistle we'd used since teenagers, same as the Wanderers used in the film 'The Wanderers'.

Before long we enter Monty's Bar on Brick lane and are greeted by the gang. There was a great painting of me this Kranksy fellow had done; it was my face during the show with the David Bowie lightening stripe going down it. I should have bought it, but just didn't want to be carting it round London all weekend. I regret it now as it was me in my golden years!

We mingled with the fans in there, including a famous East end crime authoress called Kimberley Chambers. We got on very well and have kept in touch ever since. She has written 14 crime novels up to now. We share the same sometimes wicked sense of humour.

The night went fast. So many people to chat to and sadly this was to be the last time I would ever see Terry Sue-Patt who played Benny. He was to die two years later in 2015 in his home. I never knew him as well as the older generation as I never worked with him, I know Erkan (Roland) grew close to him and it hit him hard, but we'd met at many reunions. He was full of life every time I met him and always had a tale to tell. I never saw him quiet, which is why he left a huge void in the life of anyone who knew him. Benny was one of the pioneers of the show along with Tucker and Alan. They opened the gates to the whole Grange Hill saga. Terry was a great artist too, which many didn't know about. With Kranksy he'd done many a painting. He also starred in the movie that put Gary Oldman on the map, called 'The Firm' about British soccer hooligans. In my view, the best and only soccer hooligan film. Terry was in this and played an important part. He stood out and held his own alongside Gary Oldman. We all miss Terry; I guess he's gone to open the Grange Hill school gates in the sky now.

It would be August 2017 the next gathering, the occasion this time was that Ruth Caraway was home from New Zealand. I had to make the effort as Ruth was one of my closest friends, not just from the show, but in life too. It was to be held in John 'Oakla' Holmes parent's luxury apartment in the Barbican area of London. This time Mel was to come along as she had never came to a reunion and I'd never have heard the end of it - so this was to be the one. I pulled a few strings with a train guard I knew and me and Mel travelled in 1st class all the way.

Once arrived, we headed for the Barbican and found a Latin American bar. We thought a little drink first would be a good idea before rushing into Oklahoma's apartment. After walking round in circles trying to find this place, we found it. I was a bit gutted Drummond wasn't coming as he said he was busy. Once in there, it was still great to see Ruth, Fleur who I hadn't seen either since the

Warwick pub, Lisa York and Alison, and Oakla. The biggest joke of the night was Ruth and Fleur winding me up saying I was punching above my weight with Mel. They still keep it up 2 years on. It's times like this I wished I could drink. Everyone was getting merrier and merrier whilst I had to take my time on my shandies. Yes it pissed me off, but I knew it was for the best. Better a sane Wilson than an insane one. Then, when I was feeling a little bit out of it all, as drunkenness had set in around me, the door knocked. Nobody had a clue who it could be, least of all Oakla as he expected no guests. There, to surprise us all, was Drummond; he came after all! I was so relieved. He got the biggest welcome of his life he said. Everyone was hugging and kissing him. From that moment on, I could relax properly as he wasn't drinking either so we were on the same level and laughed all night finding strange books on Oakla's parents book shelves. We find humour in the strangest of places. It was a great night. Mel got on great with the girls and they all keep in touch. They are my favourite reunions away from everyone, in a cosy home, where you can be yourself.

There was a massive reunion in 2018 for the Good Grief Trust. It was to be a reunion of many Grange Hill cast and producers from the beginning to end. All eras. Plus a handful of fans including Streaky from my old stomping ground Guernsey. The band Tight Fit sang for us all. All the money went to the Good Grief Trust, which is for people coming to terms with grief.

The day started in disaster though after I booked a hotel in White City, Oregon by mistake. This blunder was to cost me not just earache the rest of the journey but also much more money to put right, as Mel booked an executive suite in a lush hotel in Regent's Park on my card. I wasn't to arrange a hotel again I was told.

So, after all the running round and checking in, getting ready etc. we arrived at the Bluebird Cafe at the old BBC headquarters at white city. I was overwhelmed at first seeing all the old faces. I was gutted Rachel Roberts (Justine) and Fiona Mowlem (Laura) who I nicknamed Fifi the night nurse, back in 85, couldn't make it. I hadn't seen them since I'd left, although we've kept in touch on Facebook.

There were plenty of others too. Simon Vaughn made me laugh when he came over to tell Mel I was the naughtiest person he'd ever met in his life. Sadly, he and Ricky left early with Sara so I never had a proper chance to catch up. Me and Simon put old Ron Smedley our Producer, in an Uber - 93 he was. I asked him for his email and Simon joked he'd been avoiding me for over 30 years, why would he want to give me that now! It was great seeing Ron as I mentioned earlier, still going at 93 with all his faculties. One of the last of an ancient BBC breed.

Seeing Phil Redmond and his wife Alexis was special too. I used to be nervous around him when I was younger, knowing how powerful he was just scared me a bit, but not this time. Mel told them of the hotel fiasco which they found hilarious. I also told Phil how I don't drink anymore and live a clean life now. He always has, hence a lot of his writing is to warn people of the perils of drink or drugs. It was nice to tell him I've seen the light too.

Todd Carty was a joy to see again too, it has been many years since the last. We had a good chat and laugh and compared our screen characters again. Mark who played Gripper, told me recently Ziggy would of been in it from the start, had the show been set in Liverpool, but it had to be London so Tucker came first. It made sense when I thought about it.

Mel had a lovely night too; she gets on with Fleur, Lisa, and Alison so I knew she'd have a good night. Tight Fit singing 'We Are Family' at the end as everyone danced, including the fans, ended a top night organised by Linda and hosted by the amusing Mark who played Duane. It was nice later on, back at the Regent's Park hotel; a lovely view and room, but horrific price!

The last reunion of any sort was this year 2019 in the June, and it was to be on the BBC's Pointless TV show with my partner being Gwyneth Powell; the lady who held all the strings as Mrs McClusky, the head mistress. I hadn't seen Gwyneth since the day I left, so it was fantastic to catch up with her again after all these years. The show hasn't been aired yet so I have to be careful what I divulge. It all happened so quickly, as my agent Alan rang me literally 3 days before and asked if I wanted to do the show.

I had to think quickly on my feet as that particular

week I hadn't been great with my illness. Only a few days before I had run out of a cafe to breathe and calm myself down as felt a panic attack looming. I was stressed and certainly not 100% by any means. Sleeping had been a nightmare for over a month so I was taking Zopiclone every night to knock me out. Valium's were being prescribed and dropped left, right and centre to relax my moods. This was all due to something I can't talk about here; maybe one day. So when he asked me, part of me wanted to say no, I'm not up to it, but I thought no, this is a chance to overcome my recent slip from the dark world I'd found myself struggling in again. Plus I thought, it's prime time BBC. It will be good for my exposure. Show the world 'I'm still here you bastards' if I can only keep my cool.

To prepare for a show like this is impossible as you can get any topic in the world and have to find a pointless answer. I tried to go over geography as that's my weakest subject, but even that's so vast. I didn't let the thought of it stress me. It was a positive thing and all my family agreed. My pals found it hilarious, Ad van fitter Davey Cumbo commented "Possibly the most pointless man going on Pointless" but these comments never made me nervous, easier if anything as I thought "I'm gonna prove you all wrong!"

Sitting in 1st class, I listened to calming music. Once at Euston I was picked up in a huge Mercedes by a driver named Chip and driven to Elstree studios. I decided to wear a blue with white stripes down the side Cuba Vera shirt; these were the shirts worn by Italians in the 60's and 70's in New York. You see them in Goodfellas, Mean Streets and A Bronx Tale etc. I knew this looked good, so I'd feel confident. I sat outside alone smoking my e-cig, waiting for Gwyneth to arrive. I knew once I met up with her I could chat and relax more. My main worry was having a panic attack during the middle of the show. I had to keep blocking this thought out of my mind. I had a discussion with my mother and Dot's daughter Sue earlier. They both said don't take a Valium, it will cloud your judgement or make me look tired. I said I wouldn't, but, sitting outside on my own with my heart beginning to pound, I thought 'Fuck this. I need a Valium. I know I can still function on one, many times when I've been a nervous wreck in situations I've taken one and it's straightened me out, never zonked me'. I carry one Valium in my wallet at all times, just incase. I have rarely reached for it while out and about, but I feel it's better to have one and not need it than need one and not have one...

Soon Gwyneth arrived, it was great to see her and looking so well. We instantly went down memory lane; the laughs, and the people we had and had not seen. George A Cooper's funeral which she attended. How we both loved him. She worked with him more than anyone, so knew him better than anyone. He was the best caretaker the show ever had we agreed. I told her of how my Nan loved her in the likes of Z Cars, The Guardians and Father Brown - all pre Grange Hill shows. 11 years she played the tough but fair headmistress, during mainly, the Thatcher years, although I'm not comparing her in any way!

It didn't seem long until we were on, quick chat then straight into the studio. All I could think about was myself standing behind that podium and how I'm gonna get through this.

Like I say I can't go into what happened in case this story comes out and the show hasn't aired. All I can say is I got through it. A survival instinct took over and I forgot all my troubles from a few days earlier. It was time to man up and I did say to myself cometh the hour cometh the man. None of the production team would have guessed I was feeling anxious or nervous that day, like I have all my life, I hid it well. There was a lot of help from Gwyneth on the actual show I must say! After this gig, we email each other regularly. It's nice to have a new friendship from Grange Hill, and one I would never have imagined I'd rekindle.

Chapter 29
Bipolar Summary

"If you cry because the sun has gone out of your life, your tears will prevent you from seeing the stars." Rabindranath Tagore

It's a complicated illness to sum up as there are so many levels of it, so many unexplained things happened to me that I can't explain or understand myself, but do I want to know everything? The main question I ask myself is 'why?' That's the big one; why did I have suffer it all these years? They say it can be genetic, but nobody we know of in my family has had it, Born with it is a possibility, but it didn't choose to surface till I was 21. Before then I was always happy; as a child I was happy and always laughing. I can't remember feeling low or depressed as a kid ever. Many happy family memories of holidays and days out.

There were a few small signs near the end of Grange Hill, when pressure was getting to me a bit. I couldn't go anywhere without recognition for one. Tears on the isle of Wight I mentioned earlier, but not for one second do I blame Grange Hill. For the most part, I relished that way of life. So there was no signs of any mental health problems from birth through to my teens.

It was only when a chain of things started to go wrong, a downward spiral was triggered. Being arrested and the publicity with it in 89, closely followed by watching the Hillsborough disaster unfold. My beautiful Nan passing away in 1990, and me running out of money and realising following on from Grange Hill wasn't to be as easy as I thought. This all led to me going into myself, cutting myself off from society, my family and friends becoming isolated in my loft. Before I knew it, I was in another world. A world I couldn't understand; one that frightened me to the core. This led to manic behaviour, putting me in hospital for my own good and my own safety. In hospital I was not myself, I was aggressive, nasty and horrible to more or less everyone who I didn't like the look of, or looked a threat. Turning on my father I'll never understand, as he'd been nothing but good to me. We both know now I was sick and didn't know what I was doing. When I'm ill I'm not me, I turn into something I don't like or understand. That's the basic summary of the first episode.

During the 8 year gap, I was fine. I think Steve coming into my life was a big help as he got me running round making money; whether they worked or failed it was an adventure. He kept me busy. I drank and had marijuana occasionally and partied till late many times which seemingly had no effect then. Not knowing at the time though, these things were to have repercussions down the line. The main thing is that I kept myself busy. I rarely sat around and can't remember moping about dwelling on my hospital experience. It happened and I moved on; the fear of it happening again soon diminished.

Living in Spain got my confidence back fully. Working abroad in the sun seemed easier for me than in my hometown of Liverpool. At the end of the rave scene, Brookside came and that gave me deep satisfaction. It not only proved to myself I could still do it, but I felt I proved it to many others who may have written me off too.

The move to Wales seemed right at the time. I followed Steve as usual; at the time I'd have followed him to the gates of Hell if he said we could make money beyond them. The truth is it wore me down and it broke me. Without realising, the stress of writing and producing the Titanic play took it out of me, and him. He was drinking heavily towards the end. One of us was gonna break and it just happened to be me. That dreaded night on the mountain will always haunt me. Whereas the first breakdown took months to manifest to a climax, this one just erupted like Krakatoa, with a blood red sky above. It caused only pain and destruction for all I loved, in its wake. Me and Mel barely talk of it; it upsets her to look back on it. My pal Hagan said to her afterwards "Put it in a box and forget about it. It's gone." So she has. I personally don't like talking about it. It disturbs me too, what happened or what could of happened.

By the 5th and last hospital visit, it became easier for me. Yes, I still went through hell, but I could control it in the beginning, when I was aware what was happening. Once the fine line snaps, then I'm in the hands of the gods. The thing that frightens me most about this illness is not what I've done, it's what I could have done.

After being hospitalised 5 times, I believe I

understand so much more than ever now. Not through reading books on it or googling info but by simply going through it. Dealing with my own experiences, coping under strange circumstances thrown at me, overcoming the experiences. Fighting daily to get my mind (and sometimes body) back, going down to 7 stone back to 13 stone, dealing with comments and shouts in public when I've looked awful. Coming off different medications, watching other patients fail over and over, talking to patients of their experiences and picking doctors' brains over my issues. Most importantly, finding the strength to get well again and function as a normal human being; able to talk rationally, laugh, go out with my family without feeling vulnerable, work, earn money, and feel good again.

It is a cruel, sad and despairing illness. One that when it strikes me properly, causes indescribable pain for me and everyone involved. Nobody wins when it comes, only heartbreak and sorrow. There's an old saying 'I wouldn't wish it on my worst enemy.' Well that's true to a degree, but there's a few bastards out there I'd rather had it than me. I have it and there's nothing I can do about it. All I can do is take precautions so that I don't relapse again. I don't drink alcohol. I stopped smoking. I don't use drugs. All the bills are in Mel's name. I work part time now, never five days a week constant. If I lose a night's sleep I'm in the doctors ASAP to get Zopiclone tablets to make me sleep the next night. I set an alarm for my lithium every night as I know coming off them will cause another relapse as it did once.

In 2017 i saw a play in a tent in Woolton village, it was all about when John Lennon got out of his head and imagines all the people he'd loved and lost come and visit him. It was a fantastic performance by the guy who played John. But I foolishly put my phone on silent, not realising an alarm overrides this. It was a crucial scene at the end when all of a sudden a load of duck noises came quacking all around the tent. The audience were looking under their seats thinking ducks had wondered in. You see I set an alarm for 10.00 every night to remind me to take my meds. It took an eternity to turn off as Mel and my Dad saying "Turn the fuckin ducks off George" God knows how Lennon carried on but give him his due he did. So be careful when out and about if you set a reminder for meds!

 I avoid stressful places like packed bars. I limit my gambling to £10 on a Saturday. I enjoy simple things like watching the birds in the garden, walking the dog, swimming and spending time with my lovely nieces Lana, Charlotte and Bella, plus my nephew Mad Dog Junior. All these things reduce the stresses that in the past have built up and helped cause a breakdown or relapse etc. Meeting Jay and John for a coffee, or my old milkman pal Pat in Huyton village to hear his Navy tales. Simple things!

> - **'Out of your vulnerabilities will come your strength'**

Panic attacks are different, they come and go at any time and usually for a short period. I eventually shake them off but they are always very scary at the time. I go into another world. The fear is I'm going to go manic again so it's a terrifying experience; the thought it could get worse.

They happened a few years ago. One summer I was having them whilst working in hospitality at Liverpool FC, i ran out the building about to erupt and nobody helped me except for a colleague called John the Baptist who followed me, he was totally untrained in this field, so I just told the Baptist to talk to me, distract me. And he did. He just talked about his day as I breathed slowly in the fresh air until I felt well enough to continue. No management checked after to see I was ok, no aftercare. John the Baptist saved me that day. Luckily a supervisor called Tommo heard my plight and moved me over to his side to keep an eye on me. On days I felt I couldn't go in, he talked me into going and to carry on. Luckily my line manager Gary was understanding too. He'd let me go early if I felt panicky as well as allowing me to combine my acting stuff. He was repaid by front row seats for him and his Grandkids to watch me running across a stage as a deranged turkey in Jack and the Beanstalk in 2017.

I almost had another one when a crowd of extras from a film about Anne Williams all rushed in to queue up for payment after filming. There were too many. I felt claustrophobic and panicked. Luckily, Marty Mcfly the smallest guy at LFC, took me outside and calmed me. He was involved in the boxing game and I believe this helped. He had an authoritative voice but whatever he said prevented me from totally embarrassing myself, as that's how I feel when it happens; embarrassed. The bible says it 'Pride before destruction' Marty was a natural panic attack whisperer, and I've not met many. He know works for MTK Global in Scotland, chased his dream in the boxing game.

Only a few people I know can sort me out. Back in 91 on home leave from hospital I panicked in the Barry's pub, was about to run outside frightened. only one man in our gang could deal with it back then, he took me to a quiet corner and calmed me in minutes, Big Dave Galloway, he was in the army. Tough as they come. He'd seen friends die during the Gulf war so calming me down was nothing to him. He too had that authority in his voice that made me listen and realise it's all in my mind, I'm ok, without frightening me. After our chat i was fine for the rest of the night. Like I say certain people.

I applied to join the hospitality department at Everton this year. I got in and start soon. I was pleasantly surprised at the induction recently, when one of the managers after explaining job roles told all of us if we feel the need to talk to anyone due to stress or anxiety etc. that there is a club psychologist at hand every day. If we feel the need to talk. I have never experienced anyone say this in a work place. I felt like saying "Book him for me every day please" but I kept quiet. No need to reveal my cards unless I have too. Whether I use this service or not, it is a massive comfort to know it's there, and for everyone. So the times they are a changing! And for the good.

So at work, on the London Underground, waiting for buses in a busy area, in the Sea Life Centre going through the shark tunnel, walking through Church Street in town. The way I got over these panics was to work out where they were happening and then simply go into the lion's den. I re-visited all the places they happened and confronted them, saying to myself confidently "Come on then, I'm here. Do your worst!" I found they stopped. It's called facing your fear I guess. Fight or flight, and it worked for me.

Earlier this this year, in 2019, they came again. Different things were happening, stressful things, and before I knew it, panic attacks set in. I was in a cafe in Huyton village with my pal Ballowski and wanted to run outside. I contained myself as Ballowski distracted me with a sordid tale of how he wrapped toilet paper round his head once and walked into a bar like the Elephant Man, ordering a drink in his voice. This made me laugh and it took me away from my situation. On the way home, walking, I felt it happening again so I picked a colour like green and found all things green, green car, green doorway, green leaves etc. then red, blue etc. This kind of thing distracts me immediately. Your taking your mind away from what's happening, simple as that.

A couple more happened in the house. One was so severe Mel text my Mum and Dad to come immediately as she thought I was having a manic episode. Luckily i didn't but it was close. I took a Valium asap then calmed myself down by putting a YouTube video on the TV of the sea coming in gently on a beach. I lay back and breathed in and out gently till I got control again. This was after 36 hours of no sleep as I'd tried the night before without a sleeping tablet. I was on sleeping pills for all of May and June this year. So again, although a panic attack is a scary and unpredictable thing, I can control it to a degree and stop it getting out of hand. However the initial beginning of one terrifies me immensely.

Although I've had 5 spells in hospital, it doesn't end there. Every now and then I get close to a relapse, but I nip it in the bud. The past serves as an antidote. Its taught me what to do. 6 years out of hospital is, for me, a great achievement. I believe if I was going out drinking, working 9-5 every day, taking drugs, and having no exercise, then, without doubt, I would have been visiting those psychiatric places a lot more.

It was a taboo years ago and despite more people talking about it and more awareness I still feel uneasy talking to anyone about it unless they have it. It is nice when you do meet a fellow bipolar though. Every now and then I do and it's a breath of fresh air. It was great recently meeting the publisher of this book, Jason, as he is in the same boat. Just a few hours together made me feel good. He's a book writing pioneer in this subject. I also played a charity football game in Airdrie this year organised by Rossy the Bruce. Whilst there he had a guy called Graeme drive me about, turned out he had Bipolar, once we realised we both had it we spoke at length during the weekend duration. He was a breath of fresh air.

Only a few close pals understand; i can count them on one hand, the ones who visited me or who, like Steve, have seen me at my worse. We never discuss it. Unless I might bring it up there's no need. He spends most of his time running his own business near Darlington now, with his two 12 year old twins Alfie & Danny close by. So I don't see him as much, but not a week goes by when we don't speak.

I figure I've got one crack of the whip. I've seen many go young and I've seen many who let their mental illness get the better of them by either making the same mistakes over and over or giving up to easily, instead of saying to themselves 'I can beat this', 'Why should I live in a world of hell?'

Talk openly of what you're going through to family or friends. Don't be afraid, thinking they don't care or don't want to hear about your problems, because they do. One of my biggest mistakes was keeping everything inside for so many years, before and after my first breakdown. If you find it hard to talk to someone you know, then seek counselling or a psychologist. Sometimes a complete stranger can be a trusted way of letting go. I have seen many and all have helped me release information I would not want to upset my family with.

I love swimming it releases endorphins and I feel

completely relaxed afterwards. A steam and Jacuzzi after tops it off too. It's a natural high you can't buy. Lying in bed till late is no good for anyone too. I dont go jogging, it bores me , the last time I went jogging was through a riot. Set the alarm and see the morning sun. It's hard at first, but you soon get into the routine and helps sleep come easier at night. Sitting in all day will come to no good in the end, anyone would go insane. Throw David Attenborough on, any of his docs are relaxing, just his voice calms me. Simon Reeve will be step in his shoes one day. Any documentary about nature has a soothing effect I find. A good way to unwind at night are the relaxation videos on YouTube, especially the Blade Runner Ambiance one, it is so relaxing I drift before the end.

Also seek a free bus pass. If you're bipolar you're entitled to one. You can go on any bus in the UK free, plus local trains. This has saved me a fortune.

If you do find yourself in a psychiatric ward as it's got too much, it's nothing to be ashamed of. Many great minded people have been there before you, from movie stars to psychiatrists themselves. The shame lies on the other side..

It is scary at first, the fear of the unknown. Seeing other patients acting strange or in manic ways would frighten anyone. When I stop being manic in there I get frightened of others being manic. Simplest thing in the world is when someone acts up in this way, walk out the room to a quiet place.

Don't watch and stress yourself. You've got to know when to chill, play, talk, bath, shower, jerk off, to run, walk away, fight (very rare) keep quiet, sleep etc. I learnt all these things gradually over the years.

The main thing is to keep busy in these places. Any excuse to not stay cooked up in there thinking, alone all day. Walk around the grounds if they have them. If there's a garden, bask in that sun, smell the flowers, breathe in the air, listen to the birds, and escape the hospital environment.

One of my mistakes in there was kidding the doctors that I was well, I fooled them a few times so I'd be released earlier. It was a big mistake as I'd be back in sooner or later. Be honest, if you don't feel 100% tell them. You're only fooling yourself in the end. Nobody knows what you're thinking. Nobody can read your mind, no matter who in history claims they can. Don't make my mistake and hoodwink the Doc as it causes more sorrow later down the line. A relapse is almost guaranteed.

Finally, make friends in there. Company kept me going. They are the same as you and you'll find one or two that are on your wavelength, whether your age or much older as I found a few times. Once you find a companion, you can not only talk, but play games such as cards, chess, draughts etc., whatever your interest. Sitting alone in these places gives you too much time to think and for me it's a no-no. I needed my Julianne's, Alf's, the two bizarre gardeners, the caring nurse Mandy.

They all kept me going. Strange that near the end of my final hospital visit some staff in there kept telling me I should be a volunteer in psychiatric wards as I could help as good as any man, talk to people and inspire them. I decided not to for the pure reason it would remind me of my darkest days, and probably upset me. Then years later I write a fucking book about it all...

When you come out, it's not easy. It takes time to adjust again. You feel like someone's knocked the wind from your sails for a while. I won't lie, it's taken me over a year sometimes to get strong again. I got worse before I got better. There was a point I woke up every day for months on end with constant knots in my stomach. I felt constantly frightened and no medication was curing it. I thought I was to be like this for the rest of my life. It was horrific. Gradually it wore off but for a long while I felt like shit.

During a long weekend in Disneyland Paris with Mel and Kirk, I felt like this as I had not long been discharged from hospital. For 4 days my heart pounded in Paris. Kirk was only about 8. I tried not to show or speak of it to Mel, or obviously Kirk, but all the while I was a nervous wreck walking around this fantastic theme park. Even to this day I might get invited somewhere like a wedding or night out or christening and I may not feel up to it so I make an excuse. Some days are better than others. I can't feel on top of the world every day. I'm bound to have days I don't want to leave the house. Just chill, never force yourself if you really don't want to go anywhere if you're feeling not 100%. If people don't understand, that's their problem. You look after number one, they do.

Drinks are vitally important in my wellbeing. I find if I drink, say three coffees in a short space of time, I can feel giddy, light headed even to the point of a mild panic attack feeling. I have the occasional latte but no more than one that day, Also during the day herbal teas are great to help calm mild anxiety; camomile the best. I find Teapigs the best, Chamomile or Snooze. They are like something witches would have used in the middle-ages with thick camomile leaves you can see. My good friend Karen who worked on reception at LFC put me onto them. She made me one, one afternoon and after I drank it I almost fell asleep at the reception desk. Strong stuff.

The old saying of 'laughter is the best medicine' I think is not far off the truth. Ken Dodd believed this and I was fortunate enough to spend time with him after a Shakespeare play at the Liverpool Playhouse, incidentally starring Jeff Kissoon who played Mr Kennedy in Grange Hill. I took Mel and I spotted Dodd at the bar. Now I don't normally go over to celebs as I know from my own experiences if you're out you don't always want people coming over. I had to say hello to him though, he's a legend. We went over and he wouldn't let us go. When I mentioned Grange Hill, he wanted to talk about that for ages, asking questions and listening to my stories. Him and his wife Anne were very humble, funny and charming people. When it came to the after party in the Palm Sugar Club he said "No I gotta go home and feed the dog". So he never went; perfect!

A great inspirational quote I saw on a wall in May Duncan's in Everton, read:
'*Have Hope, Be Strong, Laugh Loud, Play Hard, Live In The Moment, Smile Often, Dream Big, You Are Loved, Never Give Up*'
I loved this, kind of says it all.

Has bipolar affected my career in acting? In some ways, yes. It got me in my prime at 21, knocked me sideways and I lost my focus along with my confidence. I must of turned down auditions with every agent I've ever had as i never had the confidence to go. If I can't walk out the door how can i walk into a often stressful audition. Yes, I messed about working in Spain and Guernsey seeking fun, but I was afraid to pursue my acting for a while as thought people in the business would know of my breakdown and consider me a risk. Even in 99 when I'd written the Titanic play and produced it, I was struck down again not long after. This again kept me back at a time I was feeling on top of the world. It's not the main reason I've not made a great career out of acting. Choosing to do my own thing and supporting a family are the main reasons, along with not giving a fuck about show business or the people in it, but without a doubt, the illness has had a part in it.

Yes, the thought crosses my mind that I could go in hospital again, but I move on from that thought. A thought can't make it happen. I've gotta live each day as it comes, Embrace it and be thankful I'm free, I'm sane and can function coherently with society, and, more importantly, my family.

Death doesn't bother me. I've been close a few times and I don't believe I'm wanted yet. As Kirk Douglas says in Spartacus *"I'm not afraid to die, no more than I was afraid to be born"* This illness hasn't killed me yet, my inner strength beats that. I know before it does happen the last thing I'll be thinking about is bipolar. I'll look back on the good and funny moments before I go, and there's more of them than bad. I have to go through hell before I get to heaven.

As I've got older, I have learnt who are tough. The ones who somehow carry on through utter turmoil. The Hillsborough families, or families who lost an innocent young son through knife crime and campaign through what must be total torture. I recently became friends with a man named Kieran Bimpson who lost his beautiful 3 year old daughter Francesca to a pointless arson attack, yet he carries on with his creativeness and lust for life for his family despite the awful turmoil he's endured. These are the real tough guys I have learnt later in life..

Drugs! I don't know what the percentage is of young people with fame and money who end up dabbling. For me it wasn't as important as some friends who couldn't go out without taking them. I was hyperactive, so I found marijuana calmed me at the time. Smoking it alone in my loft is when problems started. My life wasn't going as planned at the time, so it became more of a hindrance to me. Instead of feeling mellow and content as in the past, I now felt low and paranoid using it, so in time I stopped. I can't answer for every bipolar sufferer but as my condition worsened over the years, the drugs never helped me. I'm glad I take none now. My mind without is clear, not clouded or confused. I know there's people out there who use it for medical purposes and that's great if it works for them, it just doesn't for me. I've had all my fun in my younger years with all that; some great highs I won't lie but it's all over now. Some people can live my lifestyle and not be affected, but for me it had consequences in the end.

It's a good life. As Talk Talk once said 'Life's what you make it' It can be a wonderful life if you can just let go of the past and future and concentrate on the now. I could have given up years ago, succumbed to the fact I'm bipolar and have to tread carefully and stay in forever, afraid to meet and mingle. That's not in my character. I was born an extrovert type, love socialising and laughter so I'm damned if I'm gonna let some illness peg me back and stop me living my life. I want to live!

Remember, whilst all I've said in this book work for me, they may not work for everyone. Especially regarding panic attacks, as everyone handles them different. Learn your own way of handling them, but the colours is a good one if you need to distract yourself. Valium may not be strong enough to calm every individual like it does me during panic attacks or anxiety, plus its very addictive, so I'm very careful how many I take. I use them as and when needed.

My main hope with this book is that anyone who does suffer, especially in silence, might look at me and my story and find something that helps them. I've overcome the most frightening experiences I have known, and in the public eye. It may not be quick but I'll beat it in the end by small steps. Take those steps in your own time and without knowing it, you find yourself alive again and with purpose. Learn from your mistakes or history will repeat itself. Like the great doctor once told me, if he keeps on drinking he's back in, he keeps smoking the herb etc. Look at your possible causes and act on it. If it prevents hospitalisation or a life of depression then surely it's worth the sacrifice. Every man and woman at some point in their lives suffers either depression, anxiety or stress for whatever reason, whether circumstances or it just comes to them. Nobody can sail through life without some form of it. Anyone who says they haven't are simply lying.

As Sinatra once said; "Regrets, I've had a few," but my only regret is not realising earlier that I needed to change my lifestyle. Fuses were lit that could have been put out earlier if I'd known, but the circles and circumstances I was in made this hard. Hindsight is a wonderful thing.

I can't thank my family enough for the support they have given. I have been lucky to have a great support network around me. Many I know haven't. From the bottom of my heart I thank: My Mam as she has been with me every step of the way and suffered every step too.

My Dad, for eventually understanding this madness and learning how to deal with it.

My sister Zoe, God bless her, who, from a young age, had to deal and learn how to help me during many hours of need.

My partner Mel, who had my illness suddenly sprung upon her and probably knows more than any Dr how to calm me now. She has to live with my highs and lows on a daily basis.

My beautiful boy, Kirk, who luckily understands and also calms me now. Our laughter keeps me going!

Mal my stepdad for his patience during certain times I know were hard.

Verna my Dads partner for giving me sanctuary in your home and letting me feel at ease always.

I love you all unconditionally. Without your help my life would be unthinkable.

Also my closest pals (you know who you are) mainly for making me laugh and smile during truly horrendous times.

Finally, the doctors and nurses who broke through and saw past the barriers I gave them. Without them I wouldn't be here, or at least not in mind, and for that I am forever in the NHS' debt. Also all the Community Psychiatric nurses who have visited my home over the past ten years or so. My current one, Gary, has helped me on many a low period.

It wasn't easy writing this book. (Remember, this is just my story, there's nearly 60 million others out there with bipolar who have a story too) It was fun at first but when I got to the darker stuff it began playing on my mind, Taking me to places I didn't want to go again. Panic attacks returned and sleepless nights. I had to leave it for a while until I felt stronger to continue. All I hope is some may learn from it. You might see where I messed up, there's plenty of clues. Most importantly don't give up on yourself, even if you're sitting in a psychiatric hospital with nothing. There's a door that says exit in there for a reason...

It's hard to end a book like this as there is no end, so I think I've said enough about my trials and tribulations. I leave you with a simple line from my hero Bowie from the song 'Quicksand'

'I'm not a prophet or a stone-age man
Just a mortal with the potential of a superman
I'm living on' ⚡

The End

Lightning Source UK Ltd.
Milton Keynes UK
UKHW012026161020
371722UK00001B/75